Chicago

Jack Schnedler
Photography by Zbigniew Bzdak

COMPASS AMERICAN GUIDES

Chicago

Copyright © 1993, Fodor's Travel Publications, Inc.
Maps Copyright © 1993, Fodor's Travel Publications, Inc.
Compass American Guides, 6051 Margarido Drive, Oakland, CA 94618

LIBRARY OF CONGRESS CATALOGING-IN-PUBLICATION DATA
Schnedler, Jack, 1943–
Chicago / Jack Schnedler : photography by Zbigniew Bzdak.
    p.   cm.   —(Compass American Guides)
Includes bibliographical references and index.
ISBN 1-878867-29-6 (hard) : $24.95 — ISBN 1-878867-28-8 (pbk.) : $16.95
1. Chicago (Ill.)—Guidebooks. 2. Chicago Region (Ill.)—Guidebooks.
I. Bzdak, Zbigniew. II. Title. III. Series: Compass American Guides (Series)
F548.18.S35 1993
917.73'110443—dc20   93-16387
                              CIP

Series Editor: Kit Duane   Designers: David Hurst, Christopher Burt
Editors: Kit Duane, Julia Dillon   Map Design: Eureka Cartography, Berkeley, CA
Photography Editor: Christopher Burt

Production House: Twin Age Ltd., Hong Kong
Printed in Hong Kong

THE PUBLISHER WISHES TO THANK Jeff Johnson for his essay on Chicago blues; Henry Kisor for reading this manuscript for factual accuracy; and the following institutions for the use of their photographs and illustrations: **Chicago Historical Society** pp. 22, 27, 31, 34, 35, 44, 77, 83, 95, 119, 156, 194, 195, 221; **Chicago Sun-Times** pp. 40, 50, 149, 166, 184; **Kogan Collection** pp. 46, 130; **National Baseball Library Archive** pp. 265, 266; **Phyllis Kind Gallery** p. 191; **Ragdale Foundation** p. 207; **Underwood Photo Archives** pp. 15, 37, 43, 54, 58, 87, 88, 89, 90, 101, 130, 143, 257; **University of Chicago Archives** p. 73; **University of Illinois, Jane Addams Memorial Collection** pp. 125, 127; **Wilmette Historical Society** p. 23.

To Marcia and Martha

C O N T E N T S

Maps

Literary Extracts

Topical Essays

THE AWAKENING

Since mother morning wiped clean
the chaotic slate of starlight,
hard winds have forced the tree to beg.
She bends and splinters, bracing against
their steady push, her spindly brown fingers
cramped in stretch toward an impossible solace.
All of her strains toward the sun, which is
now just a pulse in the lightening sky without
the strength to poke its teasing slivers of light
through the solid gray cloak of clouds.
To move minutes, she curls her toes deep into
moist ribbons of soil. Her skin grows wet.
The lake roars in, chilling her thick ankle,
and she whistles her sudden ache toward
the skyline, with its bright confusion of
buildings and sound. The sun chuckles low in his
throat, watching her fingers freeze and crack.
Suddenly he smacks one of her glistening sides
with heat. She rises on her toes and once again
throws her tired, cold body open to her bold,
regretless love, while the lake curls away and
the wind dies to a whisper: "Tomorrow."
The tree stands taller, begins to breathe in
voices, rhythms, the blessing of sun.
She knows many things, much more than the
body suddenly flat against her, seeking shade.
She knows the lovers who stop to scratch
their hopeful names into her skin.
She knows the uncertain geography of rainfall.
And she has a name for the moan that worries gently in her hair.
It is called Chicago.

—Patricia Smith, 1991

CHICAGO FACTS

BASICS: CITY OF CHICAGO

Year incorporated	1837
Name derived from Indian word meaning	wild onion or swamp grass
Area	228 square miles (584 sq km)
Population density (per square mile)	12,209
Greatest length and breadth	25 by 15 miles (40 by 24 km)
Miles of street	3,676 (5,882 km)

POPULATION 1837 TO PRESENT

1830   1860   1890   1980   1990

50   112,178   1,099,850   3,005,072   2,783,903

Metropolitan Statistical Area population 1980   7,937,290
Metropolitan Statistical Area population 1990   8,065,633

ETHNIC COMPOSITION

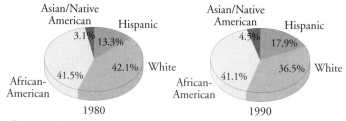

1980   1990

Note of Interest: Chicago has the second largest population of Polish peoples (937,000) in the world after Warsaw, Poland

ATHLETICS

SPORT	TEAM	HOME FIELD	LAST CHAMPIONSHIP
Baseball	Cubs	Wrigley Field	1908 World Series
	White Sox	Comiskey Park	1917 World Series
Football	Bears	Soldier Field	1986 Super Bowl
Basketball	Bulls	Chicago Stadium	1992 NBA Championship
Ice Hockey	Blackhawks	Chicago Stadium	1961 Stanley Cup

WEATHER: RECORD HIGHS AND LOWS

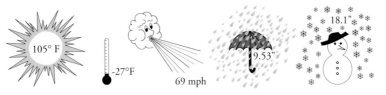

105° F	-27°F	69 mph	9.53"	18.1"
Hottest Day	Coldest Day	Windiest Day	Wettest 24 hours	Snowiest 24 hours
July 24, 1934	Jan 1, 1985	April 14, 1984	Aug 13-14, 1987	Jan 26-27, 1967

AIRPORT PASSENGERS (1990)

O'Hare	60,010,234
Midway	8,794,256
Meigs	232,596

LAKE MICHIGAN

City of Chicago shoreline length   30.7 miles
Area of Lake   22,300 square miles
Water use by Chicagoans   290 billion gallons per year
Deepest point   923 feet

NOTABLE BUILDINGS

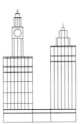

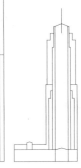

10 stories	12 stories	29 stories	110 stories	38 stories
Water Tower	Rookery Building	Wrigley Building	Sears Tower	NBC Tower
1869	1886	1924	1974	1989

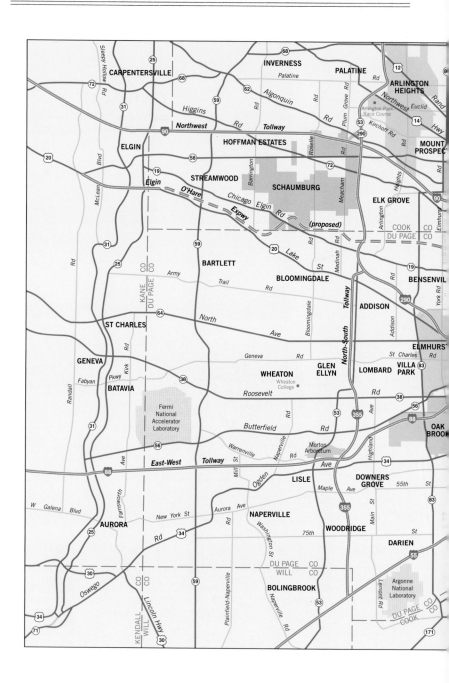

GREATER CHICAGO

0   5

miles

NORTHBROOK

WINNETKA

Willow Rd

Glenview Naval Air Station

GLENVIEW

WILMETTE

Green Bay

Central Rd

Northwestern University

SKOKIE

EVANSTON

MORTON GROVE

NILES

PARK RIDGE

Chicago O'Hare International Airport

FRANKLIN PARK

Grand Ave

RIVER FOREST

OAK PARK

CHICAGO

BELLWOOD

MAYWOOD

Eisenhower Expwy

Grant Park

CICERO

University of Illinois Chicago

BERWYN

RIVERSIDE

Burnham Park

BROOKFIELD

Comiskey Park

LA GRANGE

Chicago Midway Airport

Washington Park

University of Chicago

Jackson Park

Marquette Park

BURBANK

OAK LAWN

EVERGREEN PARK

Calumet Park

ALSIP

BLUE ISLAND

PALOS HEIGHTS

LAKE

MICHIGAN

Lincoln Park

Wrigley Field

De Paul University

Loyola University

Chicago Stadium

Lake Calumet

Wolf Lake

ILLINOIS

INDIANA

N

ACKNOWLEDGMENTS

I WANT TO THANK ALL THE PEOPLE WHO'VE HELPED ME understand and appreciate Chicago since I arrived as a wide-eyed 17-year-old from Missouri to attend Northwestern University in 1960. My colleagues at the old *Chicago Daily News* from 1965 to its death in 1978 gave me the broadest and most liberal education about the city that has become my home. There are too many to name them all, but a number of bosses who taught me a lot stand out: M. W. Newman, Ray Sons, Edward S. Gilbreth, Robert G. Schultz, Robert Signer. *Sun-Times* book editor Henry Kisor, a friend I cherish deeply, has inspired me by his recent zeal in writing wonderful books. And I'd know a lot less about Chicago without the unpredictable input of another bosom friend, Robin Robinson. The *Sun-Times* has permitted me to slip away from my travel editor's duties just enough to make this book possible, while assorted colleagues have contributed facts and ideas. The paper's own *Metro Chicago Almanac,* written by wizard reporters Don Hayner and Tom McNamee, has served as a rich lode of leads. Many other published works have launched me in rewarding directions, and many folks I've met out and around have fleshed out bare details.

From Compass American Guides, I've received the sturdy support any tremulous first-time book author needs—thanks to Christopher Burt, Kit Duane, Julia Dillon, Tobias Steed, and others. Collaborator Zbigniew Bzdak has lent valued encouragement while making me hope my verbal images can be half as vivid as his photographs.

I do wish that my father, Kurt Schnedler, could have lived to see this effort of a son in whom he invested so much care and love. Martha Schnedler continues to be the finest mother a son could want. Marcia Schnedler, wife and fellow traveler, can't imagine how much she means to me—in this project and the rest of life.

(above) The powers that be salute author Jack Schnedler's work (Underwood Photo Archives).
(following pages) Chicago's skyline is among the most impressive in the world, day or night.

INTRODUCTION
REDISCOVERING CHICAGO

NEARLY 1,600 DAYS OF GLOBETROTTING OVER THE PAST TEN YEARS as *Chicago Sun-Times* travel editor have gradually converted me into a rabid advocate for my own city, whose rough-hewn assets I'd often undervalued until I started spending so much time away from home. Now this guidebook may serve as a soapbox to spread the chauvinistic sermon that salts my conversational sallies among newly met strangers from Paris to Phuket: if you want a crash course in what the United States is all about, there's no better place to begin than Chicago. Save New York and Los Angeles for your next nightmare. Save New Orleans and San Francisco for a garnish; our Lake Michigan metropolis is the meaty main course of America, distilled to its bold and bumptious essence.

No, this text is not commissioned by the local chamber of commerce or bureau of tourism. You'll find reflected in these pages the fact that Chicago's faults and failings are as hugely all-American as its virtues and victories. "It's harsh and stony even when you're at the crest, a crusher if you dare to give your heart to it," declared M. W. Newman, perhaps the city's supreme newspaper stylist of this half-century. "You don't dare to be a loser in Chicago," added Newman, "unless you're a baseball team." (The perennially popular Cubs last won the World Series in 1908; the White Sox, in 1917.)

Newman was musing on a mournful occasion—the final issue of the late, great *Chicago Daily News,* where I'd spent the first 13 years of my career and no doubt would still be working if the paper hadn't sunk like the *Titanic* on March 4, 1978. Many other Chicago institutions have likewise gone belly-up in recent decades —from stockyards and steel mills to department stores and beloved diversions like Riverview, billed as "the world's largest amusement park" until it expired in 1967. But the city somehow absorbs the punches and rebounds with fresh prodigies, be they the world's tallest building or the planet's premier symphony orchestra.

"Only in the most indifferent does Chicago fail to awaken an ardent curiosity," was the 1919 bouquet tossed by Henry Justin Smith, managing editor in the *Daily News'* literary heyday, when Carl Sandburg even tried his hand (not so memorably) as silent-movie critic. Nelson Algren, who simultaneously adored and despised his hometown, said that living in Chicago "is like being married to a woman with a broken nose: There may be lovelier lovelies, but never a lovely so real." Norman Mailer, declaiming from the dust raised by the head-busting 1968 Democratic National Convention, pronounced Chicago "perhaps the last of the great American cities." Studs Terkel wrote that Chicago "is America's dream, writ large." Jan Morris, after a 1988 visit, waxed somewhat doubtful, recalling that Chicago once "was the heart of America in all its strength, violence, avarice, homeliness and absurdity." Now, she lamented, "Even Chicago's celebrated self-regard, itself a kind of metaphysical monument, has inevitably lost its power." Nobody today would greet a foreign visitor, as did a nineteenth-century train conductor, with: "Sir, you are entering the Boss City of the Universe."

Indeed, the last Big Boss—Mayor Richard J. Daley—has been dead and gone since 1976. His son Richard M. Daley, a resourceful politician but hardly a figure to inspire fearful awe, became mayor in 1987. But the power equation continues to shift in a city where racial minorities are now in the majority. The traditional rivalry between North Siders and South Siders is less relevant today than the jockeying among whites, African-Americans, and Hispanics. Dynamic Harold Washington, Chicago's first black mayor from 1983 until his heart-attack death in 1987, will certainly have African-American successors. Chicagoan Carol Moseley-Braun was elected in 1992 as the first black woman U.S. senator. Two of Chicago's best-known citizens are indomitable civil-rights activist Jesse Jackson and equally indefatigable talk-show wizard Oprah Winfrey.

Jan Morris may not be entirely wrong when she suggests that "few foreigners give a thought to Chicago from one year to the next." But my own travel encounters indicate that the city's image is improving in one regard: the most famous Chicagoan in far-flung corners of the world is no longer Al Capone. That moviemade mobster has been displaced for now on the marquee of global awareness by basketball's supreme maestro, Michael Jordan. No question—a slam dunk is a step up in style from a rat-a-tat-tat.

Visitors and residents amble Chicago to savor the celebrities, the architecture, the lakefront, the museums, the neighborhoods, the dining, the shopping, and the other obvious allures. With a bit of on-the-street effort, those from out-of-town can share the insights and humor of ordinary Chicagoans; despite the thickening of big-city calluses, people here remain more open to strangers than in many another metropolis. With luck, you'll leave Chicago more cheerfully inclined than

Rudyard Kipling, who wrote a century ago, "Having seen it, I urgently desire never to see it again. It is inhabited by savages." And you'll likely depart less befuddled than the daddy in Ogden Nash's whimsical verse: "I reel, I sway, I am utterly exhausted./Should you ask me when Chicago was founded I could only reply I didn't know it was losted."

A REAL CITY

I have struck a city,—a real city,—and they call it Chicago. The other places do not count. San Francisco was a pleasure-resort as well as a city, and Salt Lake was a phenomenon. This place is the first American city I have encountered. It holds rather more than a million people with bodies, and stands on the same sort of soil as Calcutta. Having seen it, I urgently desire never to see it again. It is inhabited by savages. Its water is the water of the Hughli, and its air is dirt. Also it says it is the 'boss' town of America.

—Rudyard Kipling, *From Sea to Sea,* 1889

Some winter mornings can make even the city's proudest boosters sympathize with Rudyard Kipling's harsh assessment of the city.

H I S T O R Y

TURN BACK THE TIME MACHINE a mere two centuries, and Chicago vanishes. It's a summer day in the mid-1790s, and you're standing in a swamp beside a sluggish little river the Potawatomi Indians call "Checaugou," which probably means "wild onion" or "swamp grass." In the late twentieth century, you'd be dwarfed by a skyscraper forest while dodging the relentless traffic at one end of the Michigan Avenue Bridge linking the Loop and the Magnificent Mile. But here in the late eighteenth century, the flat landscape stretching west across the endless Great Prairie looks about as empty and primeval as when the last glacier retreated 13,000 years earlier. A canvas virtually blank of civilization, it seems an unpromising setting for the "City of the Big Shoulders" soon to be born.

Yes, there is a log house near the north bank of the Checaugou, plus a scattering of other rough-hewn buildings. The homestead belongs to trader Jean Baptiste Point du Sable, who arrived around 1779 to become Chicago's first permanent resident. As the local Indians later would say, before the last of them were hustled westward in the 1830s, "The first white man to live here was a black man." Something of a mysterious figure who may have been born on Santo Domingo in the Caribbean, du Sable is mentioned in a British dispatch a few years after the Revolutionary War as "a handsome Negro, well educated and settled in Eschikagou." As an ingenious and resourceful man of commerce, this First Chicagoan makes an apt progenitor for a metropolis perpetually on the make with the civic slogan "I will!" (Columnist

Chicago's first non-Native American resident was a black man probably from Santo Domingo named Jean Baptiste Point du Sable who homesteaded on the banks of the Chicago River in 1779. (Chicago Historical Society)

This painting depicts the construction of Fort Dearborn, finished in 1804, and once called "the neatest and best garrison in the country." (Wilmette Historical Society)

Mike Royko once suggested that a truly honest Chicago motto would be "Ubi est mea?"—Where's mine?)

When du Sable sold his estate and moved to Missouri in 1800, there were just a few other traders ensconced at the mouth of the river, which emptied into Lake Michigan and also connected inland with the short Chicago Portage leading to the vast continental river system. The French explorer Louis Joliet, first European to traverse the Chicago region (along with Father Jacques Marquette), had noted presciently in 1673 that "it would only be necessary to make a canal by cutting through but half a league of prairies" to pass from the Great Lakes to the Gulf of Mexico by way of the Illinois and Mississippi rivers. The speculative fever that preceded the opening of such a canal in 1848, and the full-throttle arrival of the railroads in the immediate wake of the waterway, spawned a sudden metropolis that inspired British visitor Sara Jane Lippincott to write in 1870, "The growth of this city is one of the most amazing things in the history of modern civilization."

But first Chicago had to endure a massacre, as well as the disdain of older and more settled communities in the southern part of Illinois. In 1830, when the first town survey was plotted, the population numbered only 50. In 1837, when Chicago incorporated as a city with 4,170 residents, there were no paved streets and the tallest buildings towered all of two stories.

The Fort Dearborn Massacre, which took place at the onset of the War of 1812, stemmed from the same frontier tensions that had led to its construction in 1803 on the south bank of the Chicago River. A series of brass pavement markers around the Michigan Avenue-Wacker Drive intersection marks the site of the unprepossessing log fort. It stood directly across the river from the old du Sable homestead, which was bought in 1804 by an irascible silversmith named John Kinzie. Long known as "The Father of Chicago" by those who preferred to ignore the black man at the root of the city's family tree, Kinzie was a survivor of the Indian attack along with his nine-year-old son, John (destined to be the loser of Chicago's first mayoral election in 1837).

More than 500 warriors ambushed a procession of some 100 soldiers, women, and children who were trying to evacuate the isolated fort on August 15, 1812. Fifty-three Americans died in the massacre along the lake about two miles (3.2 km) south of the outpost, which the Indians burned to the ground the next day. One of the four stars in Chicago's flag symbolizes Fort Dearborn, rebuilt on nearly the same site in 1816 and demobilized in 1836 after the Indian threat had evaporated. The successor fort was demolished like much of the city's heritage, but logs salvaged when it was torn down in 1857 have been fashioned into a section of blockhouse wall at the Chicago Historical Society. Touch that timber, and you are reaching about as far back into Chicago's tangible past as it is possible to go.

Illinois became a state in 1818, but straggling Chicago lay almost unnoticed on its wilderness fringe far from the southern population centers along the Mississippi and Ohio rivers. The first state bank operated more than 300 miles (483 km) to the south in Shawneetown, where residents of what is now a derelict Ohio River hamlet still recount the time a delegation made the long ride down from Chicago seeking a $1,000 loan for civic improvements. Having sent investigators north, the state bank refused the loan on the ground that no place so far from Shawneetown could ever amount to anything.

A similar impression struck William H. Keating, a University of Pennsylvania mineralogist who visited Chicago in 1823. "The village presents no cheering prospects, as, not withstanding its antiquity, it consists of but few huts, inhabited by a miserable race of men, scarcely equal to the Indians from whom they are descended," wrote the non-visionary Keating.

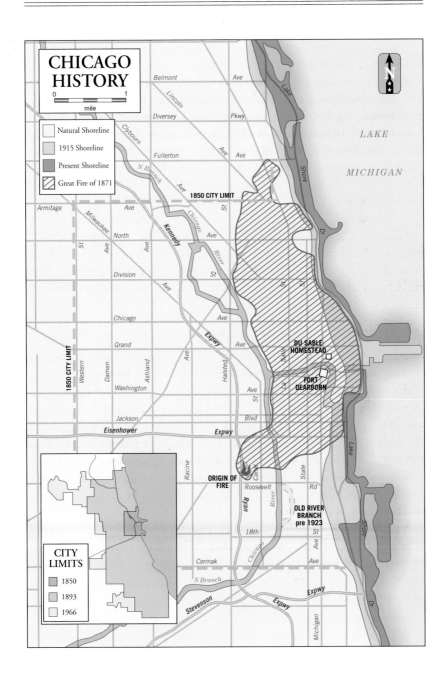

CHICAGO
HISTORY

0 _____ 1
mile

☐ Natural Shoreline
☐ 1915 Shoreline
■ Present Shoreline
▨ Great Fire of 1871

CITY
LIMITS

■ 1850
■ 1893
☐ 1966

*T*heir log or bark houses are low, filthy and disgusting, displaying not the least trace of comfort. . . . As a place of business, it offers no inducement to the settler, for the whole annual shipment of the trade on the lake did not exceed the cargo of five or six schooners. . . . The dangers attending the navigation of the lake, and the scarcity of harbors along the shore, must ever prove a serious obstacle to the increase of the commercial importance of Chicago.

But the Erie Canal was completed in 1825, opening a new Great Lakes water route from the East to Chicago, and the Illinois legislature appointed a commission in 1829 to plot a canal route between Lake Michigan and the Mississippi River. Opportunity was in the wind, and it was bringing to Chicago entrepreneurs like ebullient Mark Beaubien, who arrived from Detroit in 1826 to visit his brother and stayed to erect the city's first frame building. It housed some of Beaubien's 23 children, as well as a tavern and Chicago's first hotel, the Sauganash. Beaubien, who played the violin with passion and favored a swallow-tail coat with brass buttons on festive occasions, once declared that he "kept tavern like hell." With jolly souls like him in a location ideally suited to profit from America's impending westward boom, Chicago was poised to explode onto the national landscape.

■ CANAL AND RAILROAD BOOMS

No memento of Chicago's meteoric nineteenth-century rise from frontier mudhole to Mid-America's premier city makes a more appropriate symbol of the quick-as-lightning growth than an antique steam locomotive named the *Pioneer.* This Baldwin "4-2-0" puffer-belly, on display at the Chicago Historical Society, helped build the city's first railroad—a 10-mile (16-km) stretch of Galena & Chicago Union tracks that carried the initial load of wheat downtown from its western terminal at the Des Plaines River in November, 1848.

It was a canal rather than a railroad, however, that put Chicago on the map as a city and brought its first boom—followed swiftly by its initial bust. In 1827, the U.S. Congress authorized the digging of a canal to link the Great Lakes with the Mississippi River basin. Two years later, the Illinois legislature appointed a commission to plot the course of the Illinois & Michigan Canal. In 1830, the commissioners laid out the towns at either end of the proposed waterway: Ottawa, on the

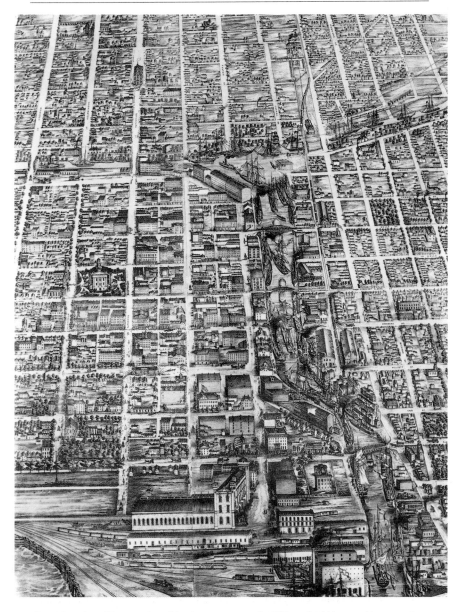

By 1857, when this engraving of the cityscape was made, Chicago had blossomed into a major city in only 20 years thanks to the railway and a canal connecting Lake Michigan with the Mississippi. (Chicago Historical Society)

The famous Baldwin "4-2-0" puffer-belly on display at the Chicago Historical Society helped build the city's first railway in 1848.

Illinois River, and Chicago, 90 miles (144 km) eastward where the Chicago River flowed sluggishly into Lake Michigan.

Chicago's original plat, which straddled the river's three branches, covered only three-eighths of a square mile (1 sq km) in a simple rectangular grid—setting a basic pattern that led one nineteenth-century visitor to call this "the most right-angle city in the United States." There was more than ample land for the 1830 population of roughly 50, and $100 was the highest price paid in the initial auction of lots that year. Then the speculators swooped in, and barely born Chicago found itself at the vortex of "the most intense land speculation in American history," as historian William Cronon called it in his 1991 *Nature's Metropolis*. Those $100 lots of 1830 were selling for as much as $100,000 by 1836 in a frenzy fed mainly by visions of wealth from the I&M Canal—which, as events transpired, wasn't completed until 1848.

It was as if "some prevalent mania infected the whole people," wrote British traveler Harriet Martineau. The scene presaged the impression of a Swedish visitor 15 years later: "It seems as if on all hands, people come here merely to trade, to make money, and not to live." Some speculators quickly became leading citizens, among them William R. Ogden, who won Chicago's first mayoral election in 1837 and amassed a big enough real-estate fortune to build a mansion on a full block of city land. The new city adopted as its motto "Urbs in Horto"—City in a Garden—although the prevalent motif on the unpaved streets was mud deep enough to swallow a horse.

The last Native Americans vanished from the Chicago area after the 6,000 remaining Potawatomis in northern Illinois were forced to sign two treaties in September 1833, ceding all their land east of the Mississippi River to the white man. The closing of the second Fort Dearborn in 1836 symbolized the end of Chicago's frontier era, even if residents were still hunting wolves that year within earshot of downtown. Emerging hallmarks of urban life included the city's first newspaper (launched in 1833 as the *Chicago Democrat*), the first brewery (opened in 1836 by German immigrants William Haas and Konrad Sulzer), and the first paid policeman (hired in 1839, by which time there were so many saloons that temperance activist John Hankins lamented, "I have never seen a town which seems so like a universal grog shop").

Chicago's knack for architectural innovation, which would make it the cradle of the skyscraper at the end of the century, manifested itself in a new kind of construction designed to meet the sudden population surge of the 1830s. The balloon frame, devised by Augustine Taylor to build St. Mary's Church in 1833, was ideally suited for rapidly growing communities. A house could be erected in a week, and the balloon-frame method—thin plates and studs running the full length of the building and held together only by nails, later called simply "Chicago construction"—spread across the nation. Except for the balloon frame, the *New York Tribune* concluded in 1855, "Chicago and San Francisco never could have arisen, as they did, from little villages to great cities in a single year."

Joseph Jefferson, destined to become a distinguished actor for whom Chicago's annual theater awards are named, visited the fledgling community by steamboat in 1837 and recorded a whirl of impressions:

> People hurrying to and fro, frame buildings going up, board sidewalks going down, new hotels, new churches, new theaters, everything new. Saw and hammer—saw, saw, bang, bang—look out for the drays!— bright and muddy streets—gaudy-colored calicos—blue and red flannels and striped ticking hanging outside the dry-goods stores—bar-rooms— real-estate offices—attorneys-at-law—oceans of them!

The speculative boom went bust that very year during the Panic of 1837, which ushered in one of the nation's early economic depressions. Chicago lot prices sank back to $100 by 1840, most local businessmen landed flat on their financial backs, and work on the I&M Canal stopped after Illinois defaulted on its debt obligations. But canal construction resumed in a couple of years, and the city began to regain its breath. One of its first ethnic neighborhoods sprang up around the canal's eastern end, populated by Irish laborers digging the waterway. Originally known as Hardscrabble, it was Bridgeport by the time Chicago annexed the area in 1863. A font of Irish-American heritage—and Irish-American politicians—for more than a century, Bridgeport is most famous as the lifelong home of the late Mayor Richard J. Daley, as well as his mayoral son Richard M. Daley.

Although the I&M Canal proved a boon to Chicago commerce, the shallow waterway was an idea whose time had come and almost gone when the first barge traversed its locks in April, 1848. By the end of that year, the *Pioneer* and other locomotives were whistling along the Galena and Chicago Union line. And the Chicago Board of Trade was newly open to broker the array of agricultural and other commodities that would flow into the world's prime rail hub in the decades ahead. The city limits encompassed only a fraction of twentieth-century Chicago, but the advent of horse-drawn street railways by the end of the 1850s boosted the growth of suburbs later absorbed within the municipal boundaries (like Lake View, Hyde Park, and Blue Island), as well as others that remain separate entities (like Evanston, Oak Park, and Lake Forest). German and Scandinavian immigrants, along with the Irish, were swelling the population of a once-again boomtown where a strong back virtually ensured employment.

A lot of that muscle between 1855 and the Civil War went into levitating the city—physically lifting most buildings from the mire by as much as a dozen feet (3.6 m) to match newly raised street grades. Like the reversal of the Chicago River to flow out of Lake Michigan four decades later, it was a marvel of civic engineering—and a necessity if urban growth was to continue. Because Chicago occupied a swamp, the streets at their natural level were quagmires most of the year. Citizens "were begot in mud, born in mud, and bred in mud," an early Chicagoan recalled. Whimsical signs marked the most treacherous passages with such warnings as "Team Underneath" and "Stage Dropped Through," while a hat plopped on the mud in one spot was labeled "Man Lost." After the elevation, strolling the streets no longer guaranteed a mudbath. The legacy of the occasional contrarian who refused to jack up his property can be seen today in neighborhoods near the Loop where a few old houses squat in yards sunk a half-dozen feet (1.8 m) below the sidewalk.

By 1856, Chicago was the hub for 10 rival rail lines and steaming mightily toward one of the brawny titles bestowed by Carl Sandburg: "Player with Railroads and the Nation's Freight Handler." The arrival of passenger service from New York the following year cut travel time between the cities to just two days from the three weeks it had taken in the 1830s. Riding high as the nation's rail capital, Chicago saw its population soar from 4,470 in 1840 to 28,000 in 1850, 110,000 in 1860, and 300,000 in 1870. By 1890, with 1.1 million residents, it had passed Philadelphia to become America's Second City—a status grudgingly surrendered to Los Angeles in 1990.

"The railroads transformed the city more crucially and vividly—and lastingly —than any other development," wrote Herman and Rick Kogan in *Yesterday's Chicago,* a sprightly illustrated history published in 1976. "They made of it a huge wholesale market from which hundreds of cities and towns could draw their wants

In its early days the city was so mired in mud that its buildings had to be literally raised to match its new paved streets, as illustrated here in the raising of the Briggs Hotel in 1857. (Chicago Historical Society)

POLITICAL CONVENTION CAPITAL

There hasn't been one in Chicago lately, not since the 1968 Democratic debacle that showed the world an ugly set of images: barbed wire and bayonets ringing the International Amphitheatre, angry chants of "Dump the Hump," the crunch of police nightsticks on the skulls of protesters and reporters, the stench of tear gas and stink bombs, the twisted face of Richard J. Daley cursing Sen. Abraham Ribicoff's attack on "Gestapo tactics in the streets of Chicago." But this brawny city securely retains its title as the capital city of national political conventions, those quadrennial circuses of the Donkeys and the Elephants. Chicago has hosted 24 Democratic and Republican conventions, starting on a high note with the 1860 GOP gathering that nominated Abraham Lincoln in the Wigwam, a jerry-built wooden arena at what is now Lake Street and Wacker Drive. Baltimore runs a distant second with 10 conventions.

As the nation's premier railway and then airline hub, Chicago has always been an obvious choice for the two major parties. And some of the most memorable conventions have been staged here. William Jennings Bryan delivered the famous "Cross of Gold" speech that swept him to the 1896 Democratic nomination in the first Coliseum, at 63rd and Harper. Republican regulars beat back the "Bull Moose" insurgents of ex-President Theodore Roosevelt to nominate William Howard Taft in 1912 at a newer Coliseum on Wabash Avenue between 14th and 16th streets. (And Roosevelt's Progressive forces held their own rump convention here later that summer.) In 1920, GOP bigwigs huddled in the original smoke-filled room at the Blackstone Hotel to swing a stalemated Coliseum convention to Warren Harding. Newly nominated Franklin D. Roosevelt broke a century of precedent in 1932 by flying to Chicago to accept the first of his four Democratic nominations in person at Chicago Stadium (where basketball's Bulls are the headline act until the new stadium is finished).

The last truly contested national convention saw Republican partisans of Dwight Eisenhower outfight Robert Taft's conservatives at the International Amphitheatre in 1952. Although a total of 10 U.S. presidents have been nominated in Chicago, Ike turned out to be the only winner among the five men chosen at the Amphitheatre, which sits on the edge of the old stockyards district at 43rd and Halsted. Adlai Stevenson came up a loser in 1952 and 1956, as did Richard Nixon on his first presidential bid in 1960. And Hubert Humphrey never recovered from the 1968 bloodletting where the whole world was watching. The twenty-first century may arrive before the planet has a chance to watch Chicago's twenty-fifth national political convention—if the parties are still staging these anachronisms by then.

of every kind. They stimulated the rise of new businesses, larger department stores, factories, plants and other enterprises of enduring significance." And, as Harold M. Mayer and Richard C. Wade observed in their 1969 *Chicago: Growth of a Metropolis*, the early railroad decisions "were written on the map in lines of iron and for more than a century have constituted fixed features of the Chicago scene." Even today, the tangles of railyards south and west of the Loop are one of the most evident landscape features from the 103rd-floor skydeck of the Sears Tower.

The web of 15 railroads converging on Chicago by 1860 made the self-styled Queen City of the Lakes a likely candidate to host the nominating convention of the infant Republican Party, a coalition that included most anti-slavery forces in a nation on the brink of bloody rupture. By then the ninth largest U.S. city, Chicago boasted the world's biggest train station, seven first-class hotels (where a luxurious room cost $2.50 a night), 50 more hotels at $1.50 a night, and 100 at $1. Meanwhile, the raising of the city continued. As Ida Tarbell wrote decades later in her *Life of Lincoln:*

> The audacity of inviting a national convention to meet there, in the con-
> dition in which Chicago chanced to be at the time was purely Chica-
> goan. No other city would have risked it. . . . When the invitation to the
> convention was extended, half the buildings in Chicago were on stilts;
> some of the streets had been raised to the new grade, others still lay in
> the mud. . . . A city with a conventional sense of decorum would not
> have cared to be seen in this demoralized condition, but Chicago per-
> haps conceived that it would but prove her courage and confidence to
> show the country what she was doing.

The City Council, led by Republican Mayor "Long John" Wentworth, appro-priated funds for a jerry-built pine-board convention hall with a capacity of 10,000 at Lake and Market streets, on the northwest fringe of today's Loop. People called it the "Wigwam," and the Republicans nominated Abraham Lincoln for president there on the third ballot. "Without attempting to convey an idea of the delirious cheers, the Babel of joy and excitement, we may mention that strong men wept like children," reported the *Chicago Press and Tribune*. Lincoln became America's most revered president, and Chicago went on to host another 23 major-party nominating conventions—including the bruising Democratic gathering of 1968, when the whole world was watching.

■ MOO-VING ON TO THE FIRE

The meatpackers of Chicago took no Christmas holiday in 1865. They were busy that December 25 with the formal opening of Union Stock Yards, destined to become one of the city's most famous—and aromatic—landmarks, as well as its largest employer for more than half a century. Writers already had branded Chicago "The Great Bovine City of the World," thanks in part to its major role in supplying beef for Union troops during the recently concluded Civil War. It was also called "Porkopolis," having processed enough hogs in 1863 to stretch in curly-tailed single file all the way to New York. Now a consortium of nine railroads and a half-dozen meatpackers was consolidating slaughterhouse operations on a square mile (2.6 sq km) of land south of 39th Street and west of Halsted, beyond that era's city limits. Its pens could house a metropolis of meat on the hoof: 20,000 cattle, 75,000 hogs, and 20,000 sheep at the peak of operations in the early twentieth century. Historian William Cronon has observed:

Longhorns, once a symbol of the settlement of the Plains, await their fate at the Union Stock Yards in 1903. (Chicago Historical Society)

Tourists might hesitate to subject them-selves to the stench and gore of the place, but all knew that some-thing special, something never before seen in the history of the world, was taking place on the south side of the city. Opinion differed about whether it should be an es-sential stop on a visitor's itinerary. Many saw in it the pinnacle of Chicago's social and economic achievement, the site, above all others, that made the city an icon of nine-teenth-century progress.

Gustavus Swift
(Chicago Historical Society)

'Great as this wonderful city is in every-thing,' wrote a British traveler, 'it seems that the first place among its strong points must be given to the celerity and comprehensiveness of the Chicago style of killing hogs.

Meatpacking magnate Gustavus Swift later boasted, "We use everything but the squeal." Carl Sandburg portrayed the city "half-naked, sweating, proud to be Hog Butcher." The yards did have their darker sides, memorably exposed in 1906 by Upton Sinclair's *The Jungle,* including the revolting neglect of sanitation and the abysmal conditions under which immigrant laborers toiled. No contemporary reader of *The Jungle* could have stomached the sight or smell of a sausage for at least a decent interval.

Meatpacking, which finally faded from Chicago with the closing of Union Stock Yards in 1971, formed merely one sinew of the city's commercial and indus-trial prowess as the nation moved into the post-Civil War era of the Robber Barons. Chicago ranked as the world's largest grain handler and the premier North American lumber market. The huge McCormick plant, on the north bank of the river between Pine and Sands streets, dominated the trade in reapers and other farm machinery around the globe. George Pullman built his prototype sleeping car in 1864, and the North Chicago Rolling Mills turned out the nation's first steel rails the following year. In 1869, the 13,730 vessels docking at Chicago Harbor exceeded the combined commercial traffic for the ports of New York, Philadelphia, Baltimore, Charleston, Mobile, and San Francisco.

Lake Street, running east and west at the northern edge of today's Loop, was Chicago's prime shopping boulevard until the late 1860s, when ex-cotton speculator Potter Palmer singlehandedly turned the spotlight toward State Street. Palmer bought a half-dozen blocks fronting on State, which was then a narrow thoroughfare lined by shanties and wooden sidewalks. He erected the elegant Palmer House at State and Monroe, where a hotel bearing his name still operates. He persuaded Field, Leiter & Co. to move from Lake Street by building them an opulent new department store along State between Washington and Randolph, where Marshall Field's now stands. Freshly widened State Street became "That Great Street," the glittering retail spine of Chicago until Michigan Avenue shifted the luxury-shopping axis north in the 1970s and '80s.

While Chicago's newly wealthy came to shop along Lake and State from their mansions to the west and north, the city's working-class majority suffered the indignities of the industrial revolution. "Unable to get away from the noise and odor of packing houses, tanneries and distilleries, the bulk of them huddled in modest pine cottages on small lots without the benefit of paved streets or sewers," according to Mayer and Wade's *Chicago: Growth of a Metropolis*. More than 200,000 Chicagoans "were jammed into these frame jungles. City fathers and visitors alike might take pride in the fact that few tenements were built and that 'thrifty workmen own the houses they live in' or can 'rent a whole house,' but filth, disease, vice and privation were the constant companions of those living in poor neighborhoods."

Cholera and typhoid, which did not spare those better off, struck with regularity because the rapidly growing city fouled its Lake Michigan drinking water with raw sewage and industrial offal carried along by the increasingly polluted Chicago River. Only by standing nature on its head and permanently reversing the river's flow at the turn of the century did health officials finally vanquish the waterborne diseases.

The moral pollution of vice was even more persistent. "The city's moral tone was lamentable," wrote the Kogans in *Yesterday's Chicago*. Political corruption ran rampant, with councilmen making quick booty in deals with contractors seeking swift action for franchises to pave streets or build bridges or dig tunnels. Too many citizens who should have known better paid scant heed to occasional cleanup movements, and even less heed to those who warned of dire things to come. Some visitors called Chicago "the wickedest city in the country," and an editorial writer reflecting on the Great Chicago Fire of 1871 felt this was proper retribution for the notorious gambling, saloons, and brothels: "Again the fire of heaven has fallen on Sodom and Gomorrah!"

In fact, more prosaic forces touched off the October 8-10 conflagration, which remains the most indelibly mythic event in the city's history. Chicago in 1871 was a densely packed community of 300,000 built principally from wood; more than two-thirds of its 60,000 structures were entirely wooden; the sidewalks were mainly wooden; most streets were paved with tar-swathed wooden blocks; and the numerous lumberyards and grain elevators were torches waiting to ignite. Meanwhile, lengthy drought had turned the city tinder-dry. Into this kindling box, as one commentator described it, Lucifer threw his match.

As was the case when San Francisco was destroyed in 1906, many prudish souls declared that the Great Chicago Fire of October 8-10, 1871, was holy retribution for the city's "wickedness." (Underwood Photo Archives)

The prime suspect, familiar to generations of schoolchildren, was a cow—not one of those hapless beef cattle waiting to meet its steak-maker at Union Stock Yards, but a milk cow belonging to Irish immigrants Patrick and Catherine O'Leary. It is a well known tale that Mrs. O'Leary went to the shed behind the family's West Side cottage on that fateful Sunday night, and that the cow kicked over the lantern while she was trying to milk the creature. But Mrs. O'Leary and her Bossie likely got a bum rap, as Don Hayner and Tom McNamee suggest in the breezy *Metro Chicago Almanac:* "The fire almost undoubtedly started in the family barn, but there is little evidence that Mrs. O'Leary was milking her cow at the time. To the contrary, in the only two interviews Mrs. O'Leary ever gave—both under oath—she said that she and her husband had gone to bed early that night. The legend of the cow may have been concocted by an imaginative newspaper reporter, and the fire's real origin remains unknown."

However ill-treated by popular legend, the O'Learys were fortunate in having their cottage escape the Great Fire, which burned its way north and east on prevailing winds through the commercial center and residential north side of the city. The death toll reached 250 or more, and 100,000 Chicagoans were left homeless by the destruction of more than 17,000 buildings. Only a handful of structures survived in the four square miles (10.2 sq km) of devastation extending from Taylor Street on the south to Fullerton Avenue on the north, and from the river on the west to the lakefront. The crenellated Water Tower, completed just two years earlier at Michigan and Chicago avenues, became the most famous (and most photographed) survivor. It sits today, dwarfed by the Gold Coast's forest of highrises, as a talisman of the city's pluck in the teeth of adversity.

In the immediate wake of the fire, a New Orleans newspaper gloated, "Chicago will never be like the Carthage of old. Its glory will be of the past, not of the present, while its hopes, once so bright and cloudless, will be to the end marred and blackened by the smoke of its fiery fate." But some entrepreneurs reopened in makeshift quarters within a matter of days amid the rubble and ashes. Realtor W. D. Kerfoot's sign announced he was back in business with "all gone but wife, children and energy." The *Chicago Tribune*, printing on borrowed presses after its supposedly fireproof building had been consumed, ran an upbeat editorial: "CHEER UP! In the midst of a calamity without parallel in the world's history, looking upon the ashes of 30 years' accumulations, the people of this once beautiful city have resolved that CHICAGO SHALL RISE AGAIN!"

Civic booster Deacon Bross, a former Illinois lieutenant governor, declared: "Within five years, Chicago's business houses will be rebuilt, and by the year 1900, the new Chicago will boast a population of a million souls. You ask me why? Because I know the Northwest and the vast resources of the broad acres. I know that the location of Chicago makes her the center of this wealthy region and the market for all its products." Bross guessed wrong by being insufficiently optimistic: the city's commercial core was back bigger and better in less than five years, with buildings erected to much more stringent fire codes. And Chicago's population, buoyed by annexing a ring of suburbs in 1889, stood comfortably above a million (1,099,805) in the 1890 census, a full decade ahead of the booster's forecast.

IROQUOIS AND EASTLAND DISASTERS

The Chicago Fire of 1871, as ravenously destructive as it was, took fewer lives (an estimated 250 to 350) than two of the city's later disasters: the 1903 Iroquois theater fire and the capsizing of the excursion steamboat *Eastland* in 1915. Both were all the crueler because they struck hundreds of families in the midst of a holiday outing.

A Christmas-season audience of 1,900 was crowded into the downtown Iroquois Theater, a new Randolph Street building advertised as "completely fireproof," for a performance of *Mr. Bluebeard* starring Eddie Foy on December 30, 1903. Shortly after the second act began, a curtain touched an arc lamp and ignited. Foy moved forward to the footlights and cried out, "Please be quiet! There is no danger!" He told the orchestra to keep playing, but the fire spread speedily across the stage set, the asbestos curtain became stuck halfway down, and the lights went out.

As the audience rushed in panic for the exits, they found several of the doors locked, while others opened only inward against the press of bodies desperate to escape. The fire blazed for no more than 15 minutes, but 602 theater-goers were killed, more than a third of them children. Firemen found 180 of the bodies in a trampled mass on the grand stairway leading from the balconies to the main floor. None of the five city and theater officials indicted afterwards came to trial, but the catastrophe did spur a sweeping overhaul of fire codes for theaters in Chicago and elsewhere.

The excursion vessel *Eastland* was packed with more than 2,000 employees and family members from the Western Electric Company, bound for a Lake Michigan

continues

cruise with a picnic along the Indiana Dunes on July 24, 1915. The crew had emptied ballast tanks to let more passengers board, making the ship dangerously top-heavy as it eased away from its Chicago River dock between Clark and La Salle streets. When the *Eastland* began to list to port, possibly because passengers were crowding that railing to watch river traffic pass, a frantic rush by hundreds more to the listing side sent the vessel rolling over in the shallow water.

Despite the valiant rescue efforts of policemen and volunteers who formed human chains, the *Eastland* death toll reached 812—Chicago's worst in any single disaster. The victims included 22 entire families. Many passengers already below decks were drowned, while others were trampled in a stampede to escape by a staircase. No specific blame for the tragedy was ever fixed, and an appeals court dismissed the last lawsuit in the 1930s. The *Eastland,* meanwhile, was righted and later went back into service as the U.S. Navy training vessel *Wilmette.* It finally was sold for scrap in 1946.

In terms of lives lost, Chicago's costliest disaster was the capsizing of the Eastland *on July 24, 1915. (Chicago Sun-Times)*

CHICAGO

Hog Butcher for the World,
Tool Maker, Stacker of Wheat,
Player with Railroads and the Nation's Freight Handler;
Stormy, husky, brawling,
City of the Big Shoulders:

They tell me you are wicked and I believe them, for I have seen your
painted women under the gas lamps luring the farm boys.
And they tell me you are crooked and I answer: Yes, it is true I have
seen the gunman kill and go free to kill again.
And they tell me you are brutal and my reply is: On the faces of women
and children I have seen the marks of wanton hunger.
And having answered so I turn once more to those who sneer at this my
city, and I give them back the sneer and say to them:
Come and show me another city with lifted head singing so proud to
be alive and coarse and strong and cunning.
Flinging magnetic curses amid the toil of piling job on job, here is a tall
bold slugger set vivid against the little soft cities;
Fierce as a dog with tongue lapping for action, cunning as a savage
pitted against the wilderness,
          Bareheaded,
          Shoveling,
          Wrecking,
          Planning,
          Building, breaking, rebuilding,
Under the smoke, dust all over his mouth, laughing with white teeth,
Under the terrible burden of destiny laughing as a young man laughs,
Laughing even as an ignorant fighter laughs who has never lost a battle,
Bragging and laughing that under his wrist is the pulse, and under his
ribs the heart of the people,
          Laughing!
Laughing the stormy, husky, brawling laughter of Youth, half-naked,
sweating, proud to be Hog Butcher, Tool Maker, Stacker of
Wheat, Player with Railroads and Freight Handler to the Nation.

—Carl Sandburg, 1916

■ QUEEN AND GUTTERSNIPE OF CITIES

Freshly crowned as America's Second City by the 1890 census, Chicago staged a world's fair in 1893 that flew directly in the face of a disastrous economic depression. The World's Columbian Exposition brought the glittering fantasy of an electrically lighted "White City" to the South Side lakefront, while a "Gray City" of unemployment and anxiety lurked beyond the fairgrounds. It was a moment that spotlighted the chasm—especially wide during the Gilded Age but always a yawning gap in Chicago's social landscape—between the grand visions professed by the powerful and the grimmer realities faced by so many others. "Chicago, queen and guttersnipe of cities, cynosure and cesspool of the world!" declaimed English journalist George W. Steevens after an 1896 visit. He surveyed the "splendid chaos" as

> . . . the most beautiful and the most squalid, girdled with a twofold zone of parks and slums; where the keen air from lake and prairie is ever in the nostrils, and the stench of foul smoke is never out of the throat; the great port a thousand miles from the sea; the great mart which gathers up with one hand the corn and cattle of the West and deals out with the other the merchandise of the East; widely and generously planned with streets of 20 miles, where it is not safe to walk at night; where women ride straddlewise, and millionaires dine at midday on the Sabbath; the chosen seat of public spirit and municipal boodle, of cut-throat commerce and munificent patronage of art; the most American of American cities, and yet the most mongrel.

This "miracle of paradox and incongruity" that amazed visitors like Steevens was wrought from a new cycle of expansion and development in the two decades following the Great Fire. The prosperity "ushered in one of the most important epochs in Chicago's history," in the words of Mayer and Wade's *Chicago: Growth of a Metropolis.* The most inspired Chicago creation of the era was the skyscraper, a distinctive urban form that has since utterly reshaped skylines from Alaska to Australia. Maitland's *Dictionary of American Slang* defined the new word "skyscraper" in 1891 as "a very tall building such as are now being built in Chicago."

Louis H. Sullivan was the maestro of the emerging Chicago School of architecture, and his description of the 16-story Monadnock Building, designed by Daniel H. Burnham and John W. Root in 1891, succinctly captured the skyscraper magic:

The opening of the World's Columbian Exposition in 1893 boosted the morale of Americans during a deep economic depression. (Underwood Photo Archives)

"An amazing cliff of brickwork, rising sheer and stark, with a subtlety of line and surface, a direct singleness of purpose, that gives one the thrill of romance." The Monadnock and a sturdy band of its landmark contemporaries still tower to delight visitors, who are left in no doubt during even the briefest downtown tour that Chicago remains a vital bastion of modern architecture.

The same businessmen financing the fledgling skyscrapers endowed a diadem of new cultural institutions that continue to offer world-class enticements: the Chicago Symphony Orchestra was born in 1891, and the Art Institute of Chicago opened the following year. A legacy of the World's Columbian Exposition was the massive neoclassical building that housed first the Field Museum of Natural History (later resettled closer to the Loop) and now the perennially popular Museum of Science and Industry. The preservation of the lakefront for public pleasure, a revelation to travelers from cities less fortunate, was sanctified as public policy in Burnham's famous Chicago Plan of 1909. "Make no little plans," Burnham urged, and the sunnier side of the city's life bears the stamp of his foresight.

The first meat train leaving a Chicago stockyard under escort of the United States Cavalry during the great Pullman (railway) Strike of 1894. (Chicago Historical Society)

But the same magnates who could be so generous to the arts typically practiced the age's industrial ethos of paying their workers as little as possible for laboring 60 hours a week or longer under conditions too often satanic. Labor unrest sparked some of the city's unhappiest episodes: the Haymarket bombing of 1886, which killed eight policemen and brought death sentences to eight socialist-anarchists in a trial of very doubtful justice; and the Pullman Strike of 1894, crushed by U.S. Army troops after the sleeping-car mogul cut wages sharply in his company town on the South Side.

The advent of Hull House, where Jane Addams began her seminal work in 1889 with impoverished immigrants on the West Side, spoke to the desperate straits of a rapidly growing tenement population. Witness this 1906 Addams description of one housing block, not far from where the Chicago Fire had begun 35 years earlier:

> The streets are inexpressibly dirty, the number of schools inadequate, sanitary legislation unenforced, the street lighting bad, the paving miserable and altogether lacking in the alleys and smaller streets, and the stables foul beyond description. Hundreds of houses are unconnected with the street sewer. The older and richer inhabitants seem anxious to move away as rapidly as they can afford it. They make room for newly arrived immigrants who are densely ignorant of civic duties.

The lowest rung on the residential ladder was reserved for blacks, who were arriving in Chicago from the South for the first time in substantial numbers. As the city's black population rose from 3,700 in 1870 to 30,000 in 1900 and to 110,000 by 1920, segregation formed a "Black Belt" ghetto stretching along State Street from 16th Street south toward 55th. A survey of this South Side area in 1913 found only a quarter of the buildings in good repair, according to *Chicago: Growth of a Metropolis,* and one-third still had outdoor toilets. "Yet rents for Negro housing were never less than for comparable white housing and commonly ran 25 percent more." Tensions fueled by rapid expansion of the ghetto during World War I touched off a race riot in July, 1919, that left 23 blacks and 15 whites dead. The riot's six days "were the worst the city had known since the Great Fire," concluded the *Growth of a Metropolis* authors. "Mobs pulled blacks from streetcars, bands roamed neighborhoods, homes were sacked and burned. Finally the governor sent in the troops. Peace was restored, but the scars could not be easily erased, for the grim affair left deep wells of guilt and remorse, hate and bigotry. Worse still, conditions did not change, and the ghetto continued to expand and fester."

Of course, there were city departments charged with such matters as sweeping the streets and maintaining the peace. But too many officials devoted their energies to self-enrichment rather than public duties in a city redoubtably corrupt even by the loose standards of the Robber Baron decades. A champion among boodlers —those who dished out the bribes—was transit wheeler-dealer Charles T. Yerkes, who finally lost his lucrative streetcar franchises at the turn of the century. Most visible among the "gray wolves," the aldermen with their hands out, were "Bathhouse John" Coughlin and Michael "Hinky Dink" Kenna, whose First Ward domain emcompassed the Loop along with the red-light district known as the Levee. Their shady legend is etched in Chicago history for the First Ward Ball they hosted each Christmas season at the old Coliseum as a Democratic fundraiser. "It's a lollapalooza," Hinky Dink said of the 1908 ball, where 10,000 magnums of champagne and 35,000 quarts of beer were consumed. "All the business houses are here, all the big people. Chicago ain't no sissy."

No sissy, indeed. This was the city that invented the smoke-filled room, that locked-door cliche of cigar-chomping politicians bent on shifty deals. It happened at the 1920 Republican National Convention, just as predicted by Warren G.

Quintessential ward politicians, Johnny "De Pow" Powers (right), boss of Chicago's 19th Ward and a conniving politico often challenged by Jane Addams, is here seen with the "Prince of Boodlers," "Hinky Dink" Kenna at a Democratic party function. (Kogan Collection)

Harding's campaign manager, Harry Daugherty. He had told the *New York Times* months earlier that the GOP convention would be deadlocked and eventually decided by a small group of men "sitting around a table in a smoke-filled room" at about two o'clock in the morning. That's exactly how Harding sewed up the nomination, in Suite 804-805 at the Blackstone Hotel.

■ CITY THAT SOMETIMES WORKS

A moon-faced New York thug named Alphonse Capone hit Chicago in 1920: Prohibition had arrived the previous January along with his twentieth birthday. Capone soon became the Babe Ruth of mobsters, riding the Roaring Twenties tidal wave of bootleg booze to wealth and worldwide notoriety. He remains to many, alas, Chicago's most famous denizen—almost a half-century after he died of syphilis following eight years in Alcatraz for income tax evasion. In fact, he survives larger than life: introduce yourself as a Chicagoan, almost anywhere from Buenos Aires to Bangkok, and the response may well include a pantomimed machine gun with a "rat-a-tat-tat" flourish. A Chicago outfit called **Untouchable Tours** stokes the legend with guided visits to such gangland meccas as the site of the 1929 St. Valentine's Day Massacre. (See "PRACTICAL INFORMATION.")

The truth is that the vast majority of Prohibition-era Chicagoans faced no closer brush with mobster violence than the inkstains from their newspaper headlines. In the peak tommy-gun year, 1926, police recorded 75 gangland slayings—less than 10 percent of the annual Chicago murder count in the 1990s, for a city with roughly the same population then as now. A great deal of more consequence was happening in the 1920s to shape the metropolis that is Chicago today. Henry Justin Smith, distinguished editor of the old *Chicago Daily News*, detailed some "symptoms of the renaissance." They included: "development of the lakefront; street, park and boulevard improvements; new bridges; straightening of an eccentric, embarrassing river branch; expansion of transportation service; track elevation program; new university buildings, especially for medical service; and a tremendous array of industrial and commercial structures, hotels, theaters, and so on."

Not that Chicago flourished as a white-gloved model of civic propriety beyond the purview of Capone and his rival gangs. The *WPA Guide to Illinois*, a splendid volume published originally in 1939, recalled the "chauvinistic clowning of Mayor

William Hale Thompson," who served three terms between 1915 and 1931, in an era "climaxed by the emergence of the 'wide-open town.' The enormous trade in alcohol and beer, gambling and prostitution, and the various 'rackets' preying on legitimate businesses moved smoothly; the conviction of a gangster was extremely rare."

The Great Depression, which began with the Wall Street Crash of 1929 and lingered almost until America's entry into World War II in 1941, brought crushing human misery to Chicago and its Cook County suburbs as elsewhere. Nearly 1,400 families were evicted from their homes in the first half of 1931 alone. The *Chicago Times* of October 3, 1931, described 1,500 huddled men waiting for food on the lower level of Michigan Avenue near Wacker Drive: "Some were young, others old, their clothes were shabby but not tattered. Everywhere the men carried huge rolls of old newspapers or lay covered by the sprawling black and white sheets." Hardest hit by the spiraling unemployment was Chicago's rising population of 250,000 blacks, then about seven percent of the city's total.

At the nadir of the Depression, Chicago managed to stage its second successful world's fair. The Century of Progress exposition, occupying 47 acres of newly created lakefront south of the Loop, attracted 39 million visitors during its 1933-34 run and wound up with a cash surplus after repaying its debts and issuing bondholders their six percent dividend. The star of the world's fair turned out to be not its futuristic architecture or glittering exhibits of technological prowess, but rather a fan dancer named Sally Rand who became a household word for artfully choreographed naughtiness.

World War II brought prosperity back to Chicago with an unparalleled surge of defense-related employment. As America became "the arsenal of democracy," Chicago rose to be its principal industrial bulwark; the $1.3 billion spent to build war plants in the city was unmatched anywhere else in the country. At the high-tech end of the spectrum, the Atomic Age awoke beneath the stands of Stagg Field at the University of Chicago on December 2, 1942, when a team of scientists led by Enrico Fermi achieved the first controlled nuclear reaction. That portentous site is now marked by a brooding Henry Moore sculpture.

Chicago emerged from the victorious war desperately short of housing, especially for its nearly 500,000 black citizens, who were effectively excluded by residential segregation from the accelerating suburban boom that began with returning veterans and continues today. "In Chicago, all the extremes and extremities of the region reach a grand climax," observed British writer David Graham Hutton in *Midwest at Noon,* published in 1946.

*W*ithin a minute or two's walk of the splendid stores and hotels and offices in the Loop, you pass the flophouses of West Madison, Canal and North Clark streets; the hiring office for casual railroad laborers ('Good Eats Provided' painted white on the windows); the terrible slums and Negro district near the stockyards; the waste lands near the railyards; the hangouts of the bums and especially of the old, wrinkled, slow-moving, pathetic bums.

In his unflattering 1950 portrait, *The Second City,* New Yorker A. J. Liebling wrote: "Chicago wore a grin that might have indicated punch drunkenness."

The city reached its peak population of just over 3.6 million in the 1950 census, a figure then 65 percent of the metropolitan area's total. It would increasingly have to learn to coexist with the suburbs; by the most recent census, the city's shrinking population of 2.8 million would represent only 35 percent of the 8.1 million in the greater Chicago area. Residentially, even as African-Americans became the city's largest ethnic group by 1990, Chicago would continue to vie for the dubious title bestowed in 1957 by Chicago Urban League President Edwin Berry: Most Segregated City in the United States.

WEARY OF CHICAGO

I am already (after 17 days of the 'Great Middle West') rather spent and weary, weary of motion and chatter, and oh, of such an unimagined dreariness of *ugliness* (on many, on most sides!) and of the perpetual effort of trying to 'do justice' to what one doesn't like. If one could only damn it and have done with it! So much of it is rank with good intentions. . . . This Chicago is huge, *infinite* (of potential size and form, and even of actual) black, smoky, *old*-looking, very like some preternaturally *boomed* Manchester or Glasgow lying beside a colossal lake (Michigan) of hard pale green jade, and putting forth railway antennae of maddening complexity and gigantic length.

—Henry James, *Letter to Edward Warren,* 1905

Richard J. Daley bestrode Chicago's body politic as the colossal Hizzoner for six mayoral terms from 1955 until his death in 1976. His Chicago was "the city that works," a resuscitated urban bruiser of new expressways, skyscrapers, and other major projects. O'Hare International Airport, which opened in 1955, soon became the world's busiest airport (a title that harried travelers might consider more of a curse than an honor). The forest of fresh skyscrapers would include the world's tallest building: the Sears Tower at the southwest fringe of downtown, topped off in 1974, and still champion at 110 stories and 1,454 feet. But two unrelated events near the dawn of the Daley era foreshadowed the shift to a post-industrial society: Hugh Hefner published the first issue of *Playboy* from his Chicago apartment in 1953, and Ray Kroc opened the first franchised McDonald's in the suburb of Des Plaines in 1955.

The search for Chicago's soul in the waning years of the twentieth century is an elusive matter. As Harold M. Mayer and Richard C. Wade noted, the spot that the

Mayor Richard J. Daley celebrates his 1955 election as mayor of Chicago at home with his family in the Bridgeport neighborhood. Future mayor Richard M. Daley is seated in the middle. (Chicago Sun-Times)

illustrious Burnham Plan of 1909 "had marked for the civic heart of Chicago is now the site of the most elaborate expressway interchange in the city. Just west of the Loop where Burnham had located a domed civic center, the Kennedy, Dan Ryan and Eisenhower come together in a baffling maze of ramps, overpasses, underpasses, entrances and exits." The expressways have cut the heart out of formerly flourishing neighborhoods and provided handy corridors for suburban flight. It is said that many current residents of Du Page and other collar counties rarely if ever come to Chicago; for them, it is an out-of-town destination almost as distant mentally as New York or Los Angeles.

Since Richard J. Daley's death, Chicago has seen its first woman mayor (Jane Byrne) and its first black mayor (Harold Washington, who died in office of heart failure in 1987). Illinois elected its first female black senator in 1992, Carol Moseley-Braun. Meanwhile Chicago entered the '90s in a kind of mayoral déjà vu with Richard M. Daley, son of Hizzoner, solidly in office and keeping his family roots in the South Side Bridgeport neighborhood as his father did. The city's economy was shifting its Industrial Age brawn to Computer Age brain more adroitly than many Rust Belt centers, but still facing a dwindling job base. Drugs and street gangs were elevating murder rates to frightening levels, and the school system was failing to educate uncounted thousands of students left adrift by broken homes and aimless parents.

So you may find that today's Chicagoans seem less ebullient than their civic ancestors were when Carl Sandburg cast them as a "bragging and laughing" breed. They may look more bent by the lacerating winter wind, and they may appear less charitably inclined toward the proliferating handout supplicants along the Magnificent Mile and other downtown thoroughfares. They may sound more cynical than ever about the politicians who are forever hiking their taxes and the public payrollers whose loafing skills remain a legend. Enough give up on their city each year that the population continues its downward slide.

But Chicago is still a vital and astonishing place, as much so today as when Mark Twain saw it in 1883: "a city where they are always rubbing the lamp and fetching up the genii, and contriving and achieving new impossibilities. It is hopeless for the occasional visitor to try to keep up with Chicago—she outgrows his prophecies faster than he can make them. She is always a novelty; for she is never the Chicago you saw when you passed through the last time." At a more personal level, on the best days, it is still the place an East Coast visitor in 1873 described as "New York with the heart left in."

ARCHITECTURE

IF CHICAGO IS THE CAPITAL OF ANYTHING, it is the world capital of modern architecture. The skyscraper, now swaggering lord of the metropolis around the globe, was born and nurtured a century ago on this swampy Midwest soil. Only New York can lay any serious claim to rival Chicago as the prime hothouse for urban life's heavenward thrust—with all its human consequences both happy and hellish—in the handful of generations since the church spire ceased to be the highest point on America's skylines. Whatever else a visitor sees and does in Chicago, here for the taking is a dazzling crash course in the complex and conflicting architectural currents that have helped shape the twentieth century's sinew and soul—from Louis H. Sullivan and Frank Lloyd Wright to Ludwig Mies van der Rohe and today's Post-Modern pluralists.

Why Chicago? It was obviously fertile ground after the 1871 fire had razed the heart of town, "and architects, sensing the opportunities that Christopher Wren had had after the Great Fire of London, came seeking work," posited the critic Robert Hughes in *The Shock of the New*, written for his provocative public-television series of 1981. These architects "found their blank slate, in more than one sense: Chicago had no traditions, no polish, and no interest in either. It was a brawling, hog-gut city, whose one rule of urban development was to grab the block and screw the neighbor." Louis H. Sullivan, the brooding genius of Chicago architecture's richest decades, said that he felt here "an intoxicating rawness, a sense of big things to be done. For 'big' was the word." To him, Chicagoans were "the crudest, rawest, most savagely ambitious dreamers and doers in the world."

Boston financier Peter Brooks observed presciently in 1880 that "tall buildings will pay well in Chicago hereafter, and sooner or later a way will be made to erect them." The safety elevator, invented by Elisha Otis in 1857, was undergoing steady refinement as a highrise prerequisite for the non-mountaineering bulk of the population. Fireproofing was making great strides with lessons learned from the 1871 fire. The floating-raft foundation and other anchoring techniques used to distribute load gave taller structures the necessary stability in Chicago's soft and sandy soil. In 1880, the tallest downtown buildings stood five or six stories. By the end of that decade, the future Loop boasted a thicket of structures towering a dozen stories or higher—including a few bold pioneers of what the pre-eminent

A collection of Chicago's most famous architecture catches the light of the setting sun.

critic Carl Condit has called "the most radical transformation in the structural art since the development of the Gothic system of construction in the twelfth century."

The innovation, essential to skyscraper technology, was the skeletal frame of iron and steel. This load-bearing grid of muscular metal lifted the burden of carrying a building's weight from the walls, where it had rested since antiquity; for the first time, an exterior wall didn't need to grow thicker as a structure rose higher. The metamorphosis of the modern building "from a crustacean with its armor of stone to a vertebrate clothed only in a light skin," as Condit aptly visualized it, was manifest in William LeBaron Jenney's design for the nine-story **Home Insurance Building**. Completed in 1885 at the northeast corner of La Salle and Adams streets, this was "the major progenitor of the true skyscraper, the first adequate solution to the problem of large-scale urban construction." Don't rush to Chicago's financial canyon to admire it, though; like too many of the city's architectural landmarks, Jenney's transitional keystone fell casualty to the wrecker's ball (in 1931). Still standing at 431 South Dearborn is his 16-story **Manhattan Building**, completed in 1890 as the first skyscraper constructed totally with a weight-carrying iron and steel frame. The possibilities for a building's facade, including walls of glass, would become virtually unlimited. One

Chicago's skyline circa 1950 before the predominance of steel and glass skyscrapers. (Underwood Photo Archives)

early hallmark, the Chicago window, featured a large fixed pane flanked by two smaller sash windows.

Meanwhile, the masters of what came to be known as the Chicago School of architecture paid homage to the old methods in three of the city's most illustrious buildings, which Condit labeled "the final monuments of the art of masonry architecture" in a tradition stretching back past the Gothic cathedrals to the ancient Romans and beyond. Still standing after various twentieth-century vicissitudes, they are Burnham and Root's **Rookery Building** (1886), Adler and Sullivan's **Auditorium Building** (1889), and Burnham and Root's 16-story **Monadnock Building** (1891), which stretched load-bearing masonry walls to their height limits. Along with Burnham's **Reliance Building** (1895) and Sullivan's **Carson Pirie Scott and Company Store** (1899, 1903-04), they form a pantheon of Chicago School glories that partisans cherish as icons of a heroic age in American architecture. "The high tides of Chicago building rose long ago," Condit wrote wistfully in 1980. His beloved Chicago School is an umbrella term for commercial structures marked by humane functionalism, skillful ornamentation, and vertical power. "A building is an act," Sullivan repeatedly declared—and he meant the act to be moral as well as aesthetic.

The Rookery's interior courtyard, magnificently restored in 1991, reflects the genius of America's most illustrious twentieth-century architect, Frank Lloyd Wright. In 1905, Wright undertook a commission to remodel the building's lobby and light court, which he executed in an elaborate but disciplined profusion of gold and ivory. It is necessary to go a bit farther afield to savor the array of Wright-designed private homes in the Chicago area, most notably **Robie House**, the quintessential Prairie School residence with its strong horizontal thrust (in Hyde Park, seven miles [11.2 km] south of the Loop), and Wright's own house and studio (in the western suburb of Oak Park). "I loved the prairie by instinct, as, itself, a great simplicity," he wrote. Even a cursory Wright circuit provides a refreshing reminder that Chicago's architectural prowess is far from solely based on its penchant for flinging up skyscrapers. In contrast to the vigorous upward thrust of Chicago School skyscrapers, the flowing horizontal planes ingrained in the Prairie School precepts of Wright and his disciples convey a solid peace and calm.

Like Wright, Sullivan was a thinking man's architect who brought philosophy as well as technology into focus. He "taught that the language of modern society is both science and romance, both fact and belief, and that the two must be wedded in one statement," wrote biographer Albert Bush-Brown in 1960. "He broadened the technology of his own day by making it poetic, and he brought it as a symbol to serve the institutions of industrial society; his art arose from his organization of the scientific ideas, technical means, utilitarian demands, and romantic beliefs of his age." Sullivan insisted that architecture embrace what became known as "functionalism." And he understood the characteristic function of the office skyscraper to be its loftiness—"the very organ-tone in its appeal," as he once wrote. "It must be tall, every inch of it tall. The force and power of altitude must be in it, the glory and pride of exaltation must be in it. It must be every inch a proud and soaring thing, rising in sheer exaltation that from bottom to top it is a unit without a single dissenting line."

Sullivan and his Chicago School followers also believed that architecture must be democratic. As the critic Hugh Dalziel Duncan has written, "Sullivan taught that democracy depended on its architects as much as on its statesmen or businessmen." But it is well worth remembering, with Duncan, that these seminal Chicago buildings "were not constructed by the city, by religious organizations, by educational institutions, or by private groups as palatial edifices. They were built by businessmen and they were built for profit. Even the Auditorium, which was the civic

Frank Lloyd Wright's famous Robie House (above) in Hyde Park is a classic example of Prairie School architecture. Its flowing horizontal planes make an interesting contrast to the pastiche of styles in the Wrigley Building and to the neo-Gothic Tribune Tower (right).

and cultural center of Chicago for many years, was built to make money. It was a civic center, a hotel, and an office building. It was financed like any other business venture on the expectation of profit." That bottom-line mindset helps explain the shameful track record of demolitions, verging on corporate vandalism, that cost the city such masterpieces as Sullivan's Garrick Theater Building (leveled in 1961 to erect a parking garage) and Adler and Sullivan's Old Stock Exchange (torn down in 1972 to make way for a nondescript office tower that soon slid into bankruptcy). Only in recent years have preservation laws provided a reasonable guarantee that landmarks highlighted in a book like this will survive to greet twenty-first-century visitors.

The commercial impetus also accounts for Chicago's boom-and-bust cycles of new architecture. The economic depression of 1893 brought a construction slump after the first flowering of Chicago School structures, as well as a municipal height limit of ten stories for new buildings to counter the over-supply of skyscraper office space. The height limit went up to 260 feet (78 m) in 1902 and fell back to 200 feet (61 m) in 1911, in step with changing business fortunes. (There are essentially no limits today, assuming that the proper setbacks and step-backs are factored into a given site.)

The Merchandise Mart, "Largest Building in the World" when it was completed in 1929, became one of several Chicago architectural superlatives. (Underwood Photo Archives)

Another burst of architectural fecundity ensued in the Roaring Twenties, styled by Condit a second "heroic age" for the city's skyline. The **Wrigley Building**, a confection sheathed in white terra-cotta to enchant by floodlight, unfurled the decade with a beguiling dose of Michigan Avenue whoopee. The Tribune Tower rose in a majesty as Neo-Gothic as the mind of resident press lord Col. Robert McCormick, and the spirit of Eliel Saarinen's second-prize design in the *Tribune's* international competition leaped south across the river to influence the **333 North Michigan Avenue** tower, an Art Deco gem designed by Holabird and Root. The Art Deco impulse—with its bold silhouettes and streamlined rectilinear forms—gave fresh vitality to other Jazz Age stalwarts such as the **Chicago Board of Trade**, topped with an aluminum statue of Ceres and opened in 1930 as the gloom of the Great Depression descended.

After two decades of economic slumber and world war, Chicago architecture awoke to find itself a handmaiden of the sleek and unadorned International Style in the person of Ludwig Mies van der Rohe, who had brought his soaring reputation across the Atlantic in 1938 and designed the new Illinois Institute of Technology campus. The Miesian motto "Less Is More" swept ornament before it, in Chicago as elsewhere. The city boasts some of his most renowned buildings, including the twin apartment towers at **860-880 North Lake Shore Drive**, the **Federal Center** in the south Loop, and the riverside IBM **Building**, his last major office design (1971). Mies and his disciples preached a gospel of naked structuralism that emphasized the telling of truth—a credo of honesty that Sullivan and his Chicago School peers had also espoused but with quite a different thrust. Decoration was an essential element of Sullivan's best buildings, while the International Style eschewed it. "No noodles," was Mies' shorthand, and that austere code ruled as skylines soared on six continents starting in the 1950s to emulate Chicago and New York.

It is tempting to label the reigning motif of Chicago architecture in the 1980s and '90s as "Gigantism"—although Post-Modernist pluralism serves as a more definitive net to cast over the astounding variety of designs that have peppered the city's skyline in reaction to the dethroned rigors of the International Style. Detail and ornament are back in good graces, along with richer colors and touches of whimsy in even some of the highest newcomers. By a recent count, Chicago can claim nine of the world's 35 tallest buildings, including the 1,454-foot (442-m) **Sears Tower**, king of the highrise hill since it went up in 1974 on the southwest fringe of the Loop—even if Sears management has now deserted the colossal

BALLET OF BRIDGES

One of the most impressive ballets a visitor is likely to view in Chicago can also be one of the most aggravating for drivers and pedestrians who happen to be in a hurry. This outdoor spectacle is the synchronized raising and lowering of Chicago River bridges to allow the passage of pleasure boats from spring through fall. Twenty of these spans cross the river in an arc running from Lake Shore Drive to the Eisenhower Expressway, and the city boasts 52 movable bridges in all. The local bridge count hardly ranks in the same big leagues with such canal-laced cities as Venice and Amsterdam, but the up-and-down performances that Chicago's bridges present when the yachts come through is like nothing you'll see in Italy or Holland.

Virtually all Chicago's movable bridges are trunnion bascules, a design so identified with the city that it is known internationally as the "Chicago style." Bascule is derived from the French word for "seesaw," and that's roughly how the bridges work, pivoting on a horizontal shaft (the trunnion). When not in action, they look like stubby workaday spans, but their profiles are endowed with touches of class. *Chicago Tribune* architecture critic Blair Kamin has written of "bridge-tender houses that seem transplanted from the boulevards of Paris; handsome ornamental railings; majestic pylons; leaded mansard roofs; delightful relief sculpture."

You'll have a few minutes to admire these details while waiting to cross when the bridges go up. Particularly notable is the **Michigan Avenue bridge**, now an official city landmark, built in 1920 as the first of its kind to carry two levels of traffic. Its neighbor to the east, the 269-foot (81.8-m) **Columbus Drive bridge**, ranks as the world's second-longest trunnion bascule design (exceeded only by a 295-foot [89.7-m] span over Spain's Bay of Cadiz).

The less conspicuous **Kinzie bridge**, spanning the north branch of the Chicago River, played a supporting role in the most invisible major disaster in the city's history. Pilings sunk into the river bed to protect the span from being hit by boats punctured one of the abandoned and little-known (at the time) tunnels that had carried freight around downtown Chicago earlier this century. The puncture ruptured in April of 1992, unleashing the great subterranean flood that brought the Loop to its knees. But that's another story, best saved for a rainy day.

The central city area has 20 drawbridges which rise and fall in synchronization across the Chicago River, much to the aggravation of motorists and pedestrians.

cloud-tickler in favor of a suburban headquarters. The 1,136-foot (345-m) **Amoco Building** (ranking seventh worldwide and reclad in speckled granite after its white-marble skin began loosening) and the 1,127-foot (343-m) **John Hancock Center** (No. 8 globally) can expect no new rivals soon in their rarefied precincts, given the office-building slow-down here in the late twentieth century. Of Chicago's Biggest Three, the Hancock is the favorite among architecture critics. For the Sears and Amoco blockbusters, "More Is Less" sums up the reviews.

The bulk of Chicago's landmark buildings, Wright's work being a principal exception, are concentrated within comfortable walking distance of each other in an orbit radiating no more than a mile (1.6 km) in any direction from the Loop. The density adds to the impact of the crash course dished up by the city's architectural banquet. It heightens what critic Duncan called "the power of these great Chicago buildings. They are a humane expression of a new way of life—the modern urban community based on money and technology. They are humane because the architects of the Chicago School have followed the teachings of their master, Sullivan. 'With me,' he said, 'architecture is not an art, but a religion, and that religion but a part of democracy.'"

Chicago—still amply endowed with crude, raw, savagely ambitious dreamers and doers—often enough fails to keep the architectural faith that Sullivan professed. But when its buildings are good, they can be very good indeed.

TOP 21: ARCHITECTURE'S CORE CURRICULUM

There are hundreds of Chicago buildings, along with some entire neighborhoods such as the nineteenth-century Pullman model town on the Far South Side, that richly reward the time and curiosity of visitors with even a passing interest in architecture. But the 21 big leaguers presented here make as good a core curriculum as any for the hurried connoisseur. These selections are by no means chiseled in concrete, and a half-dozen other compilers might produce a half-dozen variants of our must-see regimen.

For further guidance, an essential resource is the Chicago Architecture Foundation, which operates an extensive syllabus of worthwhile tours from its headquarters at 224 South Michigan Avenue (in the recently refurbished Railway Exchange Building, a D. H. Burnham and Company gem from 1904 adorned with gleaming white terra-cotta). The foundation's architectural bookstore is richly stocked.

This Top 21 sampler runs in chronological order, with the years the structures were erected, the architects, and the locations:

Rookery Building (*1886* Burnham and Root, *209 S. LaSalle*). Named whimsically for the pigeons that inhabited the temporary City Hall built on the site following the Chicago Fire of 1871, the Rookery combines exterior strength and grace with a freshly restored 1905 Frank Lloyd Wright lobby and light court that is breathtakingly exquisite.

Auditorium Building (*1889* Adler and Sullivan, *Michigan and Congress*). Roosevelt University now occupies much of this mixed-use Chicago School landmark, distinguished for its ornamental splendor. It's worth attending any performance in Louis H. Sullivan's Auditorium Theater merely to admire the lavish design details, carefully restored in the 1960s by architect Harry Weese after the derelict stage had been used as a servicemen's bowling alley during World War II.

Monadnock Building (*1891* Burnham and Root, *53 W. Jackson*). Load-bearing walls six feet thick at the base support the rhythmically projecting bays of purple-brown brick unadorned by ornamentation. The southern addition of 1893, designed by Holabird and Roche, employs the then-novel skeletal-frame construction.

continues on page 65

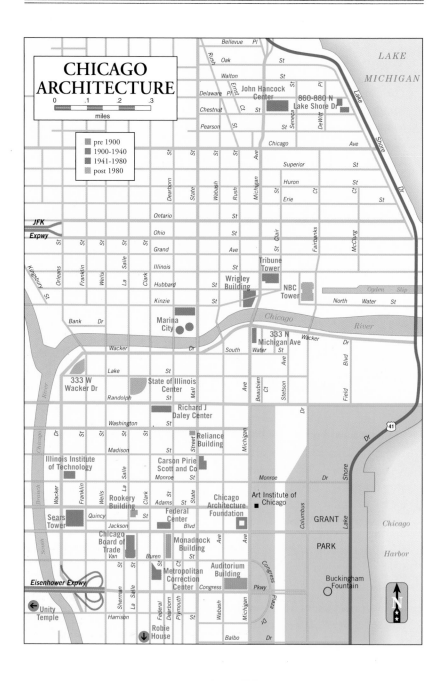

CHICAGO
ARCHITECTURE

0   .1   .2   .3
miles

■ pre 1900
■ 1900-1940
■ 1941-1980
■ post 1980

Reliance Building (*1895* D.H. Burnham, *36 N. State*). In appearance an ornamented precursor of the glass-wall design promulgated by the International Style in the mid-twentieth century, the Reliance with its slender piers and narrow spandrels ranks as perhaps the most elegant Chicago School skyscraper.

Carson Pirie Scott & Company Store (*1899, 1903-04* Louis H. Sullivan, *1 S. State*). This Loop department store, in the judgment of critic Carl Condit, is Sullivan's "unchallenged masterpiece. It is the ultimate achievement of the Chicago School and one of the great works of modern commercial architecture in the world." Sullivan's functionalism here focuses the shopper's eye on the merchandise-filled display windows.

Unity Temple (*1906* Frank Lloyd Wright, *875 Lake, Oak Park*). One of Wright's most famous buildings, this Unitarian Universalist church and parish house in a near-west suburb is an early example of reinforced-concrete use. The interior is delicately illuminated by a golden-paned skylight and clerestory windows.

Robie House (*1909* Frank Lloyd Wright, *5757 S. Woodlawn*). The University of Chicago owns this Prairie School landmark that forcefully carries Wright's horizontal motif in its broad overhanging roof and long limestone sills. The very private entrance is at the back of the house.

Wrigley Building (*1921, 1924* Graham, Anderson, Probst and White, *400 N. Michigan Ave.*). "The great bravura performance of Chicago architecture," according to Condit, the Wrigley Building should be seen floodlit after dark to fully savor "the unashamed hedonism, sheer visual drama to excite the eye." Exterior details were inspired by the Giralda Tower in Seville, Spain.

Tribune Tower (*1925* Hood and Howells, *435 N. Michigan Ave.*). The winner of a famous international competition, this Gothic Revival skyscraper design by two New York architects soars heavenward like a medieval cathedral complete with flying buttresses near the pinnacle. Embedded in its walls are stones from Westminster Abbey, the Alamo, Hamlet's castle, the Great Pyramid, the Taj Mahal, Fort Sumter, the Arc de Triomphe, and others.

continues on page 68

The staircase of the Rookery Building demonstrates both the functionalism and grace which are hallmarks of Chicago School architecture.

State of Illinois Center on the Loop dazzles the eye with sunlight and mirror-like reflections.

333 North Michigan Avenue (*1928* Holabird and Root). The first of Chicago's distinctive Art Deco skyscrapers, this slablike 35-story gem diagonally across the river from the Wrigley Building is ornamented in geometric low relief. Scenes from early Chicago history frame the windows of the fifth floor.

Chicago Board of Trade Building (*1930* Holabird and Root, *141 W. Jackson*). Outside, the Art Deco thrust is entirely vertical to anchor the south end of LaSalle Street's financial canyon. Inside, the sleekly polished three-story lobby articulates the Art Deco gospel with astonishing vigor.

860-880 N. Lake Shore Drive Apartments (*1952* Mies van der Rohe). People fated to live in glass houses can count themselves fortunate if they reside in this architecturally refined pair of towers considered exemplars of the unadorned Miesian principles. He later designed the nearby glasswall apartments at 900-910 Lake Shore.

Marina City (*1964, 1967* Bertrand Goldberg Associates, *300 N. State*). In a total departure from the severe rectilinear patterns of the International Style, Goldberg's organic approach to this much-photographed pair of circular 60-story towers features cantilevered balconies that give (in Condit's words) "the lively appearance of a vertical succession of flower petals."

Federal Center (*1964-1975* Mies van der Rohe and others, *219 S. Dearborn*). Alexander Calder's 53-foot-tall red "Flamingo" stabile adds a spark of color to this 4.5-acre Loop plaza complex of two sleekly spare glass-curtain towers rising 30 and 45 stories with a single-story post office at their feet.

Richard J. Daley Center (*1965* C. F. Murphy Associates, *block bounded by Randolph, Dearborn, Washington, and Clark*). Barebones Miesian motifs are boldly executed in this 31-story courthouse swaggerer that boasts a trio of broad bays a startling 87 feet long and 48 feet wide. The russet color of the self-weathering Cor-Ten steel continues to deepen.

John Hancock Center (*1969* Skidmore, Owings and Merrill, *875 N. Michigan*). The first Chicago giant to break the 1,000-foot mark, Big John rises in a tapering profile that—according to Ira J. Bach in "Chicago's Famous Buildings"—is "more graceful and soaring than the rectangular and paradoxically also gives the impression of maximum stability."

Sears Tower (*1974* Skidmore, Owings and Merrill, *block bounded by Adams, Franklin, Jackson, and Wacker*). Built as a bundle of nine framed tubes, each 75 feet square, the world's tallest building slims to just two tubes at its 110-story summit. Critic Richard Solomon salutes it as "an architectural icon marking the apogee of Modernism as a universal architectural style."

Metropolitan Correctional Center (*1975* Harry Weese and Associates, *71 W. Van Buren*). Even a jail can be an architectural showstopper in Chicago, as witness the knife-edged William J. Campbell U.S. Courthouse Annex (the facility's official name). Its slender triangular design rises 27 stories resembling a gargantuan computer card punched by rows of five-inch-wide windows.

333 West Wacker Drive (*1983* Kohn Pederson Fox). Among the city's new growth of Post-Modernist skyscrapers, this 36-story office tower earns very high marks for the sweeping grace of its 365-foot-long curved wall that matches a bend in the Chicago River, in contrast to its angular other faces looking onto the street.

State of Illinois Center (*1985* Murphy/Jahn, *Randolph and Clark*). Helmut Jahn's dizzying Post-Modern design of dazzling complexity, with its skin of alternating opaque and reflective glass strips, is loved by some and loathed by others (including many of the state employees who spend their days on its 17 atrium-accented floors).

NBC **Tower** (*1989* Skidmore, Owings and Merrill, *200 E. Illinois*). Art Deco returns in style with this 38-story echo of several Chicago masterpieces from the end of the Roaring '20s. It's a testament to the virtues of mining and refining the architectural past—when the result manages to be so creatively deft.

The ornate Wrigley Building may be at its best at night under floodlights.

The smoothly curved front of Post-Modernist 333 West Wacker follows the arc of the Chicago River.

CHICAGO DISTILLED

WHILE ARCHITECTURE IS CHICAGO'S MOST EVIDENT PRIDE, its justly famous buildings merely form the superstructure of this intensely American metropolis. Chicago can be boiled down to its basics—in reality and in legend—as well through its marvelously unexpected heartland lakefront, the human mosaic so rich and tangled, its gangland lore, and its lode of arts and entertainments. These facets are distilled on the pages which follow.

■ FREE AND OPEN LAKEFRONT

Planted in the middle of America, Chicago might figure to be a resolutely inland city focused on the prairies to the west. It's all the more startling for many first-time visitors, then, to discover the ocean at Chicago's doorstep. Well, not an ocean exactly, but Lake Michigan is a mighty inland sea—the world's fourth-largest freshwater lake, stretching far beyond the horizon across 22,300 square miles (57,100 sq km) to depths reaching 900 feet (274 m). As astonishing as the endless expanse of glistening Great Lakes water is the fact that the city's 30-mile (48-km) shoreline, with some notable and lamentable exceptions, has been preserved over more than 150 tempestuous years for the use and pleasure of all its citizens (and delightfully surprised out-of-towners as well).

"On Sunday afternoon, I reached a lake surrounded by green lawns; in the sunlight, the waters reminded me of silk and flashing diamonds; sailing boats were moving over them. It was the luxury of the Côte d'Azur," wrote the French philosopher-author Simone de Beauvoir some decades ago after a stroll through Grant Park just east of the Loop. "There was nothing to remind one of the squalor with its human wreckage. Crowds of people were sitting on the grass in the bright sunshine; there were well-behaved loving couples; young people had got up a game of baseball on the lawns; and children were darting in and out of bushes playing at Indians."

Other cities have shorelines that were originally pristine public playgrounds, as the public-spirited journalist Lois Wille pointed out two decades ago in *Forever Open, Clear and Free: The Struggle for Chicago's Lakefront*, still an instructive and engaging piece of background reading (reissued in 1990). "But of them all, only Chicago preserved such a magnificent stretch for its people," she noted. "Instead of warehouses and shipping docks and granaries and oil storage tanks, we have sand beaches, green lawns, beds of flowers and bicycle paths."

The commitment began in 1836, a year before Chicago's incorporation as a city, when three town fathers mapping out undeveloped tracts for sale set aside the lakefront as public ground "to remain forever open, clear and free" from construction. "With those words, they made a promise to the people of Chicago," wrote Wille. "It was a promise that this city, hustler from its infancy, born and nurtured for shipping, trading and making money, would do what no other city in the world had done. It would give its most priceless land, its infinitely valuable shoreline, to its people. The lakefront would be dedicated to pleasure and beauty, not to commerce and industry."

That promise was kept, with occasional lapses, for a century—during which time Chicago built its string of splendid lakeshore parks (Lincoln, Grant, Burnham, Jackson, Rainbow, Calumet). Wille praised these green jewels as "probably the most stunning park system in the world," with more than half its 2,800 acres created at great expense by filling in the lake. The crusaders in this ongoing campaign included such lordly figures as mail-order magnate Aaron Montgomery Ward, who succesfully fought off turn-of-the-century efforts by a boodling City Council to erect a monstrously large civic center on the downtown lakefront. Articulating the cause with uncommon eloquence was architect and urban designer

Simone de Beauvoir, upon seeing the manicured parks of
Chicago's waterfront on a warm summer day, once declared
"It was the luxury of the Côte d'Azur."
(University of Chicago Archives)

Daniel H. Burnham, whose far-reaching Chicago Plan of 1909 proposed the shoreline chain of grassy islands and shaded lagoons that the city partly created before World War II ended the work. "The lakefront by right belongs to the people," wrote Burnham. "It is a living thing, delighting man's eye and refreshing his spirit." He wanted the shore "made so alluring that it will become the fixed habit of the people to seek its restful presence at every opportunity."

The sylvan aura that graces so much of the Chicago lakefront's 30 miles (48 km) makes the commercial intrusions of the last half-century seem even more unwelcome. These steel and concrete invaders include a sprawling water-filtration plant just north of Navy Pier, and a smaller such facility between 75th and 79th streets on the South Side; Soldier Field, home of the football Bears with its asphalt lagoon of parking lots, at the south end of Grant Park; Meigs Field, a landing strip for private planes, east of the football stadium; the highrise cluster of Illinois Center commercial buildings, Outer Drive East, Harbor Point apartment towers, the 1,136-foot (345-m)-tall Amoco Building to the northeast of the Loop; and the ribbons of new or widened roadway that cut off access to the lake for many miles.

Lincoln Park's North Avenue Beach (above), is one of Chicago's many waterfront parks at which the city's residents find relief from the pressures of urban life. Daniel Burnham, who first proposed the Chicago Plan of 1909 to preserve the lake shoreline for the public, wrote: "The lakefront by right belongs to the people. It is a living thing, delighting man's eye and refreshing his spirit."

Most egregious violator of Burnham's dictum that the lakefront belongs to the people is massive McCormick Place-on-the-Lake, North America's largest convention center with 1.6 million square feet (148,000 sq m) of exhibition space. It squats brazenly on the shore between 21st and 23rd streets, redeemed visually only by the realization that it is less of an eyesore than the original Mc-Cormick Place, which was destroyed by fire in 1967. Undeniably the linchpin of Chicago's profitable convention trade, the center leapt Lake Shore Drive in the 1980s when an annex was erected on railroad land to the west. Aggravating the scene for believers in the open-lakefront dream is the ugly and formidable tangle of ramps and viaducts that connect the Stevenson Expressway with Lake Shore Drive immediately south of McCormick Place. A full mile (1.6 km) of shoreline is effectively inaccessible to pedestrians here.

A visitor aiming to appreciate Chicago's nonpareil lakefront, occasional warts and all, would be remiss in failing to see it at least once from a waterborne perspective. A half-dozen companies operate sightseeing cruises of varying lengths on Lake Michigan and the Chicago River from spring into fall. The quality of on-board commentary varies as well, and there are specialty itineraries including lunch and dinner excursions. Particularly worthwhile is the **Architecture River Cruise** program offered by the Chicago Architecture Foundation, with departures from North Pier near where the river flows out of the lake.

Landlubbers who wish to explore the lakefront at their leisure on foot or bicycle will find that the North Side's five miles (8 km) of Lincoln Park hiking and biking paths make the most congenial venue. **Grant Park** is a field of dreams for museum-going pedestrians, who can begin at the Art Institute, then stroll south to the Field Museum, Shedd Aquarium, and Adler Planetarium. Some other stretches of lakefront are tough going for walkers and cyclists. The most thorough way to sample the shore's allures in a single day is by automobile with frequent stops at chosen attractions. Driving the 124 blocks of Lake Shore Drive from Hollywood Boulevard in the north to Jackson Park in the south provides a grand tour of Chicago's shoreline.

However you get about, your journey may be spiced by a music festival, ethnic gathering, marathon race, or some other activity in one of the lakefront parks. That pleasure-for-the-people focus, promoted since the mid-1970s by the city's post-Richard J. Daley mayors, "has repopulated much of the parkland from dawn to dark," observes Gerald D. Suttles in the new foreword to the 1990 edition of Wille's book. Suttles thinks these events, most notably the perenially thronged festival Taste of Chicago, "have grown to the point that during much of the summer portions of the lakefront resemble a suburban franchise row of restaurants. Yet the crowds are genial and diverse. It is possible, of course, that they are a little numbed by high caloric intake, alcohol, and rock-and-roll music."

Daniel H. Burnham, who preached that the lakefront belongs by right to the common man, presumably would have approved of these latter-day festivities—even while he winced at the noise levels.

■ HUMAN MOSAIC

Both pride and shame are clearly reflected in Chicago's intricate human mosaic. The pride radiates from the city's vital and ongoing role, beginning with the arrival of Irish canal workers in the 1830s, as an economic and social crucible (if not always a melting pot) for immigrants from around the globe. Chicago remains "the most ethnic and culturally diverse of all American cities," according to Richard Lindberg, author of the splendid 1993 *Passport's Guide to Ethnic Chicago*.

Polish neighborhoods remain to this day part of the city's varied human mosaic. This photo of a Polish ecclesiastical goods store was taken in 1872. (Chicago Historical Society)

He locates "the soul of Chicago" not in the bustling Loop or glittering Gold Coast, but in the "ethnic enclaves and side streets seldom previewed by conventioneers and out-of-town guests." The newest waves of immigrants enriching the mosaic include a host of Asians (Koreans, Filipinos, Thais, Vietnamese, Indians, and others); East Europeans and Russians (Jewish as well as non-Jewish); and Hispanics from a dozen Central and South American lands.

As for the shame, it lingers in Chicago's long record as one of the most residentially segregated U.S. cities, a racial blot that still shapes the lives of African-Americans here even after a generation and more of fair-housing laws. The *Chicago Reporter,* an incisive publication focused on race relations, concluded in its twentieth-anniversary issue in 1992 that "blacks, Hispanics, Asians, and American Indians have made solid gains in some quarters. But our reporting also uncovered many disappointments, exposing an expanded and increasingly isolated underclass." Civil-rights laws and slowly changing attitudes have done much to banish "raw, overt racism," the magazine said. "But more subtle forms of racism and discrimination abound" in the Chicago area; one basic reason is that "many whites

(above) This Ukrainian Village store might have been a neighborhood shop in the nineteenth century.

(opposite) The kinta cloth worn by this mother and her son are reminders that ethnic pride plays a role in today's Chicago neighborhoods.

continue to view blacks as physical threats." And spiraling poverty keeps many locked in the ghetto.

Visitors to Chicago, whatever their color or ancestry, are unlikely to venture into the city's most blighted neighborhoods—any more than they would stroll the slums of Rio de Janeiro or Bombay. But they will leave Chicago the poorer for it if they do not bother to gain some sense of how crucial the African-American heritage (along with the traditions and energies of other ethnic and racial groups) has been in making the city what it is today. They also need to understand that population shifts of recent decades have turned Chicago into a city (like others in America) where the minorities now form the majority, circled by a swelling sprawl of suburbs in which the faces remain overwhelmingly white. Only 36.5 percent of the 2.8 million Chicagoans counted by the most recent census are white Americans. African-Americans make up 41.1 percent of the city's population, surpassing white Americans for the first time, while 17.9 percent are Hispanic (the fastest-growing category), and 4.5 percent are Asian or Native American.

More detailed breakdowns from that census make evident "the dilution of European culture" in Chicago described by Lindberg. "Racial fears predicated over real or imaginary concerns about neighborhood safety, the proliferation of gangs and drugs, and a resulting decline in property values compelled the children and grandchildren of many first-generation Europeans to abandon the same inner-city neighborhoods their parents and grandparents inhabited years earlier," he writes. Those shifting realities "inevitably upset the political equilibrium that guided Chicago's destiny since the time of the Civil War."

Indeed, the 1990 census found a single European ethnic group representing an absolute majority of the population in only one of Chicago's 77 officially designated communities (Archer Heights on the Southwest Side, 54.6 percent Polish). By contrast, blacks form a population majority in 31 of those 77 neighborhoods, Mexicans in two others, and Chinese in one. The largest single ethnic group, whether a full majority or not, is African-American in 39 city neighborhoods, Polish in 14, Mexican in nine, German in seven, Irish in three, Puerto Rican in two, and one each of Chinese, Italian, and Russian. Chicago still dyes its river green on St. Patrick's Day, but mostly for the memories. The city's biggest parade, for some years now, has been the black Bud Billiken Day procession on the South Side. Richard M. Daley may well be Chicago's last Irish-American mayor,

Asians account for a good portion of the city's newest wave of immigrants, and, as always, it is the elderly who have the greatest difficulty adjusting to their new life in America.

and Harold Washington surely will have been only the first of many African-Americans in that office.

Meanwhile, despite the fact that a good many African-Americans became suburbanites in the 1980s, most suburbs in the Chicago metropolitan area still have a very pale complexion (even if few remain lily-white). Of 252 suburban communities listed in the census, only 13 have a black majority, and blacks are the largest single ethnic group in no more than 27. The number of suburbs with a sizable middle-class African-American population amounts to a handful, most notably Park Forest, Evanston, and Oak Park. One subtle barrier, spotlighted by the *Chicago Reporter,* is the fact that "Chicago area banks deny home mortgages to high-income blacks at a rate higher than to middle-income whites and Hispanics. That's not economics; it's fear."

Today's pattern of residential segregation would appear dismayingly familiar to any black Chicagoan returning after 50 years—or even 100. The West Side has become a racial ghetto since World War II, but the bulk of the city's African-Americans are confined within 20 contiguous South Side neighborhoods comprising a vast expansion of the "Black Belt" that grew along the spine of State Street starting before the turn of the century. From the 1930s until the Civil Rights era, residents called their ghetto "Bronzeville," and it grew to be a virtual "city within a city," as St. Clair Drake and Horace R. Cayton wrote in a 1947 *Holiday* article, "a community of grim contrasts, the facets of its life as varied as the colors of its people's skins . . . a life that to its inhabitants is crippling." Four years later in the same magazine, the poet Gwendolyn Brooks called Bronzeville "something that should not exist—an area set aside for the halting use of a single race." Her compelling article sought to demonstrate "that here resides only what is ordinary: human struggle, human whimsicality, and human reach toward soul-settlement, toward peace if not happiness, sufficiency if not fortune."

Bronzeville also nurtured the best of jazz between the world wars at such clubs as the Dreamland, the Royal Gardens, the Schiller Cafe, and the Elite. It was fertile ground for pioneering black entrepreneurs like Jesse Binga, who founded the first black-owned bank at 35th and State streets in what was known as the "Black Downtown." Its voters, pawns for decades in the plantation politics of Chicago's Democratic Party machine, sent Oscar De Priest to Washington in 1928 as the first African-American popularly elected to Congress since the Reconstruction era. Bronzeville's heyday, along with many other facets of the black experience in Chicago and around the nation, is illuminated at the Du Sable Museum of

African American History, 740 East 56th Place, which devotes an entire room to the achievements of Harold Washington. The Gap, Chatham, and Avalon Park are only three among a number of comfortable black residential neighborhoods.

To grasp how sharply other facets of Chicago's human mosaic have shifted in the last generation or two, head for the Pilsen neighborhood on the Lower West Side. The name reflects the fact that this was Chicago's Czech heartland for 100 years beginning in the mid-nineteenth century. It was the power base of Anton Cermak, the city's only Czech-American mayor, shot to death in Miami in 1933 while traveling with President-elect Franklin D. Roosevelt. The Czechs migrated west along Cermak Road in the 1950s and '60s to the suburbs of Cicero and Berwyn, as Pilsen evolved into the Mexican-American enclave it is today. Mexicans make up nearly two-thirds of Chicago's burgeoning Hispanic community, which is expected to total one-fourth of the city's population by the year 2000.

Neighborhoods are forever changing, but most retain the fierce sense of community that *Ethnic Chicago* author Lindberg believes is more prevalent here than anywhere else in America. And that continues to impact African-Americans, in his view: "Though Chicago blacks have lived and worked in the community since the frontier days, they are still viewed suspiciously as the new, unwanted arrivals in a social order that until only recently saw fit to exclude them." So pride and shame mingle today as before in the Chicago mosaic, even while minorities become majorities.

An African-American couple being escorted to a safe area during the Race Riot of 1919. (Chicago Historical Society)

Fortunately, Michael Jordan has displaced Al Capone as Chicago's most world-renowned resident.

Chicago may be the sports-fan capital of America.

■ THE MOB AND THE MYTH

Hawkers in Hollywood and Beverly Hills sell maps to the movie stars' homes. In Chicago, you can shell out five bucks or so for a map and guide pinpointing the famous (more truly, infamous) sites from the city's Gangland heyday in the Roaring '20s Prohibition era. You can be taken for a ride by Untouchable Tours on a two-hour bus rumble past gangster hideaways and hit spots. You can buy posters and postcards emblazoned with the portrait of a scarfaced bootlegging entrepreneur named Al Capone. And you may leave town with the impression that history's most celebrated Chicagoan is this skull-busting kingpin of a thug who happened to be in the right place with the requisite ruthlessness when legal liquor dried up in the 1920s. Syphilis finally killed Capone in 1947, but he was resurrected by the fascination of movies and television (not to mention the rest of us) with tough guys toting tommy guns who raked in tons of money. Chicago tourism can't shake its addiction to his bloody saga.

The Mob (a.k.a. Syndicate or Outfit) continues to be a malign force in the Chicago area as elsewhere, working a variety of vice, extortion, protection, and other rackets. But the once potent political influence of the mobsters appears to have waned substantially in Illinois over the last couple of decades, while the exploits of these aging hoodlums no longer command oceans of ink in the local press—merely puddles. That dwindling media curiosity may be directly related to the sharp drop in Chicago gangland slayings, which long furnished "Body Found in Trunk" headlines as a front-page staple. The last year when mobster murders reached double figures (with 12) was 1978, and the entire 1980s saw only 30 such killings, with just one apiece in 1987 and '89. Farewell to "rat-a-tat-tat" and all that.

Thus a visitor's imagination is left free to roam, on the wings of such accounts as Herbert Asbury's vivid *Gem of the Prairies,* back to the Gangland wars of Prohibition (522 slayings in the 1920s, peaking at 75 in 1926). "So well had publicity done its work," Asbury wrote in his 1940 informal history of Chicago's underworld, that "the famous seven-ton armored car, with the pudgy gangster lolling on silken cushions in its darkened recesses, a big cigar in his fat face, and a $50,000 diamond ring blazing from his left hand, was one of the sights of the city; the average tourist felt that his trip to Chicago was a failure unless it included a view of Capone out for a spin. The mere whisper: 'Here comes Al,' was sufficient to stop traffic and to set thousands of curious citizens craning their necks along the curbing."

When Capone arrived from Brooklyn in 1920 as a budding 20-year-old bruiser, Chicago already had a long and dishonorable history of organized crime dating virtually to the city's incorporation in 1837. It boasted a scarlet reputation in the second half of the nineteenth century as a Gomorrah of prostitution and gambling centered in a succession of red-light districts: the Sands, Conley's Patch, and the Levee (site of the Everleigh Club, for a decade the nation's most luxurious and notorious bordello). In an era of rampant civic corruption, it was sometimes hard to distinguish Chicago's mobsters from the greedy politicians and rapacious financiers.

Reigning underworld overlord when Prohibition took effect at the start of 1920 was "Big Jim" Colosimo, who operated a notorious cabaret at 2126 South Wabash in the heart of the old Levee. "His massive figure, clad in snow-white linen and a suit of garish checks, blazed with diamonds," wrote Asbury. "He wore a diamond

Gangster Al Capone, wearing his trademark hat, dark glasses, and smoking a cigar, listens with amusement as an attorney explains the government's case against him for income tax evasion in 1931. But the IRS had the last laugh when the notorious gangster was sentenced to Alcatraz, where he stayed for eight years. (Underwood Photo Archives)

ring on every finger, diamond studs gleamed in his shirt front, a huge diamond horseshoe was pinned to his vest, diamond links joined his cuffs, and his belt and suspender buckles were set with diamonds. He bought diamonds by the hundreds from thieves and needy gamblers, and cherished them as other men cherished books and paintings."

Colosimo was shot to death in the lobby of his club on May 11, 1920, and the man behind the decade's first major Gangland killing was almost certainly his nephew and henchman Johnny Torrio, who took over his lucrative domain and brought Capone to Chicago. Colosimo got the first of the flower-bedecked funerals that became the underworld fashion in the 1920s. His active and honorary pallbearers included three judges, a congressman, a state representative, nine city aldermen, and an assistant state's attorney. That reflected the insidious hold organized crime long maintained over public officials in all branches of government. Several Chicago suburbs in the 1920s became basically Mob fiefdoms, including Capone's base of Cicero. Wags said the way to tell when you'd crossed the Chicago line into that western suburb was simply to sniff: "If you smell gunpowder, you're in Cicero."

That *Gangland Chicago* map-guide pinpoints the site of Colosimo's slaying and other headlined Mob murders of the Prohibition period: Dion O'Banion, a rival of the Torrio-Capone gang, shot point-blank in 1924 by three assassins pretending to pick up a funeral arrangement at his Schofield Floral Shop, 738 North State; Hymie Weiss, O'Banion's hot-headed successor, gunned down in 1926 by Capone's men on State Street outside the same flower shop, with some bullets hitting the cornerstone of Holy Name Cathedral across the way; "Machine Gun" Jack McGurn, blasted in the head in a bowling alley at 805 North Milwaukee Avenue, on February 14, 1936. Whoever ordered McGurn's murder

"Machine Gun" Jack McGurn with Captain of Detectives John Stege waiting to be booked for murder in connection with the St. Valentine's Day Massacre, 1929. Charges were later dropped when McGurn produced an alibi. (Underwood Photo Archives)

St. Valentine's Day Massacre 1929, the purported work of Jack McGurn, who was "rubbed out" himself seven years later in 1936. (Underwood Photo Archives)

possessed some sense of history, because this Capone torpedo had been the reputed mastermind of the legendary St. Valentine's Day Massacre exactly seven years earlier. Six members of the Bugs Moran gang and one bystander were lined up against a wall and machine-gunned on February 14, 1929, in the S.M.C. Cartage Co. garage at 2122 North Clark. That sanguinary spot today is occupied by the tranquil side yard of a senior-citizens' home.

Capone's gross income by the late 1920s was estimated at $70 million or more a year. He liked to be called "the Big Fellow," and perhaps he began to take himself too seriously, as longtime *Chicago Daily News* reporter and correspondent Robert J. Casey suggested in a whimsical 1951 *Holiday* magaine article titled "The Bullet Barons." He once flew into a rage because some reporter, implicating him in a murder, misspelled his name as "Caponi." The federal government targeted him as "Public Enemy Number One," putting Eliot Ness on his case, and Capone eventually came to trial in 1931 on charges he had filed no income tax returns for the years 1924 through 1929.

CHICAGO LAWYER WINS MUSSOLINI IN GANG WAR

Chicago, Feb. 25-28, 1928:—An important agreement regarding the prosecution of Italian gangsters and criminals who escape from the United States to Italy, and involving concessions on some points of Italian law regarding extradition, was reached between Premier Benito Mussolini and Assistant State's Attorney Joseph Nicolai of Chicago yesterday in Rome. Mr. Nicolai had a long interview with Premier Mussolini on Matteo Ambrosini, alleged slayer of Mrs. Francisca Greco in Chicago four years ago. Ambrosini escaped to Italy and was arrested by the police of Naples when he landed there on Dec. 28. Attorney Nicolai immediately left for Rome to prosecute the case, but has been informed, however, that he cannot appear in the trial, as that is against the Italian criminal code, but he has been assured that Ambrosini will be punished.

Attorney Joseph Nicolai of Chicago. (Underwood Photo Archives)

The world's most famous gangster was "put in his place by the federal income-tax experts," wrote Casey, "and his trial was to show him to be only a false face—a stupid oaf who had seized the hooch-distributing machinery by force and held it by threat." Convicted on five of the 23 tax-evasion counts, he spent nearly eight years in federal prison before being released from Alcatraz in 1939 with physical and mental symptoms of untreated syphilis. There were rumors he would resume command of his ex-empire. "Bunk," said former associate Jake "Greasy Thumb" Guzik. "Al's nuttier than a fruitcake."

After eight years of seclusion on his Palm Island estate off Miami, Capone died on January 25, 1947, at age 48, of an apoplectic stroke complicated by pneumonia. His funeral "was extremely modest," wrote Francis X. Busch in his book *The Enemies of the State*. His body "was shipped by rail to Chicago. In a casket that an appraising reporter said 'could not have cost a dime over $2,000,' covered with 'only a sprinkling of gardenias and orchids,' the erstwhile emperor of gangdom was lowered into a grave in the family plot in Mount Olivet cemetery. There were no bands, no crowds, no politicians. Only his closest relatives and a handful of the old gang."

The marble monument engraved with the Capone name still stands in Mount Olivet on the city's Far Southwest Side. But the remains of all the family including Al were moved some years ago to Mount Carmel Cemetery in the western suburb of Hillside, where it takes a careful eye to spot the small black gravestones arranged around a piece of granite. His far more visible legacy is described in Perry Duis' introduction to the 1986 reissue of *Gem of the Prairie*: "Probably no other city in America has labored more than Chicago under a worldwide impression that it was filled with crime and violence." Al Capone T-shirts, anyone?

■ CULTURE: HIGHBROW TO HIP-HOP

Local cultural tastes were perhaps less refined when infant Chicago, still three years away from becoming a city, saw its first professional performance in 1834. The featured artist promised to "draw a red-hot iron across his tongue, hands, etc.," according to Don Hayner and Tom McNamee's fact-packed *Metro Chicago Almanac*, then "partake of a comfortable warm supper by eating fireballs, burning sealing wax, live coals of fire and melted lead."

Not even a full-throttle rock concert offers the prospect of such sizzling pyrotechnics today, but just about anything else is conceivable across the vast spectrum of Chicago's arts and entertainments. From highbrow to hip-hop, this is no Secondary City. The Art Institute of Chicago and the Chicago Symphony Orchestra rank at the top of their classes worldwide, while Lyric Opera of Chicago boasts a remarkable record of recent critical and financial success. The city's panoply of live theater is often livelier than the best Broadway can muster. Chicago blues, the guitar-driven daddy of rock 'n' roll, keeps the musical faith with earthy honesty in scores of clubs around town. Jazz maintains a vital and varied presence in spots like **Andy's** and **Joe Segal's Jazz Showcase**, while Buddy Charles plays on as a nonpareil piano-bar legend at the Drake Hotel's **Coq d'Or**. The world beat rhythms of the Caribbean, Latin America, and Africa are increasingly heard. (For more details see "PRACTICAL INFORMATION.")

Okay, so Chicago is no Hollywood. But it could have been, except for the inconvenient fact of too-far-north geography that cut severely into the number of comfortable outdoor shooting days. Essanay Studios, founded in 1907 by George K. Spoor and pioneer movie cowboy Gilbert M. "Bronco Billy" Anderson, was a giant of the early film industry. Hundreds of silent movies were made on the Essanay lot in the 1300 block of Argyle on the North Side, starring such luminaries as Charlie Chaplin, Francis X. Bushman, Gloria Swanson, Wallace Beery, and Ben Turpin. Swanson and Beery were wed at Essanay in 1916. Then moviemaking's young men went west to the more equable climate of Southern California, although Chicago has become a popular on-location venue in the last couple of decades. *The Blues Brothers,* shot here in 1979, was the most hard-driving of the recent made-in-Chicago genre.

The electronic media likewise had Chicago heydays. This was radio's soap-opera capital through the Great Depression and World War II, beginning with

Chuck Close's "Portrait of John" at the Art Institute of Chicago.

CAVALCADE OF CHICAGO MOVIES

Not all movies with a Chicago setting involve gangsters and tommy guns, although Hollywood has made plenty of bullet-ridden epics over the decades. Here's a cavalcade of first-rate films that take place entirely or partly in Chicago; the more recent were shot mostly on location. This two-thumbs-up list is chronological.

The Front Page (1931). Smooth early talkie and the original film version of the Ben Hecht-Charles MacArthur newspaper tale, starring Adolphe Menjou and Pat O'Brien.

Little Caesar (1931). Pioneering gangster film that set the mold, with Edward G. Robinson in the role that forever defined him.

Scarface (1932). Another Chicago mobster vehicle modeled on Al Capone's career, subtitled *The Shame of a Nation* to mollify censors. Paul Muni, Ann Dvorak, George Raft.

His Girl Friday (1940). Faster and funnier remake of *The Front Page,* with the ace Chicago reporter turned into a woman. Rosalind Russell, Cary Grant.

Call Northside 777 (1948). Chicago newspaperman helps a washerwoman prove her son did not kill a policeman. James Stewart and Lee J. Cobb.

Wabash Avenue (1950). Breezy Midwest remake of *Coney Island,* with Betty Grable as a world's-fair shimmy dancer chased by two suitors played by Victor Mature and Phil Harris.

Carrie (1952). Film version of Theodore Dreiser's massive novel about country girl who loses her innocence in Chicago while ruining the wealthy man who loves her. Laurence Olivier, Jennifer Jones.

The Man With the Golden Arm (1956). Frank Sinatra is splendid as a Chicago poker dealer who beats the drug habit in this screen version of the Nelson Algren novel.

Al Capone (1959). Fascinating Rod Steiger portrayal of the Chicago underworld kingpin, with semi-documentary script.

Compulsion (1959). Orson Welles in fine cameo role as lawyer Clarence Darrow for adaptation of Meyer Levin's play about the Leopold-Loeb murder case. Dean Stockwell and Brad Dillman.

A Raisin in the Sun (1961). Film version of Lorraine Hansberry's powerful stage drama about the dreams of a black Chicago family. Sidney Poitier, Ruby Dee, and Claudia McNeil.

Gaily, Gaily (1969). Ben Hecht's farcical and melodramatic memoir of his early career on a Chicago newspaper. Brian Keith, Beau Bridges, and Melina Mercouri.

The Sting (1973). Two con men (Paul Newman, Robert Redford) stage an elaborate revenge on a bigtime gangster in Chicago of the Roaring '20s; the film won an Academy Award for best picture.

A Wedding (1978). Robert Altman mile-a-minute satire filmed at a lakefront mansion in Chicago's North Shore suburbs. Carol Burnett, Paul Dooley, Mia Farrow.

The Blues Brothers (1980). Car chases, anyone? John Belushi and Dan Aykroyd as the manic, music-minded brothers in black.

My Bodyguard (1980). Captivating drama of 15-year-old Chicago boy's hassles at school. Chris Makepeace, Adam Baldwin, Matt Dillon.

Ordinary People (1980). Family agony and tragedy in a well-heeled, tight-strung North Shore home. Best Picture Oscar in 1980. Mary Tyler Moore, Donald Sutherland, Timothy Hutton, Judd Hirsch.

Ferris Bueller's Day Off (1986). North Shore suburbanite (Matthew Broderick) plays hooky for a day's tour of Chicago to cheer up a friend.

About Last Night (1986). Salesman for Chicago grocery wholesaler meets art director for Michigan Avenue ad agency in comic love story. Rob Lowe, Demi Moore, James Belushi.

The Untouchables (1987). Kevin Costner as Eliot Ness and Robert De Niro as Al Capone, with Sean Connery as Ness's Scottish-American sidekick and 1920s' Chicago as the background star. In gangster movies, the more things change, the more they stay the same.

Essanay Studios was founded in Chicago in the early 1900s when movie making was an outdoor art. Not surprisingly, the vagaries of Chicago's climate caused them to relocate to Los Angeles. However, many early motion pictures were made here starring such one-time luminaries as Francis X. Bushman, Beverly Bayne, Wallace Beery, and Ben Turpin. (Chicago Historical Society)

"Just Plain Bill" in 1932. In television's tender years of the early '50s, the so-called "Chicago School" briefly claimed fame for low-budget creativity and intimacy with shows such as "Kukla, Fran and Ollie," "Garroway at Large" with Dave Garroway, and "Studs' Place" with Studs Terkel. Network television swiftly steered away from low-budget creativity and drifted away from Chicago. The city's reigning TV titan is Oprah Winfrey, who shoots her tell-all talk show from Harpo (that's "Oprah" spelled backwards) Studios on the Near West Side. It's a tough ticket to get into Winfrey's studio audience.

If you hanker to hear Chicago blues on its home turf, prime time is the May or June weekend when the free-admission **Chicago Blues Festival** puts dozens of performers on three stages in lakefront Grant Park. The clubs run at top tempo as well that weekend, but there's a daunting array of choices for hearing this juiced-up music live any time of year. No fewer than 144 spots are listed in the 1992 edition of *The Original Chicago Blues Annual* magazine, ranging from the New Checkerboard Lounge and dozens of even grittier settings in black neighborhoods on the South and West sides where white faces may feel very much out of place, to more genteel downtown and North Side stages such as B.L.U.E.S, **Blue Chicago**, and **Kingston Mines**. Muddy Waters, who brought his music north from the Mississippi Delta to become the most celebrated Chicago bluesman, has been dead a decade now, but the spirit of his "Hoochie Coochie Man" and "Got My Mojo Workin'" crackles through the rhythms and lyrics of his modern-day successors.

At the highbrow end of the scale, the illustrious **Chicago Symphony Orchestra** entered the 1990s with a hard act to follow—its own. In 22 years under the baton of Sir Georg Solti, the Chicago musicians were widely heralded as the world's best symphony orchestra. Solti led them on 11 triumphant foreign tours during a golden era that also brought two dozen Grammy Awards and a bundle of lucrative recording contracts. When Solti finally stepped down, Daniel Barenboim's first season as musical director (in the orchestra's centennial year) was marred by a strike in the fall of 1991. Whatever international critics may declaim as the decade unfolds, an evening with the Chicago Symphony remains a glorious experience—whether at Orchestra Hall on Michigan Avenue from September through May, or outdoors in the summer at the Ravinia Festival on the suburban North Shore.

West across the Loop in the Civic Opera House, **Lyric Opera of Chicago** performs the amazing feat of selling more than 100 percent of its tickets year after

Every late May or early June, Grant Park hosts the admission-free Chicago Blues Festival.

CHICAGO BLUES

Chicago blues fans would find irony in the geographic shifts of the club scene in this self-proclaimed "Blues Capital of the World."

A music form born on the Mississippi Delta, the blues made its way to Chicago in the 1930s, accompanying the plantation workers as they migrated from Mississippi and Louisiana to Chicago to answer the call for cheap industrial labor. Then in the 1940s—in the words of Joe Seneca's elderly bluesman in "Crossroads"— "Muddy Waters invented electricity." Soon the music that had been strummed on front porches in the Delta was being played through amplifiers on electrified instruments. Black nightclubs on the city's south and west sides that catered to a working-class clientele became jumpin' juke joints.

Guitarist Buddy Guy, whose South Loop club Legends is one of Chicago's finest blues bars, recalls the years after his arrival in Chicago in the late 1950s. A South Sider back then could walk up and down both sides of 47th Street for a ten-block stretch and find one club after another with live blues.

A few decades later, the music that had provided an entertainment staple for black nightclubs was no longer in fashion. Younger, hipper blacks were dancing to Motown and, more recently, urban contemporary tunes. For this newer generation, the blues represented a lifestyle they'd just as soon forget.

Getting down at Andy's.

By the '70s, the blues in Chicago was becoming a North Side phenomenon, as interest waned on the South Side except in a few historic clubs within shouting distance of the University of Chicago. With the "houserockin' blues" of Chicago-based Alligator Records paving the way for a new audience of white, upper-middle-class fans, a night on the town meant blues and beers to young college grads who'd been introduced to the music as part of campus life.

The musical migration to the North Side bars was in a sense just as significant in the evolution of the blues as the movement from the Southern states. Today, many bands are integrated, but most clubs that feature live blues are patronized primarily by young urban white audiences.

Make no mistake, though: the blues is not becoming a museum piece, to be studied as some primitive American folk art. It is a living, growing art form, with a legion of devoted fans and new, up-and-coming stars more technically proficient—if less knowledgeable about the roots of the music—than their Southern ancestors.

Each year, the City of Chicago throws a huge blues bash at its lakefront playground in Grant Park. The Chicago Blues Festival takes place in late May or early June. Committee members work virtually year-round to assemble a collection of talent that is both representative of all sub-genres of the music and conducive to listening by large crowds. The three-day festival might draw up to 400,000 people, who come early to picnic in the park and stay to boogie to the city's homegrown

Buddy Guy still plays to enthusiastic crowds at his nightclub, Legends.

music as the sun sets over a breathtaking view of the skyline.

The Chicago club scene is a hit-or miss proposition for the blues. Hit the more trendy bars, and you'll miss the ambiance that should go with the music. The **Kingston Mines** and the **Wise Fools Pub**, two clubs in the chic Lincoln Park neighborhood on the North Side, both have good records for developing local followings for up-and-coming artists. Their schedules are often printed months in advance, though: when it comes to adventuresome bookings, forget it.

B.L.U.E.S. and its younger, bigger brother, B.L.U.E.S. Etc., suffer from the same swinging-singles disease as Kingston Mines and Wise Fools, but their music is up to snuff. The little B.L.U.E.S. club on Halsted is a particularly good place for out-of-towners to get a feel for the music. It was the first North Side blues bar that did not feel compelled to serve a steady diet of bands fronted by a male vocalist-guitarist. And B.L.U.E.S. Etc. is big enough to draw nationally known out-of-town blues artists on the weekends.

One place that's guaranteed to put a smile on a visitor's face is Rosa's, located off the beaten path in a Hispanic neighborhood on the West Side. The club, run by an elderly woman from Italy and her son, bills itself as "Chicago's friendliest blues bar." There's no disputing that slogan, just as there's no quarreling with the innovative booking strategy.

Legends may be Chicago's best blues club, rated according to both music and atmosphere. While the scene is hottest when co-owner Buddy Guy is fronting his own band, there are plenty of other reasons to patronize the club. Where else, for example, could you find the city's finest harmonica players dueling in a "Harp Attack," or veteran blues artists paying tribute to departed musical greats? The knowledgeable clientele make it possible for management to book talented but little known out-of-towners who wouldn't draw flies on the North Side. And if arena bands are out slumming after a show in town, Legends is one of their prime hangouts.

For those who insist on the authenticity of a real South Side blues club the best choices are probably the **Checkerboard Lounge** and **Brady's Liquors & Lounge**. The down-to-earth, comfortable atmosphere inside these clubs is often compromised by a sense of danger in the streets outside. But management makes a point of ensuring the safety of customers by seeing them safely to their cars and keeping a constant eye out for trouble.

So if you've got the blues, or want to get them, Chicago is still ready to satisfy your needs. Only the locale has changed.

—Jeff Johnson, essayist on the blues for the *Chicago Sun-Times*

year. Lyric manages that bit of box-office prestidigitation, under the wing of general manager Ardis Krainik, by reselling tickets that have been returned by season subscribers. It's sometimes possible to buy those returns at the Opera House on the day of performances, which run from September through January. Lyric attracts a world-class cast of singers, and its adoption in recent years of English-language supertitles flashed above the stage makes operatic story lines less inscrutable to the uninitiated. The smaller **Chicago Opera Theater**, critically acclaimed but struggling financially in recent years, does its productions entirely in English at a cozy North Side church auditorium.

Perhaps Chicago's most remarkable arts-and-entertainment saga of recent decades has been the birth and flowering of the premier regional-theater scene in America. David Mamet is the best-known playwright to spring from this dramatic renaissance, and **Steppenwolf** is the most celebrated among the 100-plus professional companies—the bulk of them non-profit either by intent or in practice. Annual theater attendance in the Chicago area totals somewhere around 3 million, higher than for any of the city's professional sports teams.

Students rehearse A Midsummer Night's Dream *in the court adjoining the Chicago Art Institute, 1927. (Underwood Photo Archives)*

Highly regarded companies besides Steppenwolf include **Goodman, Remains, Victory Gardens,** and **Wisdom Bridge.** Half-price tickets to many productions are available at Hot Tix booths in the Loop and elsewhere run by the League of Chicago Theaters. It may not be true that New Yorkers now fly to Chicago for a weekend of theater, but the trip would be well worth their while.

And they should save time for the city's most venerable cultural landmark, the **Art Institute of Chicago,** founded in 1879 and moved into its present Michigan Avenue building guarded by a beloved pair of bronze lions to herald the 1893 World's Columbian Exposition. Some of its wealthy patrons in the Robber Baron era fancied a controversial new school of French painting, thanks to which the Art Institute possesses an Impressionist collection as fine as any on either side of the Atlantic. Georges Seurat's beguiling "Sunday Afternoon on the Island of La Grande Jatte" is the institute's signature work, worth a visit all on its own. The museum houses treasure troves in many other fields of fine and decorative arts, including the exquisite trading room of the Old Stock Exchange. The Art Institute is nicely complemented by the **Museum of Contemporary Art,** as well as a busy gallery scene and a splendid ensemble of public sculpture. Most familiar of the outdoor works is Pablo Picasso's enigmatic, untitled lion-dog-bird-woman on the Loop's Daley Center Plaza. Most emblematic may be Claes Oldenburg's 100-foot (30-m)-tall "Batcolumn" that towers along Madison Street's ex-Skid Row—"a five-story nightstick," as one protester called it, for a bruising metropolis where a fire-eating act would still fit right in. (See page 103 for photo.)

Chicago Art Institute patrons admire one of its works, "Paris Street on a Rainy Day," by Gustave Caillebotte.

Claes Oldenburg's "Batcolumn."

HEART OF THE CITY

"THINGS FALL APART; THE CENTER CANNOT HOLD," wrote William Butler Yeats. The great Irish poet was speaking cosmically, but his centrifugal image fits the decline of all too many American downtowns in this half-century of rampant suburbia. Some metropolitan areas in the Sun Belt grew up without any real heart to begin with—all sprawl and no center. Some older cities in the Snow Belt saw their cores wither and rot in the decades after World War II—to the point where no cosmetic surgery could delay or disguise the wasting illness. That's mostly not so for Chicago, where all roads have always led to the **Loop**—even before there came to be an actual Loop created when the cable-car lines spun their web around downtown in the 1880s, indeed even before the city was chartered in 1837. Today's visitors, once whisked into town from O'Hare International Airport, can feast richly on the city's smorgasbord without ever going more than a brisk walking distance—two miles (3.2 km) maximum—from the traditional civic hub at State and Madison streets.

Not that the Loop itself has escaped the bruising changes that have transformed this profoundly segregated metropolis, where the central city lies beyond the mental horizon of many suburbanites (who now outnumber city dwellers almost two to one). Along State Street, there aren't enough major stores left to shop till you drop—or even till you stagger. But in daytime hours, at least, the Loop's pulse still races with activity. And the real revelation for an out-of-towner seeing Chicago after an absence of 10 or 15 years is the rejuvenation (or juvenation for the first time, in some instances) of the Loop's periphery. South, west, and north—even east a bit to the lake—from the rusty girdle of elevated tracks, there is a wealth of new or relocated businesses (shops, restaurants, nightspots, museums, galleries, and other attractions) in such areas as South Loop, New East Side, River North, and Streeterville. North Michigan Avenue has seized State Street's retailing banner and flies it skyscraper-high. These and other close-in quarters—some now populated by honest-to-god residents—are the expanded heart of Chicago, where the judgment made seven decades ago by a visitor named D. H. Lawrence still holds: "It seemed to me more alive and more real than New York." And Lawrence was here in fog and rain, when "muddy-flowing people oozed thick in the canyon-beds of the streets." Imagine it on a sunny day.

■ THE LOOP

Chicago's Loop will never again be quite the magnet it used to be—which is a sad fact if you're a downtown visitor on the prowl for shopping or nightlife. **State Street,** that onetime Great Street lined for decades with the densest concentration of department stores anywhere, is down to its last two major retailers. And the survivors, Marshall Field's and Carson Pirie Scott, both came under out-of-town ownership in the 1980s—although Field's has declared its faith in the Loop's future with a $110 million "Renaissance on State Street" renovation.

The spine of the Loop in its heyday from the 1880s through the Eisenhower era, State Street also dazzled as Chicago's Great White Way, a brightly lighted theater and entertainment strip that set a lively tempo for the toddling heart of town. Now the Loop on many nights might be mistaken for a morgue, with a handful of old-line restaurants hanging on, and only an occasional live performance in State Street's gloriously restored Chicago Theater and a few other venues (plus those seasonal heavyweights, Chicago Symphony Orchestra and Lyric Opera, on the eastern and western edges).

But the Loop, to borrow a phrase once tagged to the Broadway theater scene, is a fabulous invalid. It's still alive and kicking, energized by the hives of corporate and government offices that occupy the thickets of skyscrapers flung up in the last couple of decades. The **La Salle Street** financial canyon is more than ever the Wall Street of the Midwest after the explosive expansion of its facilities for stock and commodities trading in the feverish Reagan years. The hulking new **Harold Washington Library Center** anchors the Loop's south end looking ever so much like a fortress of knowledge. Development has stretched the city-core boundaries in all directions—even creating a New East Side to defy the hoary local joke that "East Side" lies somewhere below Lake Michigan's waters. And people are moving to the Loop's fringes in large enough numbers that the central city's residential population nearly doubled between 1980 and 1990. In daylight hours Monday through Friday, today's Loop is a bustling and diverting place that also happens to be a nonpareil outdoor museum of modern architecture.

Strictly speaking, the Loop's boundaries are defined by the girdle of elevated train tracks shadowing Wabash, Van Buren, Wells, and Lake streets—the nexus of the century-old "L" rapid-transit system that novelist Nelson Algren called Chicago's "rusty iron heart." Stand beneath the lattice of steel at one of the 90-degree

"L" curves while a couple of Chicago Transit Authority trains make the turn, and you'll be assaulted by a mega-decibel screech hardly less deafening than a heavy-metal concert or an O'Hare runway. In practice, today's Loop extends beyond the tracks to the Chicago River on the north, a bit across the river on the west, Congress Parkway on the south, and beyond Michigan Avenue to Grant Park and the lakefront on the east. Covering not much more than a square mile (2.6 sq km), it's easily explored on foot, while a car in the Loop is a millstone that should be quickly dumped in a parking garage.

One logical place to begin is ground zero—State and Madison, starting point for the city's street addresses. Boosters long billed this as "the world's busiest inter-section," the spot where the New Year's Eve midnight countdown rivaled the hoopla in New York's Times Square. These days, it isn't even the Loop's busiest in-tersection, with State Street having been closed since 1978 to all motor traffic ex-cept buses in a quasi-mall experiment that has been less than a wild success.

While window-shopping at Carson Pirie Scott on the southeast corner, savor the intricately ornamented cast-iron panels that frame the glass. Their spidery leaf and floral designs are the creation of Chicago School stalwart Louis Sullivan for what is considered one of his most masterful buildings. "This rich but delicate pattern gives an unusually luxurious effect to an entrance already distinguished by its semicircular shape and its location at the corner of the building," observe Ira J. Bach and Susan Wolfson in *Chicago on Foot*.

One of the Loop's most famous landmarks is the clock of Marshall Field's at State and Randolph streets.

Magnificently restored Marshall Field's, just to the north between Washington and Randolph streets, now boasts an 11-story atrium flanked by glass elevators and anchored by a cast-iron water fountain that was in the original turn-of-the-century floor plans but never built. Field's has a cherished spot in the memories of count-less Chicagoans for its lavish Christmas displays

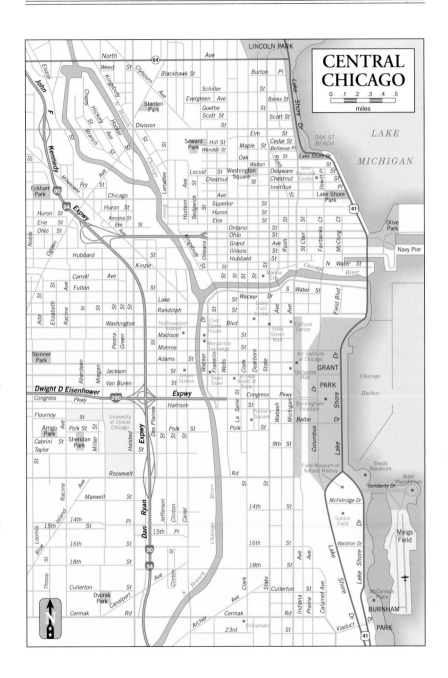

and its adherence to the first Marshall Field's old-fashioned credo, "Give the lady what she wants."

On Monroe Street between State and Wabash, the **Palmer House** is grande dame among Loop hotels (newest being the Stouffer Riviere, which debuted in 1992 on Wacker Drive). The first Palmer House opened only 13 days before the Chicago Fire of 1871 burned it to the ground. The second, torn down to make way for the present 23-story structure in 1925, is said to have been the first hotel to offer guests elevators, telephones, and electric lights. In the Loop's heyday, the Empire Room of the Palmer House was a legendary big-band nightspot; now it's a setting for Sunday brunch.

West of State Street another block south at 17 West Adams stands the **Berghoff**, a don't-miss dining spot if you relish a pinch of history and a dash of beer-hall jollity with your sauerbraten or wienerschnitzel. Launched as a beer garden at Chicago's world's fair in 1893, the Berghoff ranks as the city's oldest functioning restaurant. Expect lines for lunch and early dinner, along with high noise levels, hard-boiled service, and respectable Teutonic fare. An ideal solvent is Berghoff's own draft beer, light or dark. If the Berghoff lines look too long, hiking a block and a half south brings you to another venerable Loop survivor, Binyon's, where platoons of judges and lawyers tuck into such specialties as turtle soup. Binyon's is shadowed on narrow Plymouth Court by the 16-story Chicago Bar Association building, a 1990 Tigerman McCurry design with a whisper of Gothic Revival thrust and detail.

Some of those legal heavyweights ply their profession in the two **Federal Center** highrises that flank Dearborn between Adams and Jackson as testament to the mature majesty of Ludwig Mies van der Rohe's late work. Completed in 1975, these steel-and-glass swaggerers overlook a sizable plaza embellished with Alexander Calder's red "Flamingo" stabile. It is the southernmost of three plazas fronting on the west side of Dearborn that give this architecturally premier Loop thoroughfare a more open and airy feeling than is afforded by most skyscraper canyons. First National Plaza, site of that bank's A-shaped headquarters rising 60 stories, is graced by a late-in-life Marc Chagall architectural mosaic, "The Four Seasons." Richard J. Daley Plaza, home of Chicago's **Picasso** (now a beloved civic treasure, whether it be woman, bird, beast, or whatever) is a likely place to witness the urban theater of a protest rally, as well as the setting on a dozen summer and fall weekdays for a farmers' market. How do you like those apples?

Like the Eiffel Tower in Paris a century ago, the Chicago Picasso took some getting used to—an adjustment that began with the 1967 unveiling by Mayor Daley. There were gasps from the crowd on the plaza when the mayor pulled a white streamer that dropped the blue fabric from the statue. Then Daley began clapping, and he told the audience of 50,000: "We dedicate this celebrated work this morning with the belief that what is strange to us today will be familiar tomorrow." One of Gwendolyn Brooks' later poems to the Picasso speaks to its mission: "Art hurts. Art urges voyages—and it is easier to stay at home, the nice beer ready."

Lining Dearborn at the southern extremity of the Loop are four century-old gems of the Chicago School: the **Monadnock Building** (Burnham and Root, 1891, for the original southern half); the **Fisher Building** (D. H. Burnham, 1896); the **Old Colony Building** (Holabird and Roche, 1893), and the **Manhattan Building** (Jenney and Mundie, 1889-91). Now an apartment complex, the 16-story Manhattan was briefly the world's tallest commercial building when it went up as one of the first complete steel-and-iron frame structures. The rounded corner bays of the Old Colony were a device of the time used by architects to create highly desirable corner offices.

If you're old enough to remember ticker tape, **La Salle Street** (the Loop's western spine, two blocks beyond Dearborn) may have a familiar look. This is where Chicago staged its triumphal parades to salute military heroes, astronauts, the very occasional championship sports team, and other luminaries back when the magnitude of such processions could be measured in the tons of confetti left behind. Buttressing the south end of the financial canyon is the **Board of Trade Building**, completed in 1929 just in time for the Great Depression, with a gilded aluminum statue of the Greek grain goddess Ceres perched at the 45-story summit. The Art Deco interior by Gilbert Hall deserves a leisurely look, and the visitors' gallery is open each weekday for a view down on the apparent bedlam of the futures markets. Running south behind the Board of Trade is the three-building **Exchange Center** (Chicago Board Options Exchange, One Financial Place, Midwest Stock Exchange), built in 1983-84 as testimony to that decade's speculative boom and clad in polished red granite. A landscaped plaza softens the setting to the west, and the complex houses the Everest Room restaurant, where both the 40th-story view and Alsatian chef Jean Joho's cooking rank with the finest in town.

Even more exquisite than the Board of Trade lobby, Frank Lloyd Wright's gold-and-ivory ornamentation of the light court inside the **Rookery Building** (209

PEERING INTO THE FUTURES

One of Chicago's most animated shows can be watched free of charge each weekday from 8 A.M. to 2 P.M. It's not a theatrical performance as such, although the actors are colorfully costumed and wildly expressive. Nor is this a sporting event, despite the fact that it features high-stakes winning and losing. The players sometimes seem frantic past the point of bedlam, and the rules appear more arcane than cricket to uninitiated spectators peering down from the visitor galleries. But what you're watching is actually a time-tested bastion of free enterprise that was formed by 82 merchants in 1848 to stabilize grain prices. This is the world's oldest and largest futures market, the Chicago Board of Trade—"The Pit" of Frank Norris's 1903 muckraking novel and the stuff of headlines on today's financial pages.

Occupying a 45-story Art Deco skyscraper at the foot of LaSalle Street's financial canyon, the Chicago Board of Trade now has two trading floors. Both are outfitted with the tiered octagonal wooden pits that look a bit like risers for a church choir or senior-class photo, and computerized quotation-board displays whose ribbons of lighted figures could be mistaken for the giant sports-book scoreboards at Las Vegas casinos. The original Agricultural Commodities floor deals in orders for wheat,

continues on page 112

An active day on the floor of the Chicago Board of Trade.

Every day at the Commodities Exchange is a tribute to Chicago's captains of commerce, whose busts adorn the entrance to the Chicago Mercantile Exchange.

corn, soybeans, cotton, beef, and a variety of other farm products (including those ever-popular pork bellies). The newer Financial Futures floor does business in U.S. Treasury bonds and notes, stock indexes, municipal-bond indexes, and other instruments.

Only the 1,400 Board of Trade members have the right to trade on the exchange floor, which is why a full seat was selling for about $360,000 in 1992 (and as much as $550,000 in 1987). Each pit deals in a specific commodity, whether wheat or Treasury bonds, and where the traders are standing indicates the future delivery month in which they are dealing. The rules require traders to use "open outcry" in making their buy or sell offers—thus the waves of shouting (actually a very controlled form of chaos). Sellers call out quantity first, then price; buyers do the reverse. The animated hand gestures help to clarify the bids in the din of voices; the palm of the hand facing out indicates a trader is selling, while an inward palm is an offer to buy. Other finger and hand signals indicate the price being bid and the number of futures contracts involved. Traders wear badges color-coded to denote their floor privileges and bearing an acronym of no more than three letters by which their trades are recorded. Exchange rules require jackets and ties on the floor; but the lightweight, loose-fitting trading jackets (in the distinctive colors of various brokerage firms) look more like tear-away football jerseys than formal business attire.

The main function of the futures markets, as the presentation in the visitor galleries takes pains to assert, is first to determine the value of the myriad commodities and instruments traded, and then to transfer the risk of price fluctuations over the months ahead. Those seeking protection from unwanted price changes are known as hedgers, while the risk-takers who fuel the markets are the speculators. From the days of "The Pit" to the present, those who speculate have been the high-rolling stars—and the market-cornering scoundrels—in the Board of Trade's storied history. Like the wheeler-dealer Curtis Jadwin in the Norris novel, the speculator is "a sort of creature of legends, mythical, heroic, transfigured in the glory of his millions."

If you become an instant fan of the trading tumult, there are also viewing galleries that overlook the floors of the Chicago Board Options Exchange, 400 South La Salle Street (linked to the Chicago Board of Trade by a pedestrian bridge, and dealing in stock options); the Midwest Stock Exchange, 440 South La Salle Street (the world's fifth largest stock exchange); and the Chicago Mercantile Exchange, 30 South Wacker Drive (known as "The Merc" and even more boisterous than the Board of Trade).

South La Salle) fully reflects its original 1905 glory after a recent restoration (see "ARCHITECTURE"). The iconoclastic Wright, incidentally, had his own contrarian view of the Loop and its heavy traffic. "The automobile is going to ruin this city," he told a newspaper reporter in the 1920s. "This is a dreadful way to live. You'll be strangled by traffic." Asked by the reporter what should be done, Wright replied, "Take a gigantic knife and sweep it over the Loop, cutting off every building at the seventh floor. If you cut down those horrible buildings, you'll have no traffic jams. You'll have trees again. You'll have some joy in the life of this city. After all, that is the job of the architect—to give the world a little joy."

Rising in stark counterpoint three blocks west of the Rookery's dulcet delicacy is the unadorned muscle of the **Sears Tower**—a 110-story behemoth that might have left even Wright speechless. Wait if possible for a clear day, then ride the hyper-speed elevator to the 103rd-floor skydeck (or a newer 100th-floor observatory annex used on busy days) for world-class panoramas from the world's tallest building. Sears Tower's souvenir shops stock every conceivable Chicago-branded souvenir—a surfeit of park-it-in-the-closet-back-home items.

North up Wacker Drive, the sleek twin towers of the **Chicago Mercantile Exchange** (with yet another visitors' gallery to marvel at the trading frenzy) look north across Madison Street to the **Civic Opera House**, built by the speculative shark Samuel Insull in 1929 just before his financial house of cards toppled. It has been home since the 1950s to the phenomenally successful Lyric Opera of Chicago. West across the Chicago River stands another fine 1920s' Art Deco skyscraper, the **Riverside Plaza Building**, with a wonderful ceiling mural by John Warner Norton in the lobby concourse leading to the Northwestern rail station. An echo of the building's original ownership by the old *Chicago Daily News,* it depicts with figurative license the process of putting the newspaper to press.

Passing Lake Street, which preceded State as Chicago's prime commercial boulevard in the mid-nineteenth century, Wacker Drive turns east to follow the river at the 36-story **333 West Wacker Building,** one of city's finest Post-Modernist skyscrapers of the 1980s. It's three-fourths of a mile (1.2 km) east to Michigan and Wacker, where pavement markers outline the first Fort Dearborn of 1803-12, taking an imaginative visitor back to the virtual dawn of the white man's time in Chicago. This was also roughly the natural Lake Michigan shoreline, so that the New East Side developments beyond Michigan Avenue rise on landfill

(following pages) A clear day offers spectacular vistas from the 103rd floor observatory of the 1,454-foot (442-m) Sears Tower.

from earlier this century. These eastward neighbors include the architecturally desultory **Illinois Center** mixed-use complex built over disused railyards, three large hotels (Hyatt Regency Chicago and the newer Fairmont and Swiss Grand), the Sporting Club (a workout wonder with a 100-foot [30-m]-high indoor climbing wall), the 1,136-foot (345-m) **Amoco Building** (Chicago's second tallest structure, reclad in granite after its original white marble panels began loosening like bad teeth), and the 42-story **Prudential Building** (officially One Prudential Plaza and now a relative pygmy, but the city's tallest building for a decade after it went up in 1955).

Grant Park, the greensward buffer between Loop and lake, presents a grab bag of pleasures: **Richard J. Daley Bicentennial Plaza**, with ice skating in the winter and roller skating and tennis in the summer; **Petrillo Music Shell**, the setting for summer classical concerts under the stars (or rainclouds) as well as annual blues, gospel, and jazz festivals; two rose gardens and a spread of prairie wildflowers; Taste of Chicago, the start-of-summer food and music mega-festival; beloved **Buckingham Fountain**, a Beaux Arts confection of pink Georgia marble that plays a computer-coordinated symphony of water and colored lights during the summer. Straight west from the fountain, flanking Congress Drive at the park's western edge, stand two of the city's most vigorous sculptures, "The Bowman" and "The Spearman," Native Americans on horseback by the Yugoslav master Ivan Mestrovic.

Lining Michigan Avenue's west side are such jewels as Adler and Sullivan's 1889 **Auditorium Building,** rescued from a generation of decay after World War II; the **Railway Exchange Building,** a white terra-cotta beauty designed by D. H. Burnham and Co. in 1903 and now housing the Chicago Architecture Foundation, an essential resource for books and guided tours; and the **Chicago Cultural Center,** formerly the main public library, where the lively **Museum of Broadcast Communications** is only one of several notable attractions. Around the corner, on the second floor at 50 East Washington, is the **Savvy Traveller,** the city's top store for travel books and paraphernalia.

Back in Grant Park, between Monroe and Jackson, the **Art Institute of Chicago** merits as much time as you can manage until feet and eyes beg for mercy. The museum's staggering array of Impressionist and Post-Impressionist canvases testifies to the vision of Chicago patrons such as Mrs. Potter Palmer and Martin A. Ryerson, who were willing to take a flyer on these radical French artists in the 1880s when New York collectors disdained them. Thus Chicago has Seurat's "Sunday Afternoon on the Island of La Grande Jatte," Toulouse-Lautrec's "At the Moulin Rouge," as well as priceless Cezannes, Renoirs, Monets, Gauguins, and Van Goghs. The treasures of the Art Institute, from Old Masters to Chinese bronzes, are a feast too rich for a single meal—like the Loop itself even in these latter days.

■ SOUTH OF THE LOOP

Some of Chicago's richest—and raunchiest—heritage lies immediately south of the Loop in a mile-and-a-half (2.4 km) of much-redeveloped territory stretching from Congress Parkway to the Prairie Avenue Historic District and McCormick Place-on-the-Lake convention center. The first Chicago suburbanite, hardware dealer Henry B. Clarke, built a Greek Revival home here in 1836 that still stands as the city's oldest building. Merchant princes erected a string of mansions that made Prairie Avenue the poshest Chicago address in the two decades following the Great Fire of 1871. The city's first residence lighted by electricity was businessman John Wesley Doane's mansion at 1827 South Prairie. Four hundred guests attended a lavish party on November 10, 1882, to celebrate the new wonder, which the *Chicago Tribune* described the next day: "The Edison electric incandescent lights made the house brilliant in the extreme. From the ceiling to the door was spread an awning of light. On the hearths shone forth electric lights so arranged as to imitate a glowing fire." It marked the birth of a revolution in the after-dark life of Chicagoans.

At the same time, the brothels and gambling dens of the notorious **Levee vice district**—which earned Chicago its reputation as a modern Gomorrah—thrived from the 1880s through the World War I period a few blocks to the west along Dearborn and Clark Streets. Most opulent of the Levee's brothels was the **Everleigh Club**, which opened in 1900 at 2131-33 South Dearborn Street in a flourish of mahogany staircases, Greek statuary, and potted palms. Champagne was the only drink served at the Everleigh Club. Of its proprietors, one newsman wrote, "Minna and Ada Everleigh were to pleasure what Christ was to Christianity." Minna was said to tell her girls: "You have the entire night before you, and a single $50 client is more desirable than five $10 ones. Less wear and tear." After authorities closed the Everleigh Club in 1911, the sisters retired on their fortune to New York; long-lived Ada died at age 94 in 1970, 22 years after Minna.

In a more edifying vein, the lakefront south of the Loop saw splendid cultural and educational attractions—Field Museum of Natural History, Shedd Aquarium, Adler Planetarium—rise astride the shoulders of the industrialists' philanthropy as symbols of civic self-confidence on landfill (now Burnham Park) that also hosted the 1933-34 Century of Progress. That Depression-defying world's fair is best remembered for Sally Rand's fan dancing, which might have been at home in the old Levee. Her striptease in the Streets of Paris exhibit was broken up as many as five times a day by police; thanks to the publicity, she was earning $3,000 a week

A Sunday stroller in Grant Park with a smile as big as her hat.

(opposite) Sally Rand's fan dance act during the 1933-34 Century of Progress Exposition landed her in court where Judge J. B. David threw the case out declaring, "Some people would like to put pants on horses." (Chicago Historical Society)

by the end of the fair. Refusing the city's request to close Rand's act, Judge Joseph B. David declared: "Some people would like to put pants on horses. This court holds no brief for the prurient or ignorant. Let them walk out if they wish. If you ask me, they are just a lot of boobs come to see a woman wiggle with a fan or without fig leaves. But we have the boobs, and we have a right to cater to them." Rand continued to perform in Chicago and elsewhere into her 70s. "It's better than doing needlepoint on the patio," she explained.

John Wesley Doane's mansion and the Everleigh Club fell long ago to the wrecker's ball, along with much else glorious and grim, as the area south of the Loop became a backwater. The makings of an entire new neighborhood have sprung up since the late 1970s in what had been mostly an urban wasteland of derelict commercial buildings and railyards. Residential and mixed-use developments in this Burnham Park/South Loop community include **Printer's Row**, **Dearborn Park**, and **River City**. The urban pioneers—yuppies and other neighborhood frontiersmen—who've moved into these lofts, apartments, condominiums, and townhouses enjoy a short commute to Loop offices along with the extracurricular allures of the central city, including handy access to Chicago Bears' football at lakefront Soldier Field just south of the Field Museum.

Whether they've yet created a genuine neighborhood is a debatable point on which a strolling visitor may begin to form an opinion. A skeptical perspective comes from *Chicago: City of Neighborhoods,* by Dominic A. Pacyga and Ellen Skerrett: "Dearborn Park was intended for families, but it is actually occupied by singles and by couples with few or no children. While it is an economic success, Dearborn Park is neither a neighborhood nor a suburb." The authors urge "a more conscious effort to humanize urban renewal. Chicago cannot survive as a city of highrises and townhouses." They lament a lack of "third places" where people can socialize outside the home and office—taverns, grocery stores, drugstores, hardware stores.

Some of these amenities have sprouted since *Chicago: City of Neighborhoods* was published in 1986, and one axis of the reborn district is the two blocks of Dearborn Street running from Congress south to the old Dearborn Station at Polk Street. In the late nineteenth and early twentieth centuries, this was the locale of a vigorous Chicago printing industry that rivaled New York's. The print shops eventually went broke or went elsewhere, but the rugged brick loft buildings with their fine detailing remained, ready to take on new lives through the recent conversions.

One—**Grace Place**, at 637 South Dearborn—has come back as a loft church (shared by Grace Episcopal and Christ the King Lutheran congregations) with the parish hall on the ground floor and the sanctuary upstairs, in a striking adaption by Booth/Hansen & Associates. These innovative architects, responsible for much of the Printer's Row renovation, also did the adaptive work on the 14-story **Pontiac Building** (542 South Dearborn), a Chicago School pioneer of 1891 vintage that is Holabird and Roche's oldest surviving skyscraper here.

One South Loop hotel worth an admiring look even if you're not a guest is the **Chicago Hilton and Towers**, overlooking Grant Park on Michigan Avenue between Balbo Avenue and Eighth Street. First called the Stevens and then the Conrad Hilton, this was once the world's largest hotel with nearly 3,000 rooms and an 18-hole miniature golf course on the roof. The rejuvenated Hilton positively gleams these days following a $185 million overhaul in the mid-'80s that reduced the room count to 1,620. Ex-yippies can pause and reflect near the Balbo corner at the plate-glass windows that were cracked in 1968 on a legendary Democratic convention night perfumed by tear gas. As Nora Sayre reported in Britain's *New Statesman,* "Outside the Hilton, a nice little old lady and I were suddenly hurled against the wall when 100 policemen seized their blue wooden barricades to ram the crowd (mainly onlookers and the press) against the building with such force that many next to me, including the old lady, were thrust through plate-glass windows. People sobbed with pain as their ribs snapped from being crushed against each other."

North across Balbo, the **Blackstone Hotel** claims fame for the original smoke-filled room, Suite 804-805, where Republican kingmakers bestowed their 1920 nomination on Warren G. Harding, who proved to be one of America's most forgettable presidents. The Blackstone hosts the highly regarded Joe Segal's Jazz Showcase, as well as the Mayfair Theater, where the comedy whodunit *Shear Madness* began running in 1981 as the Chicago answer to London's *Mousetrap.* A block east at 754 South Wabash, Buddy Guy's **Legends** books a mix of big-name blues talent. In the same Michigan Avenue block as the Blackstone are two notable small museums. **Spertus Museum of Judaica** spans 3,500 years of Jewish history in galleries ranging from an artifact center with hands-on archeology to the Zell Holocaust Memorial. The **Museum of Contemporary Photography,** part of Columbia College, was founded in 1967 as an offshoot of that center-city institution's highly regarded photography curriculum. Either can be an hors d'oeuvre for the Field Museum, Shedd Aquarium, and Adler Planetarium three-quarters of a mile (1.2 km) south on the lakefront where Grant Park melds into Burnham Park.

Marshall Field, founding father of the department store and publishing family, endowed the present **Field Museum of Natural History,** which is said to be the largest Georgia marble building in the world—yet another among the myriad "biggest" brags mustered by the Windy City. The museum moved north in 1920 from its original Jackson Park location in the Fine Arts Building constructed for the 1893 World's Columbian Exposition and now occupied by the Museum of Science and Industry. From dinosaur skeletons and stuffed elephants to a pharaoh's tomb and a premier collection of art by Pacific Ocean peoples, the natural and civilized worlds are unveiled here. The McDonald's on the ground floor is not an ethnographic exhibit; those are real Big Macs, a museum fast-food concession to popular taste.

John G. Shedd, a Marshall Field & Co. board chairman, gave the money to build **Shedd Aquarium**—yes, the world's largest indoor aquarium. Shedd's headline attraction, the enormous Oceanarium for marine mammals, has drawn huge crowds since its 1990 opening while also grappling with controversy over its capture of beluga whales, two of whom died here in 1992 after receiving anti-parasite medication. The aquarium's Coral Reef tank is a 90,000-gallon kaleidoscopic marvel of tropical fish and other sea creatures. The short walk east along Solidarity Drive (bespeaking the clout of Chicago's large Polish-American community) to **Adler Planetarium** provides spectacular views of the Loop skyline. The intriguing sculpture directly in front of the planetarium is Henry Moore's 1980 bronze, "Sundial." Sears, Roebuck & Co. executive Max Adler funded the star-gazing mecca, which presents sky shows daily in its domed Zeiss projection theater and displays a superb collection of antique astronomical instruments.

It's best to drive or take a taxi south to **Prairie Avenue Historic District,** where a few mansions survive to evoke the halcyon days when Field, George Pullman, Philip Armour, Potter Palmer, and their entrepreneurial peers made this Chicago's neighborhood of choice. The estimable Chicago Architecture Foundation maintains **Glessner House,** a 35-room bastion of rough-hewn granite that is the only remaining building in the city designed by the Romanesque Revival master Henry Hobson Richardson. Built in 1886, it has been lovingly restored inside in the English Arts and Crafts style favored by the Glessners with some of their original furnishings. One negative review did come from Mont-

The Field Museum of Natural History is said to be the largest Georgia marble building in the world.

gomery Schuyler, a nineteenth-century architecture critic who wrote, "The whole aspect of the exterior is so gloomy and forbidding and unhomelike that but for its neighborhood, one would infer its purpose to be not domestic but penal."

During the Christmas season on Prairie Street, Marshall Field would invite a dozen of his department store executives to dinner at his since-demolished mansion. "There would be plenty of wine and liquor, though the host took none," according to Finis Farr's lively 1973 *Chicago* history. "After dinner, when the cigars were fuming and the brandy lay in the glasses, Field would announce the bonuses, and praise those who had performed well during the year. He would also announce the firing of one man, with the remark that 'After January first, Mr. So-and-so will no longer be with us.' And that dead-looking left eye reflected no more sympathy than its fellow." Thus it was in the Gilded Age of unbridled capitalism.

■ WEST ACROSS THE RIVER

Although it boasts one of Chicago's most illustrious histories, the two-story **Hull House** looks like a red-brick interloper, wedged along Halsted Street against the gray concrete masses that form the University of Illinois at Chicago. In truth, the parvenu here is the university, whose moonscape campus landed on the Near West Side's Harrison-Halsted neighborhood in the 1960s and wiped out a sizable chunk of a close-knit Italian community that fought hard but failed to keep urban renewal at bay.

The wrecker's ball leveled most of the 13 buildings in the Hull House complex, where Jane Addams did her remarkable settlement work beginning in 1889 to give so many immigrants a better shot at the American dream. But the original Hull House was preserved as a museum, where visitors are reminded that this center-city area a bit west of the Chicago River was long one of the city's most vibrant and varied melting pots. Addams herself described the ethnic richness at the turn of the century: "Between Halsted Street and the river live about 10,000 Italians. In the south on 12th Street are many Germans, and side streets are given over to Polish and Russian Jews. Still farther south, thin Jewish colonies merge into a huge Bohemian colony, so vast that Chicago ranks as the third Bohemian city in the world." Northwest were French Canadians, with Irish to the north and beyond that a few "well-to-do English speaking families" along with one man "still living in his own farmhouse."

Addams spent the last 46 years of her life at Hull House, which she called "my place of work and residence." The Nobel Peace Prize she won in 1931 honored her decades of effort for international amity, women's suffrage, child-labor laws, better schools, improved public sanitation, and a host of other worthy causes. A shrewd businesswoman, Addams was also an impulsively generous soul with an assortment of eccentricities: she couldn't pass a hanging picture without straightening it. And a friend who traveled regularly with her reported that Addams always dressed completely in the hotel room closet, even arranging her hair perfectly in the semi-darkness. Of her Hull House, a prosperous Greek-American merchant remembered from his boyhood visits that "we walked into it as though we walked into our own house, and in that

Jane Addams, winner of the 1931 Nobel Prize for her 46 years of service to poor immigrants at Hull House. (University of Illinois at Chicago, Jane Addams Memorial Collection.)

nurturing warmth that animated everything and all, there sounded in our ears the soft words and sentences of the young women of the house, the only soft and kind words we immigrant boys heard in those days."

Little Italy's remnant west of the university is the only real ethnic community left in this once-variegated territory running west to Ashland Avenue from roughly Roosevelt Road in the south to Fulton Street in the north. But the campus, along with the large medical complex west of Ashland, has undeniably brought growth and stability to the area. Intrepid homeowners have restored fine old houses in the Jackson Boulevard District and elsewhere, while new townhome developments

ROSES IN CHICAGO

*I*n those early days we were often asked why we had come to live on Halsted Street when we could afford to live somewhere else. I remember one man who used to shake his head and say it was "the strangest thing he had met in his experience," but who was finally convinced that it was "not strange but natural." In time it came to seem natural to all of us that the Settlement should be there. If it is natural to feed the hungry and care for the sick, it is certainly natural to give pleasure to the young, comfort to the aged, and to minister to the deep-seated craving for social intercourse that all men feel. Whoever does it is rewarded by something which, if not gratitude, is at least spontaneous and vital and lacks that irksome sense of obligation with which a substantial benefit is too often acknowledged. . . .

We were also early impressed with the curious isolation of many of the immigrants; an Italian woman once expressed her pleasure in the red roses that she saw at one of our receptions in surprise that they had been "brought so fresh all the way from Italy." She would not believe for an instant that they had grown in America. She said that she had lived in Chicago for six years and had never seen any roses, whereas in Italy she had seen them every summer in great profusion. During all the time, of course, the woman had lived within ten blocks of a florist's window; she had not been more than a five-cent car ride away from the public parks; but she had never dreamed of faring forth for herself and no one had taken her. Her conception of America had been the untidy street in which she lived and had made her long struggle to adapt herself to American ways.

But in spite of some untoward experiences, we were constantly impressed with the uniform kindness and courtesy we received. Perhaps these first days laid the simple human foundations which are certainly essential for continuous living among the poor: first, genuine preference for residence in an industrial quarter to any other part of the city, because it is interesting and makes the human appeal; and second, the conviction, in the words of Canon Barnett, that the things which make men alike are finer and better than the things that keep them apart, and these basic likenesses, if they are properly accentuated, easily transcend the less essential differences of race, language, creed, and tradition.

Perhaps even in those first days we made a beginning toward that object which was afterwards stated in our charter: "To provide a center for a higher civic and social life; to institute and maintain educational and philanthropic enterprises, and to investigate and improve the conditions in the industrial districts of Chicago."

—Jane Addams, *Twenty Years at Hull-House,* 1910

The immigrants who flooded into the neighborhood of Hull House worked long hours and lived in miserable conditions, yet they often met adversity with pluck and good humor. (University of Illinois at Chicago, Jane Addams Memorial Collection)

have sprung up as well. Slicing through the area are intersecting expressways, which meet in a spaghetti-bowl tangle of ramps and overpasses just northeast of the university. You may still hear it called Circle Campus, an earlier name the administration has banished; it's now the University of Illinois at Chicago.

It's worth taking at least a brief stroll among the stark ensemble of university buildings designed by Walter A. Netsch Jr., a Skidmore, Owings and Merrill partner whose previous credits included the Air Force Academy in Colorado Springs. Netsch's UIC design motif was communications, focused on an open amphitheater descending from the center of a concrete Great Court, which forms the roof of six lecture halls. Chicago weather has conspired to dampen Netsch's hope that the amphitheater would serve as an outdoor forum for debate, drama, discussions, and political rallies. Its extent of use by UIC's 25,000 mostly commuter students varies widely with the season. The 28-story University Hall, housing administration and faculty offices, spreads as it rises so that it is 20 feet (6 m) wider at the top than the base. Best place to get a feel for campus life, if you can find your way among the labyrinth of pillars and walkways, is the teeming Student Center. Many undergrads are the first generation in their family to attend college, and they have the same things on their minds as students elsewhere—including where to find real-world work.

The tastes of Little Italy, to the southwest of the campus, include sit-down pasta and other robust fare in bursting-at-the-seams places like Tuscany, Rosebud Cafe, and Vernon Park Tap; stand-and-stuff-your-face sandwiches at Al's No. 1 Italian Beef; and the warm-weather treat of flavored syrup on shaved ice from the sidewalk stand of Mario's Italian Lemonade. For a casual visitor, the food spots and the green street-lamp banners proclaiming "A Touch of Italy" are the only obvious clues to the enclave's Mediterranean roots. You'd probably need to move in for a while to penetrate the ethnicity that remains, and you'd discover that many former Little Italy residents come back each Columbus Day to celebrate mass at **Our Lady of Pompeii Church**, on the corner of Lexington and Lytle streets.

Now in the university's southern shadow, one of Chicago's trademark attractions in the first half of this century was the raucous Maxwell Street open-air bazaar, where Jewish merchants sold goods of all kinds from stalls and pushcarts in a tumult reminiscent of New York's Lower East Side. Among distinguished alumni of the Maxwell Street neighborhood were Supreme Court Justice Arthur Goldberg, "King of Swing" Benny Goodman, and actor Paul Muni. "In its heyday, the

Summer festivals bring out the cooks. You can almost smell the barbecued Italian sausage.

street represented the trappings of free enterprise," writes Richard Lindberg in the new *Passport's Guide to Ethnic Chicago.* He adds that "the liveliest debate in town was not in Bughouse Square, where orange-crate orators espoused socialism, but between buyer and seller haggling over the price of a pair of knickers on Sunday morning at Maxwell and Halsted." The famous flea market hangs on as a scruffy shadow of its onetime vigor and may fall victim to UIC expansion. The busiest time is Sunday morning anytime after six o'clock, but what you've heard about the vintage Maxwell Street is better than anything you'll see (or find to buy) today.

The people of Maxwell Street Market may have been poor, but they were indefatigable entrepreneurs: their world was a confusion of stalls, boxes, wagons, and pushcarts, all offering goods at prices that could be reduced through spirited haggling. (Kogan Collection)

Immediately north of the university, the dozen and more Greek restaurants packed along Halsted between Adams and Van Buren are virtually all that's left of a **Hellenic community** so sizable a century ago that the area was known as the Delta (after the triangular letter in the Greek alphabet). Each restaurant has its partisans, and you'll hear in all of them the cry of "Opaa!" as waiters brandish the *saganaki,* a flaming cheese appetizer created not in Athens but here in Chicago. Tucked among the cheerfully noisy restaurants are a few shops like the Athenian Candle Company, which also purveys incense; the Pan Hellenic Bakery, for baklava or spinach pie to go; and the Athens Grocery, stocked with feta cheese and vats of plump Greek olives. You can taste the commercial flavor of Greece along Halsted, but the residential community has dispersed throughout the Chicago area.

Visitors heading west from the Loop to Greektown on Madison Street get a visual wallop from an astonishing public sculpture. It's Claes Oldenburg's "**Batcolumn**," a latticework baseball bat that stands 100 feet (30 m) tall outside the Social Security Administration Center across the street from the Presidential Towers apartment complex along the former Skid Row. A couple of blocks south, Amtrak riders set foot in Chicago at Union Station, where a recent renovation has restored a measure of the gleam from railroading's golden era. The wholesale meat and produce warehouses along Randolph Street at Desplaines occupy the site of the 1886 Haymarket Affair, when eight policemen and two bystanders were killed by a bomb thrown during an outdoor rally called to protest brutality against workers at the strikebound McCormick Harvester Works. Eight anarchists were convicted of murder, despite a lack of evidence they'd had any part in the bombing; four were hanged and a fifth committed suicide by exploding a dynamite cap with his teeth. A policeman's statue honoring the dead officers stood until 1970 at the bombing location. After it was twice toppled (with the radical Weathermen claiming credit the second time), the sculpture spent four years at Police Headquarters before finding its current home in the atrium of the Police Training Academy, 1300 West Jackson Boulevard.

And if you think fire departments lack a sense of irony, head for block-long DeKoven Street, east across the Dan Ryan Expressway from the university. The red-brick **Chicago Fire Academy,** where fledgling firefighters get their training, was built in 1960 at 558 West DeKoven, on the very site of the O'Leary family house and barn where the Great Fire of 1871 started. "**Pillar of Fire**," an elegant bronze sculpture by Egon Weiner, marks the location of the barn where the fire apparently began—but most probably without any cow kicking over a lantern.

Patrick and Catherine O'Leary's humble frame house survived the conflagration, which raged northward on strong winds. A prosperous Bohemian later built a two-story brick residence with a white marble front where the O'Learys had lived. Now it must be one of the safest places in the city for a fire to break out.

■ NORTH OF THE RIVER

Cradled in two arms of the Chicago River, the near-Loop enclave now called River North looked like a loser in the 1970s. Settled first by Irish laborers in the 1840s, it had hummed in the half-century after the Chicago Fire of 1871 as a hive of factories built mostly of sturdy red brick, with a patina of mansions dressing up its eastern fringe. Then the industrial enterprises began giving way to warehouses between the world wars, and the handsome dwellings found themselves slumming as rooming houses. In the 1960s, the Cabrini-Green highrise public housing just to the northwest cast a shadow of poverty and crime, as most of the remaining warehouse and factory operations pulled up stakes.

Left intact were the solid shells of all those derelict lofts, which turned out to be an irresistible lure for artists and other creative spirits in search of cheaper quarters with ample elbow room. The artful arrivals soon reached critical mass to generate River North, Chicago's answer of the 1980s to New York's raffish SoHo quarter. Some called it SuHu, playing off the concentration of galleries on Superior and Huron streets—while one wag suggested WeeWee (west of Wells Street). The district became a hothouse of studios, galleries, restaurants, and clubs, so fashionable by the start of this decade that restless artists were staking out more pristine (and less pricey) neighborhoods to the west. Meanwhile, the retailing triumph of North Michigan Avenue was giving a trickle-down boost to development along Wabash, State, Ontario, and other stretches on River North's eastern edge.

River North's boundaries extend roughly to Chicago Avenue on the north and Rush Street on the east, a territory of not much more than a square mile (2.6 sq km) best explored on foot. Although no longer an urban frontier, it still sees frequent comings and goings of businesses and attractions: a second **Berghoff's**, clone of the landmark Loop restaurant, materializes at 436 West Ontario in the last block before the river; the stimulating **Peace Museum** vanishes from 430 West Erie and aims to find a new home in the neighborhood. Sharply higher rents and the economy's overall malaise are increasing the number of empty windows.

But nobody is about to move the **Merchandise Mart,** which has been anchored since 1930 on the river's north bank between Wells and Orleans. This 25-story blockbuster—call it Art Deco on steroids—began life as the world's largest building (superseded a decade later by the Pentagon). It still ranks as the biggest commercial structure anywhere, with 4.2 million square feet (378,000 sq m) of floor space devoted to home and office furnishings as well as other design products. Department store magnate Marshall Field III erected the mammoth mart as a national center of wholesale showrooms and offices, but the Great Depression was already entrenched by the time the facility opened in 1931, and Joseph P. Kennedy picked it up at a bargain price in 1945. The general public is barred from wandering around the showrooms in the mart or the mid-'70s Chicago Apparel Center just to the west, but guided visits are available through the Tours at the Mart program. Tourists are also welcome to admire the south lobby's Jules Guerin murals depicting the history of trade around the globe. And they're more than welcome to spend time and money in the mart's new two-level shopping mall and international food court. One of the Apparel Center's two towers is topped by the Holiday Inn Mart Plaza, notable for the splendid skyline panoramas from its 525 guest rooms.

The Merchandise Mart, a wholesale outlet for furnishings and design products which was built in 1930, still ranks second only to the Pentagon as America's largest office structure.

East along the river past the sleek Japanese-owned Hotel Nikko, the circular twin towers of Marina City are a fixture among Chicago's postcard images three decades after Bertrand Goldberg designed the distinctive mixed-use complex with its flower-petal balconies. At the outset of the '90s, the commercial space that Goldberg hoped would make Marina City virtually a self-contained community had deteriorated into a ghost town. That was a source of rising anxiety for condominium owners in the 60-story towers, where apartments shaped like a blunt wedge of pie have always presented a decorating challenge.

Ludwig Mies van der Rohe's final office design, the 52-story IBM **Building**, presents the instructive contrast of a firmly rectilinear profile just to the east of all-curves Marina City. Miesian pilgrims can revere a bust of the master Modernist in the lobby of the IBM, which has garnered deserved praise from architecture critics for the superb proportions of its precisely detailed curtain wall of dark aluminum and bronze-tinted glass. But the IBM is the bane of pedestrians for the winter winds that whip across its plaza—not quite a hurricane, but enough to topple an unwary wayfarer. On the worst days, management sets up a chain of ropes to aid unfortunates battling the headwinds between Wabash and State streets. The rappeling is Chicago's variant of mountain climbing—on a horizontal plane.

A hike north up State behind the IBM Building passes one of Chicago's best wurst joints, teeming Gold Coast Dogs, on its way to River North's sleekest piece of new architecture. The 515 North State Street building, headquarters of the American Medical Association, went up in 1990 as the first major commercial design in this country by Japan's Kenzo Tange. The glass-and-aluminum curtain walls of the 30-floor tower are pierced near the top by a four-story, see-through cutout. Lunchtime picnickers can find a congenial venue on the building's landscaped plaza—not a bad place to munch a Gold Coast hot dog. Across State Street at 11 West Grand, the **Jazz Record Mart** claims the largest stock anywhere of jazz and blues titles.

The art milieu of an earlier era is manifest along State between Ohio and Ontario in the yellow-brick **Tree Studios Building**, constructed in 1894 by Judge Lambert Tree to provide 17 artists with working space arranged around an interior courtyard that remains a small oasis of urban calm for anyone who ventures through its Ohio Street entrance. Some artists still reside at Tree Studios, now owned by the Medinah Temple Association, whose **Medinah Temple** fronting on Wabash Avenue to the east represents the Shriners' notion (circa 1912) of a

Moorish mosque, complete with onion domes, crescents, and Islamic motifs in the grillwork and stone trim. The circus is a yearly crowd-pleaser in the temple's 2,000-seat auditorium.

Food as entertainment forms one motif of a stroll west on Ontario from Rush to Wells. Ghosts of marionettes whisper inside the former McCormick Mansion, now the setting for Lawry's The Prime Rib, where today's showbiz features a spinning salad bowl, and beef trolleys almost as formidable as an armored personnel carrier. Chicagoans of a certain age recall fondly the puppet theater that enlivened the mansion during its Swedish incarnation as the Kungsholm. The Romanesque Revival fortress on the northwest corner of Ohio and Dearborn is a nightclub with a checkered past. Built in 1892, it housed the Chicago Historical Society until 1931, did Depression-era time as a Moose lodge, and was briefly home of the famed Bauhaus School of Design in the '40s. In the last couple of decades, it has watched several nightclubs arrive and depart; as of this writing, the entertainment complex styles itself Excalibur.

South across Dearborn, that Neo-Georgian Revival structure is a **Commonwealth Edison** substation, a 1989 design by Tigerman McCurry to echo the 1929 power facility it replaced. The design was also devised to be compatible with the neighboring Hard Rock Cafe, a 1985 Tigerman McCurry commission. The world may not have needed another Hard Rock Cafe, but this one continues to pack in suburbanites and tourists as well as the occasional wayward Chicagoan. For a double dip of rock nostalgia, step west to the next-door Rock-N-Roll McDonald's, so called because its memorabilia-crammed interior takes customers on a nostalgia bender back to the rock heyday of the 1950s and '60s. The Big Macs are merely a side dish here to the flashing pinball machines, red '63 Corvette, and life-size white sculptures of the four Beatles on parade. For slightly more serious dining in the '50s time warp, it's two more blocks west on Ontario to Ed Debevic's, a whimsical and very popular reincarnation of an Eisenhower-era diner where you needn't be ashamed of ordering meatloaf.

West and north of all this pop culture lies the heart of River North's **gallery quarter** along Erie, Huron, and Superior as well as north-south Franklin and Orleans streets. Many of the 50-plus galleries here schedule openings of new shows for Friday evenings, a prime time to stroll and browse while sipping the jug wine that's often part of the program. Widely available in the neighborhood is *Chicago Gallery News,* which lists exhibits, hours, and other useful details for

SuHu hopping. Reliable Italian and Mexican fare with a Chicago twist is dished up respectively at Scoozi! and Hat Dance, two noisy Huron Street outposts of the Lettuce Entertain You empire. A place with a more venerable pedigree is the Green Door Tavern, 678 North Orleans, a bastion of burgers, chili, and other stick-to-the-ribs fare since 1921, in a frame building that went up a year after the Chicago Fire of 1871.

Back east on Superior at State Street, the hats of several former cardinals hang from the ceiling of **Holy Name Cathedral,** which has served the Roman Catholic Archdiocese of Chicago since it was erected in 1874 to replace a smaller late-Victorian church destroyed in the Chicago Fire of 1871. The archdiocese remains one of the most influential powers in the Chicago area, serving 2.5-million Roman Catholics, although it is having to close some inner-city churches because of shifting population. The parking lot opposite the cathedral on the west side of State was occupied in the 1920s by a row of shops, including Schofield florists, where mob chieftains Dion O'Banion and Hymie Weiss were gunned down by Al Capone's hitmen during the Prohibition wars.

Another post-fire church, the **Episcopal Cathedral of St. James,** at Wabash and Huron, has a typical English Gothic exterior of the 1870s. But the interior, carefully restored in 1985, is a revelation for its wealth of Arts and Crafts Movement stencil work, executed in 1888 in 26 colors focused on stylized plant motifs. That period treasure is an exemplar of the mixed bag of surprises in evolving River North, where twenty-first century visitors may well find yet another neighborhood permutation.

The Bull's mascot sits atop Ed Debevic's restaurant in Near North.

■ MAGNIFICENT MILE

Amid the North Michigan Avenue building boom of the last two decades, the Old Chicago Water Tower has stood its ground as the civic talisman that miraculously survived the Great Fire of 1871. But the circling skyscrapers have contrived to shrink this mock-Gothic good-luck charm once vilified by Oscar Wilde as "a castellated monstrosity with pepper boxes stuck all over it," so that the cream-yellow **Water Tower** at first glance now resembles a runty mascot best suited to adorn souvenir postcards and coffee mugs. Hard to believe, but the 154-foot (46-m)-high tower was the tallest Michigan Avenue structure north of the Chicago River as recently as 1920. That was the year when widening of the thoroughfare and the opening of its double-deck bridge gave birth to "the Magnificent Mile," which eventually dethroned downtown State Street as Chicago's premier shopping district in the 1970s and fueled the recent lakeward development in Streeterville to the east.

This is the patch of 1990s' Chicago where it's easiest to slip into the tourist groove, as you meld into the throngs of giggling suburban teen-agers, badge-marked conventioneers, and other promenaders. You can hop a horse-drawn carriage, ride a London-style red double-decker bus, cough up some coins for sidewalk musicians, play miniature golf indoors, tuck into a trademark deep-dish pizza, and round up a wad of brochures complete with discount coupons. The Magnificent Mile does lack the spacious grandeur of the Champs-Elysees, and the Water Tower hardly manages the gravity of the Arc de Triomphe, but Chicago's avenue far surpasses its legendary Paris counterpart in the serious matter of shopping.

For a multimedia gloss on local attractions, there's the "Here's Chicago" show in the Chicago Avenue Pumping Station east across Michigan Avenue from the Water Tower. Vintage photographs at "Here's Chicago" may help you envision the accelerating rise of the Magnificent Mile along what had been a residential thoroughfare known as Pine Street until World War I. First came the Drake Hotel at the avenue's north end in 1920, then the Wrigley Building (1924) and the Tribune Tower (1925) less than a mile (1.6 km) to the south, followed by a scattered crop of highrise hotels and other structures. A Chicagoan writing in the *Saturday Evening Post* was dazzled enough to boast that Michigan Avenue made New York's Fifth Avenue seem "hardly more than a side street." Well-heeled motorists liked to promenade their fancy new cars down the avenue during the automobile boom of the 1920s, defying that era's 15 mph (24 kph) speed limit when traffic allowed.

But the Water Tower still had elbow room until the 1,127-foot (343-m) **John Hancock Center** swaggered into the neighborhood in 1970 as catalyst for the sky's-the-limit construction frenzy that has transformed Michigan Avenue into a grand canyon of conspicuous consumption. The 875-foot (266-m) behemoth that goes by its address of 900 North Michigan Avenue and the 859-foot (261-m) whopper called Water Tower Place currently rank second and third in the boulevard's skyscraper sweepstakes, which seemed to run on the principle "More is more" before cooling in the economic chill that ushered in the '90s. For gleam-in-the-eye shoppers, the Magnificent Mile is the place in Chicago that really matters: Bloomingdale's, Saks Fifth Avenue, Neiman-Marcus, Lord & Taylor, Marshall Field's, and a host of designer-label specialty shops from Burberry's to Tiffany's including a traffic-stopping F.A.O. Schwarz toyland that opened in 1992 just north of the Water Tower. Never mind that 15 mph (24 kph) is a rush-hour fantasy as Michigan Avenue traffic jams grow more intractable by the year. When the myriad tiny white lights twinkle on the avenue's procession of trees in the Christmas season, there is still enough magnificence to go around.

Aiming to recapture some of the avenue's old magic from the Grinch of commercialism, the local merchants' association created a holiday tree-lighting ceremony in 1992. Slated for the Saturday before Thanksgiving each year, it features a procession of horse-drawn carriages, double-decker buses, costumed Christmas characters, and musicians parading south down Michigan from Oak Street to the Wrigley Building as the twinkling Italian lights are turned on block by block. Carolers and mayoral remarks cap the event, intended to put some human spirit back into the concrete canyon.

The Water Tower is closed to the public and occupied by the administrative staff of the Chicago Office of Tourism, while that body's brochures and a mound of other free literature are dispensed at the Pumping Station. Paid admission to "Here's Chicago," which puts on a better show than the average booster extravaganza, also affords a look at the functioning waterworks that occupy part of the station. Although not a heart-stopping thrill, all those pipes and valves do provide a clue that the Water Tower was erected not to edify latter-day tourists but as part of essential improvements in the city's water system. The tower disguised a 138-foot (42-m)-high standpipe that equalized the pressure of water pumped through the station from a new Lake Michigan tunnel and intake unit (a forerunner of the circular cribs that hover on today's offshore horizon). *Edwards' Chicago City Guide for 1869-70* reported that:

> The good people of Chicago suffered great affliction in the character of the water that they used. It was a dirty fluid taken from the edge of the lake and often abounding with scaly inhabitants of the great deep whose presence in the houses and on the tables recalled the Egyptian plague of the fishes. But engineering skill has overcome that difficulty, and now gives us the finest water in the world, deep from the bottom of the lake.

Touché, Vittel, and Evian—although nobody is bottling Chicago Tap with a designer label.

To the Water Tower's west, where the Magnificent Mile's prosperity now oozes, blossomed Chicago's equivalent of Greenwich Village in this century's early decades. It was described in a 1929 book, *The Gold Coast and the Slum*, by Harvey Warren Zorbaugh:

> *If* one gets off the bus at the Water Tower and rambles the streets within a half-mile radius of it, one discovers, tucked away in dilapidated buildings, quaint restaurants, interesting art shops and book stalls, tearooms, stables and garrets with flower boxes, alley dwellings, cards in windows bearing the legend 'Studio for Rent.' For this is the 'village,' Chicago's Latin Quarter, dubbed by the newspapers 'Towertown' because it lies about the foot of the Water Tower.

In Towertown's heyday before World War I, it was home to writers the likes of Sherwood Anderson, Ben Hecht, Carl Sandburg, Edgar Lee Masters, and Alfred Kreymborg. Towertown has vanished from the local gazetteer today, but a few ghosts linger on some of the blocks heading west to the current River North galleries quarter.

North of the Water Tower and F.A.O. Schwarz, God keeps a foothold on the west side of Michigan at Chestnut by grace of the **Fourth Presbyterian Church**, built in 1914 in Gothic Revival style for a blueblooded congregation whose spiritual descendants attend today. At lunchtime or on Sunday afternoon, you may be fortunate enough to find a concert in progress. But Mammon is firmly entrenched

The Water Tower, shown here through a screen of falling snow on a wintry evening, was once the highest structure in Chicago, and survived the Great Fire of 1871.

in the final two blocks before Michigan fades into Lake Shore Drive at Oak Street: Bloomingdale's anchors the upscale shopping in the 66-story 900 North Michigan Avenue tower, which also contains the highly rated Four Seasons Hotel; and One Magnificent Mile rises 58 stories at 940-980 North Michigan with Polo Ralph Lauren, Chanel, Giacomo, and their kin on three levels at the base. Around the corner, the block of Oak Street stretching west to Rush Street is a browser's bonanza of wall-to-wall boutiques, galleries, and salons.

The **Drake,** a low-rise these days at 13 stories but a grande dame among the city's luxury hotels, has a splendid Art Deco neighbor to the south across Walton Street. It's 919 North Michigan Avenue, a Holabird and Root skyscraper formerly known as the Playboy Building and before that as the Palmolive Building; it went up in 1930 just as the Great Depression brought a hiatus of almost two decades in major Chicago commercial construction. The mast atop the building supported an aerial navigation beacon, which was a landmark of the night sky for decades but went dark in the '70s once twice-as-tall neighbors dwarfed it. Condo cliff-dwellers in the upper stories of the Hancock Center the next block south complained that the powerful beam cast a blinding light into their apartments. It's bad enough waking up above the clouds, as Hancock inhabitants occasionally find themselves doing on low-ceiling mornings, without having your private life in the spotlight. On a clear day, the views from the center's 94th-floor observatory are, if anything, better than from the higher Sears Tower eyrie a mile-and-a-half (2.4 km) to the southwest.

Take a suburban mega-mall, stand it on end, add a sleek hotel plus pricey condominiums, and you have Water Tower Place, the marble-clad fortress that is Hancock's next-door neighbor to the south. This was a mid-'70s prototype for the vertical shopping mall, replete with atrium and other mesmerizing accoutrements, that makes visitors from the outlands feel as though they'd brought suburbia with them. You could spend the better part of a day—and a lot of people do—filtering through Water Tower Place's two department stores (Lord & Taylor and Marshall Field's) and seven levels of specialty shops (including stylish Rizzoli International Bookstore and Gallery). Through a separate entrance on Pearson Street, elevators whisk guests to the 12th-floor lobby of the Ritz-Carlton Hotel, which vies with the Four Seasons for top ranking locally.

Mall-aise can easily set in along North Michigan Avenue if you have an allergy to recreational shopping. One antidote is the perspective a newspaper writer brought in 1927 to its first generation of swanky shops: "Scattered up and down

Michigan Avenue are many exclusive shops furnished in the latest Louis XV, Spanish, and Italian styles. Unlike most museums, these have no admission fee; but a cover charge is added to the price of each purchase." Approach the vertical malls as though they were well-stocked interactive exhibits in the art of conspicuous consumption.

If the skyscraper life is beginning to pall, the west side of Michigan Avenue's two blocks from Erie to Ohio brings low-rise relief and a nice mix of allures: Stuart Brent Books, a Chicago literary fixture with a proprietor of vigorous opinions; next-door Garrett Popcorn Shop (but buy your fresh-popped bag after leafing through the bookstore); Terra Museum of American Art, a trove of American Impressionist paintings; Crate & Barrel, the five-story headquarters store of this housewares heaven; Hammacher Schlemmer, the guru of gadgets; and a number of galleries including the long-esteemed Richard Gray. Deep-dish stalwarts Pizzeria Uno and Pizzeria Due lie in wait just a block or two inland.

COYOTE, AS PET, MAKES A HIT IN CHICAGO

News item February 11, 1920: When Mrs. L.M. Watson of Hayden, Colorado, a former Chicago girl, visited the shopping district along Michigan Avenue, she took her constant companion and pet, "Sir Coy," a full blooded coyote captured by her husband at Bags Hole, Colorado, and given her as a wedding present. The coyote made a tremendous hit, as the photo shows. Mrs. Watson is the lady with the hat and fur on.

(Underwood Photo Archives)

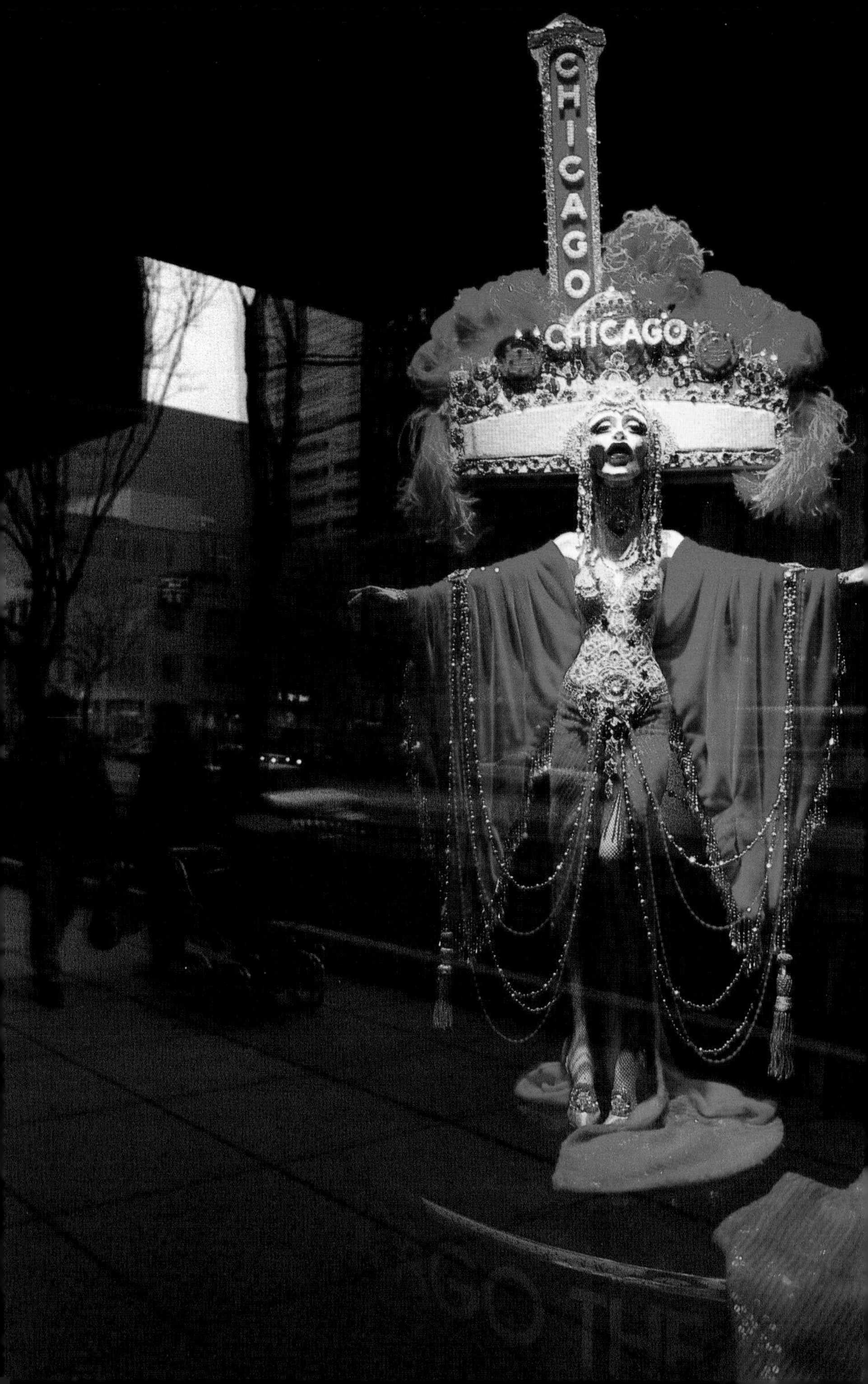
CHICAGO
CHICAGO

The **Wrigley Building**, overlooking the Chicago River on Michigan Avenue's west side somewhere near the homestead site of pioneer settler Jean Baptiste Point du Sable, may bring to mind a wedding cake with its swirls and squiggles of terra-cotta decoration. Nonetheless, this is one of the city's most beloved icons, a romance more plausible once you've seen its shimmering white transformation when the floodlights go on after dark. Across the avenue to the north, the **Tribune Tower** provides more exterior entertainment and edification than a score of less flamboyant buildings: a facade imbedded with chunks of stone from the Alamo, the Taj Mahal, and a host of other landmarks around the globe; oversized reproductions of famous *Chicago Tribune* front pages etched in copper; a glass-fronted studio for the Tribune Company's WGN radio station; and a cap of full-fledged flying buttresses that evoke Europe's Gothic cathedrals. The Gothic Revival design by Hood and Howells won an international competition in the early '20s—although the great Louis Sullivan was not impressed. "It is an imaginary structure—not imaginative," said Sullivan in the last year of his life. Of the Tribune building's flying buttresses, he complained that the designers had crowned the tower with a monstrous spider. The crown on its 41-story northward neighbor, the recently renovated Hotel Inter-Continental Chicago, is a prominent mosque-like dome bespeaking an earlier life as the Medinah Athletic Club. Off the lower level of Michigan Avenue between the Wrigley Building and Tribune Tower, Billy Goat Tavern claims fame as the greasy inspiration for John Belushi's "cheesebugga, cheesebugga" sketches on "Saturday Night Live." Stick to the beer.

East of the Tribune Tower, in the Streeterville territory that began as a shanty-town perched on landfill a century ago, the 38-story NBC Tower is an invigorating 1989 arrival from Skidmore, Owings & Merrill, echoing some of the city's best Art Deco buildings from the 1920s. Its newer neighbor, the massive **Sheraton Chicago Hotel and Towers**, boasts a terrace cafe perfect for watching pleasure-boat traffic ply the river on a sunny day. It's also a cozy rest-and-recovery spot after tackling the varied enticements of North Pier Terminal, a former commercial pier now given over to the tourist trade as a festival marketplace with a nice mix of diversions. **City Golf Chicago** garnishes its putting course with miniatures of local landmarks; **Chicago Children's Museum** engages youngsters with such touch-and-feel exhibits as "The Stinking Truth About Garbage"; **Chicago Maritime Museum** includes a fascinating section on Lake Michigan shipwrecks. There are several noisy restaurants in the complex, and a chapel as counterpoint. The Chicago Architecture Foundation's ultra-informative river cruises depart from the pier.

Window display along Michigan Avenue's Magnificent Mile, Chicago's premier shopping district.

Farther east past the three-lobed Lake Point Tower apartments, spun in the late '60s by Mies van der Rohe students from a skyscraper project he'd proposed for Berlin in 1921, stretches **Navy Pier**. A former Navy training facility and University of Illinois branch campus, the 3,000-foot (904-m)-long pier is due to emerge from a thoroughgoing renovation. It has been the site in recent years of the prestigious International Art Exposition. The formidable municipal water-filtration plant to

---

CAPTAIN STREETER'S DOMAIN

Chicago's gallery of rogues, which would need a couple of Art Institutes to hang its innumerable portraits, contains few characters more engaging or determined than George Wellington (Cap) Streeter. This rascally showman, who'd gone bust as a circus and theater owner, defied law and order as well as his high and mighty neighbors for more than three decades from a lakefront shantytown that he styled "the District of Lake Michigan" and claimed allegiance only to the federal government. Cap eventually lost his turn-of-the-century domain, but lived to be 84, and even Mayor William Hale Thompson turned out for his funeral. East of Michigan Avenue, some of the city's priciest real estate bears his name today as the Streeterville neighborhood.

The Streeter saga began here in 1886 when Cap and his wife, Maria (Ma), got their broken-down steamboat stuck on a sandbar several hundred feet from that era's shoreline, roughly due east of where the John Hancock Center towers today. As Lois Wille tells the tale with gusto in *Forever Open, Clear and Free: The Struggle for Chicago's Lakefront,* Streeter filled in and staked out 186 acres of sand and debris around the derelict vessel, which he dismantled in 1889 to build a shack he christened "The Castle." One day, according to Wille's account, a wealthy Lake Shore Drive property owner told Streeter, "You've got to get out of here. This is my land. I've got riparian rights." The leathery Cap barked back, "I've got squatter's rights and the right to eminent domain. Now git." He squirted tobacco juice at the businessman's feet, while Ma waved her ax and a pistol.

Declaring himself governor of "the District of Lake Michigan," Cap sold beer on dry Sundays and performed marriages. There were pitched battles over the years with police and a number of deaths, but he held out until 1918 and weathered into a local celebrity. "He clung on through hard times and good, growing constantly in pride, aware that the newspapers had made him a public figure," wrote Henry Justin Smith and Lloyd Lewis in *Chicago: The History of Its Reputation.* They found him "always glad to be interviewed, but holding a long Springfield rifle, with a bayonet, on his arm as a threat to the constables." He was a Chicago original.

the north of Navy Pier is fringed by Olive Park, a landscaped grace note that affords superlative views of the lakeshore skyline. Immediately to its west nestles one of Chicago's smallest public beaches, Ohio Street Beach, where sunbathers face a northern exposure that will quickly remind them it's a long way to the nearest tropical strand.

Ontario, the next street north from Ohio, is thick with restaurants but has lost some of its cachet as a gallery strip to River North and other more westerly precincts. And it stands to lose the **Museum of Contemporary Art** when that cutting-edge institution opens new galleries with a sculpture garden a few blocks north at 234 East Chicago Avenue later this decade. The MCA's current location, 237 East Ontario, was the first U.S. building wrapped by Christo. There'll be a challenge to your perceptions in whatever special exhibition the museum happens to be hosting, and its permanent collection ranges from Surrealism to Pop Art with an emphasis on Chicago artists. There are fine examples of antic canvases from the local "Hairy Who" school by Ed Paschke, Jim Nutt, Roger Brown, and others.

Sailors at the Navy Pier near Grant Park.

■ GOLD COAST

Neighboring blocks are sometimes worlds apart in Chicago, and visitors can get a choice example of how swiftly the landscape shifts by making the brisk four-minute walk from Astor and Goethe (German tourists note: it's "GO-thee" here) to State and Division. Astor Street is elegant and architecturally distinctive enough to be the heart of a namesake historic district. One of the city's creme de la creme addresses since the 1880s, it is lined with mansions built by several generations of Chicago's major movers and shakers. Astor speaks in a cultivated and well-heeled whisper, modulated by the discreet crinkle of old money.

The language is loud, lubricious, and boozy on the action-packed block of Division Street from State west to Dearborn. For the last three decades, this has been Chicago's prime nocturnal meat market, a vortex of elbow-to-elbow singles bars where the pickup lines vary from year to year but the point of the boy-meets-girl exercise remains the same. One concession to this decade's AIDS crisis is the Condoms Now boutique operating almost directly across the street from Butch McGuire's, which opened in 1961 as the city's first full-fledged singles bar. This raucous block is at its best—or worst—during Chicago's annual St. Patrick's Day binge, when it helps if you can stomach green beer and battalions of drunks.

Astor runs a half-mile (.8 km) down the Gold Coast, where a nouveau-riche invasion of apartment skyscrapers since the 1970s has somewhat sapped the sylvan atmosphere along the shaded streets. But property values appear to be holding up nicely; the average sales price of Gold Coast mansions is approaching a million dollars. A stroll up Astor makes a soothing change of pace for shoppers who have overheated their charge cards in Michigan Avenue's highrise malls to the south. As for those singles bars, which hover near the Gold Coast's southern extremity, they can be approached in the spirit of the anthropologist. An urban archeologist might be better equipped to pick through the decline and fall of Rush Street, the once naughty but now dispirited nightlife strip that runs diagonally into State State just south of the Gold Coast proper.

Real-estate and department-store magnate Potter Palmer and his wife, Bertha, began the Gold Coast land rush in 1882 by deserting the South Side to build their $1 million castellated residence at 1350 North Lake Shore Drive on the eastern outskirts of a neighborhood settled by German immigrants in the 1840s and Swedes in the 1860s. The Palmer castle, described by an architecture critic as "a mansion to end all mansions," spurred a quintupling of land values over the next decade on the Gold Coast (roughly bounded by the lake, North Avenue, La Salle Street, and Oak Street).

The Palmers' entryway set a tone of conspicuous opulence with its soaring octagonal space three stories high, hung with Gobelin tapestries, strewn with tiger skins and Oriental rugs, and set off with a massive fireplace. The mansion's most

peculiar feature was an absence of outside doorknobs or keyholes on any of the doors, which had to be opened from the inside by a servant. Bertha Palmer became the undisputed queen of Chicago society, as well as a prime patron of the new-fangled and controversial French Impressionist art. She entertained labor leaders and social reformers along with industrialists and socialites. And, as Finis Farr recounted in his 1973 *Chicago* history, "in the cavernous kitchens of the mansion, Mrs. Palmer conducted a cooking school for society girls. Why should a rich girl learn to cook? There were several reasons, according to Bertha Palmer: For one thing, a young woman needed practical knowledge to direct a husband's household property. . . . But suppose the young couple should be so pushed for money they could afford only one servant. Then it would be a good thing if the bride could prepare meals, on that servant's twice-monthly day off."

Mrs. Bertha Palmer launched a cooking school for debutantes in her mansion, as she believed girls needed practical knowledge to properly manage a staff—or fill in should the cook quit. (Chicago Sun-Times)

A rich chunk of Chicago heritage was lost when the old Palmer place fell to the wrecker's ball in 1951 to make way for a 22-story apartment tower—after Chicagoans were allowed a chance to tour the erstwhile castle for 50 cents. The neighborhood's surviving Gilded Age mansions include the three-story Venetian Gothic townhouse designed by Holabird and Roche at 1258 North Lake Shore; a Georgian Revival design by that firm at 1260 North Lake Shore; the vine-covered townhouse row built by Potter Palmer at 36-48 East Schiller; Burnham and Root's trio of sandstone and red-brick rowhouses at 1308-1312 North Astor; and the Romanesque Revival residence at 1443 North Astor.

Even more notable, though hardly typical of the era, is the **James Charnley House** (1365 North Astor), officially the work of Adler and Sullivan but almost certainly an 1892 creation of the young Frank Lloyd Wright, then a draftsman for that famous firm. There's hardly a hint of Wright's later Prairie School revolution in the blocky three-story townhome built around a skylighted central stairwell and garnished with a second-floor balcony.

The most luxurious Gold Coast apartment building of its day, and still a handsome structure, 1550 North State Parkway originally boasted a single 15-room apartment on each of its 12 floors renting for $8,400 a year—in rock-solid 1912 dollars. Designed with a Beaux Arts facade by the distinguished Benjamin Marshall, it had five servant's chambers per apartment, as well as a grand salon and petit salon, an orangerie, two dressing rooms in the main bedroom "so that a valet can enter the gentleman's dressing room without passing through the bedchamber," and a range with three broilers "so that steaks and fish need never be prepared on the same broiler." Today's apartments at 1550 are smaller, and the three-broiler ranges have gone the way of the valet.

In a league of its own is the rambling residence of the **Roman Catholic Archbishop of Chicago,** just south of Lincoln Park at 1555 North State Parkway. No fewer than 19 chimneys sprout from this Queen Anne pile set on spacious grounds; it is the oldest surviving structure in the Astor Street District, dating to 1880. The sacred dwelling had a profane neighbor of some notoriety in the 1960s when Hugh Hefner and his nubile bunnies cavorted in the Playboy Mansion, 1340 North State. After Hefner took his Playboy philosophy to California, the School of the Art Institute bunked its students in the 1899-vintage Georgian residence for a number of years before it went back on the market. At 1209 North State, Art Moderne has its moment at the Frank Fisher Apartments, a brick design of 1936 by Andrew Rebori with terra-cotta detailing by artist Edgar Miller.

The James Charnley house on the Gold Coast.

THEM WAS THE DAYS

*W*ith her truthfulness, her rigid sense of honor, her fearless outlook, she seemed to him to collect in herself all that was the most admirable in his countrywomen. But he saw in her something more than the perfect type of the American girl, he felt that her exquisiteness was peculiar in a way to her environment, and he was assured that no city in the world could have produced her but Chicago.

But at last the train steamed into Chicago and he exulted when he saw the long streets of grey houses. He could hardly bear his impatience at the thought of State and Wabash with her crowded pavements, her hustling traffic, and their noise. He was at home. And he was glad that he had been born in the most important city in the United States. San Francisco was provincial, New York was effete; the future of America lay in the development of its economic possibilities, and Chicago by its position and by the energy of its citizens, was destined to become the real capital of the country.

"I guess I shall live long enough to see it the biggest city in the world," Bateman said to himself as he stepped down to the platform.

His father had come to meet him, and after a hearty handshake, the pair of them, tall, slender, and well-made, with the same fine, ascetic features and thin lips, walked out of the station. Mr Hunter's automobile was waiting for them and they got in. Mr Hunter caught his son's proud and happy glance as he looked at the street.

"Glad to be back, son?" he asked.

"I should just think I was," said Bateman.

His eyes devoured the restless scene.

"I guess there's a bit more traffic here than in your South Sea island," laughed Mr Hunter. "Did you like it there?"

"Give me Chicago, dad," answered Bateman.

They passed out of the crowded streets in the Loop and drove along the lake till they came to the imposing house, an exact copy of a château on the Loire, which Mr Hunter had built himself some years before. As soon as Bateman was alone in his room he asked for a number on the telephone. His heart leaped when he heard the voice that answered . . . .

> "When may I see you?"
> "Unless you have anything better to do perhaps you'll dine with us to-nite."
>
> ❖ ❖ ❖
>
> At dinner, at which beside himself and Isabel no one was present but her father and mother, he watched her guide the conversation into channels of an urbane small-talk. . . . The dining-room was a fitting frame to her fragile beauty, for Isabel had caused the house, a replica of a palace on the Grand Canal at Venice, to be furnished by an English expert in the style of Louis XV. . . . She spoke now of the *Musicale* to which she and her mother had been in the afternoon, of the lectures which an English poet was giving at the Auditorium, of the political situation, and of the Old Master which her father had recently bought for fifty thousand dollars in New York. It comforted Bateman to hear her. He felt that he was once more in the civilised world, at the centre of culture and distinction; and certain voices, troubling and yet against his will refusing to still their clamour, were at last silent in his heart.
>
> "Gee, but it's good to be back in Chicago," he said.
>
> —W. Somerset Maugham, *The Fall of Edward Barnard*, 1921

Not for the extremely squeamish is the **International Museum of Surgical Science**, a 32-room survey course in medical history inside the headquarters mansion of the International College of Surgeons at 1524 North Lake Shore. From trepanning and blood-letting to kidney-stone crushing and pre-anesthesia amputations, the detailed exhibits serve as a graphic reminder of how physically painful life could be prior to the medical revolution of the past century. Museum artifacts include one of Florence Nightingale's white-lace nursing caps, the first stethoscope, an early iron lung, and a cast of the Emperor Napoleon's death mask. The equally handsome neighboring stone mansion to the north houses the consulate of Poland—an incongruously aristocratic setting for a nation in economic tatters.

East beyond the eight lanes of Lake Shore Drive (the Outer Drive, in local parlance) stretches a thin strip of sand that is Chicago's most fashionable beach. On a sunny summer afternoon, Oak Street Beach resembles a giant casting call for one of those beer commercials where every body is lithe and youthful, beautifully bronzed, and perfectly proportioned. Volleyball, Frisbee-flipping, and other landlubber diversions are more popular than swimming and wading, because Lake

Michigan water can be chilly even in August. A more cerebral shoreline alternative is the Chess Pavilion, just south of North Avenue, where the boards are set in concrete and you bring your own chess pieces. In January or February, when storm-driven waves have sculpted fantastic ice forms at water's edge, the beach provides a bracing outdoor art show for well-bundled walkers.

Chess game at the "Chess Pavilion" on North Avenue Beach.

(opposite) The good times roll on a summer day at one of the Gold Coast's lakefront parks.

A Jewish coppersmith and his family pose before their shopfront, circa 1900. (Chicago Historical Society)

NEIGHBORHOODS

TO A SOCIOLOGIST OR A NOVELIST, Chicago's neighborhoods could merit months of exploration. The residential communities radiating from the city's heart have always been the city's soul. From the earliest days, they defined the ethnic and economic boundaries of an intricate urban mosaic that reflected the successive waves of immigrants from across Europe and elsewhere. Many neighborhoods were self-contained universes, revolving around one's own block of bungalows, where the complexities and frustrations of big-city life could be reduced to a human scale. James T. Farrell's *Studs Lonigan* trilogy of the 1930s, set in the South Side Irish Catholic neighborhood of his youth, is only one well-known example of the riches mined by writers over the years from this lode. While these tight-knit communties nurtured, they could also narrow—and the tenacity of Chicago's neighborhood patterns surely bears some relationship to the city's pervasive residential segregation.

There are now fewer Chicago neighborhoods where shared ethnic roots provide the social binding, and the heritage has shifted to non-European in a good many of them. Gentrification has brought changes positive and negative to an increasing number of areas on the central city's fringes, where the rehab challenge (at affordable prices) lures young professionals. Poverty and crime have blighted other parts of the city. But a great many of the communities, as Dominic A. Pacyga and Ellen Skerrett observe in their wide-ranging *Chicago: City of Neighborhoods*, are "remarkably resilient, and they continue their day-to-day life rather successfully, even in the face of dramatic economic changes."

Not all Chicago neighborhoods and sub-neighborhoods have sharply defined borders, and names even change from time to time. Several of the half-dozen itineraries that follow roam to several neighborhoods, and a stickler might argue that Old Town should be in the "HEART OF THE CITY" chapter, since it is hardly much farther from the Loop than the Gold Coast. It's a judgment call. Some of the city's most idyllic neighborhoods are omitted because they remain essentially residential, for example, Sauganash, Edison Park, Chatham, and Beverly. All the areas that are covered can provide eye-opening glimpses of the real Chicago—past and present, warts and all.

■ OLD TOWN

Henry Meyer is long gone, along with the cows and chickens he kept. But the frame farmhouse he built in 1874 on what was then a meadow still stands as a private residence at **1802 North Lincoln Park West,** not much more than two miles (3.2 km) north of the Loop. Enlivened by the artfully carved wooden trim that typifies the neighborhood's stock of homes built immediately after the Chicago Fire of 1871, this is one among myriad surprises to reward the visitor who pokes up and down the shaded streets and cul de sacs of Old Town. Although not the oldest, Old Town is indeed one of Chicago's most venerable communities. It was first settled around 1850 by German immigrants, many of whom became farmers who grew potatoes and cabbage in the fields north of North Avenue. A newspaper account of a parade down Sedgwick Street in 1879 reported festivities that included a costumed "Duke Ulrich" who reviewed the marchers while suspended from a clothes basket and was "kept alive by large potations of lager-beer which he drew up in a dinner pail with a string."

The neighborhood—originally called North Town—remained strongly German into the first decade of this century, when North Avenue was known as "the German Broadway." Then it saw an influx of Hungarians and Russian Jews in the World War I era, followed by other ethnic groups that eventually erased all but the patina of Germanic character, which can be savored today only in rare throwbacks like the Golden Ox restaurant (just west of Old Town proper at North and Clybourn). Gone from the neighborhood is the tradition of saloonkeeper aldermen, last and most famously exemplified by Mathias "Paddy" Bauler, who ran the 43rd Ward's Democratic affairs for close to a half-century until the 1970s from his saloon at North Avenue and Sedgwick Street. "Chicago ain't ready for reform," was Bauler's most famous observation, and he also liked to tell reporters, "I'll talk about anything, as long as the statute of limitations has run out."

The vicissitudes of the Great Depression left many of Old Town's nineteenth-century wooden houses showing serious wear and tear by 1948. In that year a civic-spirited group of residents formed the Old Town Triangle Association, which ever since has played a key role in reinvigorating the community. During City Council hearings that led to the **Old Town Triangle** area's designation as a landmark district in 1976, the pastor of St. Michael's parish testified that "the real strength of Chicago lies not in the Sears Towers, or the Hancock Centers, but in

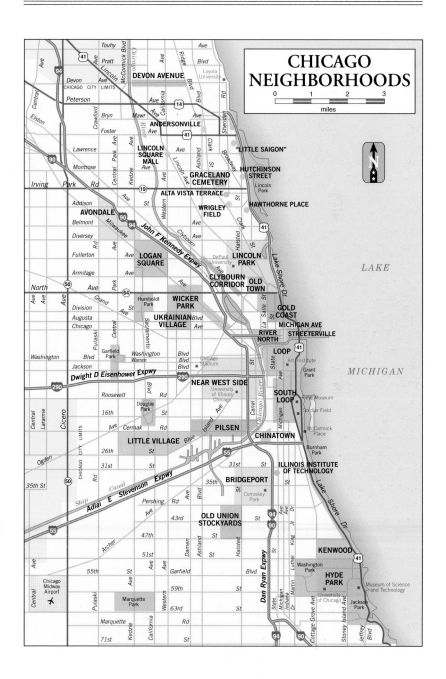

the neighborhoods such as this one. Chicago, to be humanly alive, must sustain little homes inhabited by the common man." In fact, the skyrocketing of Old Town property values since the 1960s has driven out many low- and middle-income families—the economic dark side of urban renewal in Chicago and elsewhere.

St. Michael's, as rich in history as any Chicago church, has been the heart and soul of the neighborhood since German Catholics built their first house of worship at North and Hudson in 1852 for a mere $730. The second St. Michael's, completed in 1869 in red brick with a 200-foot (60.8-m) tower, was gutted by the Chicago Fire. But its double brick walls formed the core of the grander present church, which boasts a monumental altar of carved wood capped by a figure of the patron saint with sword and jeweled crown. It is said that you are within the boundaries of Old Town if you can hear the pealing of St. Michael's' five bells.

The church's nearest religious neighbor, within eyeshot a block to the north, is the **Midwest Buddhist Temple**. A testament to Old Town's ethnic diversity, the temple was built in 1972 with a shingled gable roof that echoes traditional Japanese designs; the centerpiece of its shrine is a small, standing gold Buddha. The temple devotes one weekend each summer to a lively Ginza Festival open to the public. It's the only vestige of Old Town's former Little Tokyo, which was dispersed (mainly to the suburbs) in the 1960s and '70s by the construction of the Sandburg Village residential complex to the south of North Avenue.

Two blocks west of the Japanese temple stands the 1874 **Meyer farmhouse**, on a block of Lincoln Park West that is a virtual museum of vintage residences erected when the neighborhood rebuilt itself in the 1870s and '80s. The most distinguished provenance belongs to the five two-story brick rowhouses at **1826-1834 North Lincoln Park West,** designed in a simplified Queen Anne motif in 1884-85 by the great architect Louis Sullivan. Few such examples of the Chicago School master's early work survive anywhere, and these townhouses bear the imprint of his hand in their intricate terra-cotta ornamentation. Brewer Frederick Wacker, a leader of the German community, employed a Swiss architect in 1874 for the brick-and-clapboard home with the faintly Alpine air at **1838 North Lincoln Park West.** Its carved gingerbread trim is a premier Old Town Triangle example of that art form. The smaller neighbor at 1836 North Lincoln Park West was originally the Wacker coach house at the back of the lot. In the 1880s it was moved forward and remodeled as a mother-in-law house (a small semi-detached cottage) by Charles Wacker, later the first chairman of the Chicago Plan Commission.

A Northwest neighborhood typical of many surrounding the Loop District.

Some streets in the Old Town Triangle District run for only a block or two, cut off to discourage through traffic, but almost all deserve at least a bit of meandering. Leafy St. Paul Street stretches for a single block, as does Concord Place, while Fern Court manages about a block and a half. Intersecting St. Paul at midblock is one of the city's most distinctive enclaves, **Crilly Court,** which could pass for a tranquil side street in London's West End. It was developed in 1885 by contractor Daniel F. Crilly with two-story rowhouses on the west side of the court and a four-story apartment building on the east. The names carved above the entrances to the apartments are those of Crilly's children: Edgar, Erminnie, Oliver, and Isabelle. One early tenant was Eugene Field, a children's poet and pioneering newspaper columnist. Crilly Court and its immediate neighbors were early beneficiaries of the post-World War II rehabilitation drive that helped make Old Town Triangle a coveted address. These buildings are now condominiums.

Sustenance for weary walkers is available at two time-tested Sedgwick Street spots that well predate Old Town's gentrification. **Marge's,** at the corner of Sedgwick and Menomonee, traces its roots to a saloon opened more than a century ago. It prospers today as an admirably old-fashioned tavern, even if the neighborhood yuppies are sometimes a bit thick on the ground. A block south at Sedgwick and Eugenie, **Twin Anchors** has drawn a steady stream of customers since 1932 for its barbecued baby back ribs; Frank Sinatra is said to be a finger-licking fan. Another congenial place that defies trends and fashion is the no-frills **Old Town Ale House,** at 219 West North Avenue.

The ale house's famous neighbor is that fountainhead of contemporary comedy, **Second City.** Ever since Mike Nichols and others set up satirical shop in 1959, Second City's distinctive brand of ensemble and improvisational humor has thoroughly reshaped American notions of what's worth a laugh. Its legion of famous alumni includes Alan Arkin, John Belushi, Bill Murray, John Candy, and Joan Rivers. Even after four-plus decades, Second City revues manage to be fresh more often than stale, and weekend shows in the 290-seat main room can be a tough ticket. A reverent nod is appropriate as you enter the Second City building at 1616 North Wells: the richly detailed ornament on its facade is an architectural treasure rescued from the much-mourned Garrick Theater when that Adler and Sullivan landmark was demolished in 1961 to make way for a Loop parking garage.

Wells Street went through a meteoric flame-out in the 1960s and early '70s as a counter-culture ghetto synonymous with "Old Town." It's two blocks from North

Avenue south to Schiller Street blossomed into a smaller, tamer version of San Francisco's Haight-Ashbury. This was the place to buy love beads or a roach clip while mingling with fellow flower children. Once the hippies went away, tourists had nothing to gawk at besides other tourists, and the aura soon withered. Wells today is just another commercial strip of shops, restaurants, and a couple of music clubs. Its longest-lived retailer, **House of Glunz,** has been selling fine wines for more than a century at Wells and Division. The aura of the neighborhood's German heyday lingers here amid the stained-glass windows, antique bottles, and murals depicting wine-making. A visit makes an evocative final stop to cap an Old Town exploration.

■ NEAR NORTHWEST

On the early stretches of its run northwest from downtown, **Milwaukee Avenue**—which long served as Main Street for Chicago's huge population of Polish descent—speaks a lot of Spanish these days. Along this commercial spine of the Wicker Park and Logan Square neighborhoods, a definite Hispanic flavor dominates the area between Division Street and Fullerton. Gentrification is making its mark as well with the rehabilitation of sturdy old homes in these communities, while hundreds of artists migrating away from the high rents of fashionable River North have set up their studios and galleries in Wicker Park and Bucktown immediately north. Urban pioneers are also moving into the farther-south **Ukrainian Village** enclave, which is graced with several splendid Orthodox churches. And there is still a Polish retail corridor on Milwaukee Avenue, concentrated in four blocks of the Avondale community between Diversey and Belmont.

A few Polish institutions remain in the old neighborhood to the south, including the **Polish Museum of America** at 984 North Milwaukee. One highlight of its substantial collection is a 13-by-27-foot (4-by-8.2-m) stained-glass window, "Poland Reborn," that was designed in Krakow for the Polish pavilion at the 1939 New York World's Fair. A small cluster of cooperative art galleries on the fringe of River West to the south includes ARC (Artists, Residents of Chicago), woman-run Artemesia, Randolph Street Gallery, and the School of the Art Institute's Gallery 2.

West of Damen Avenue between Chicago and Division, Ukrainian Village's ethnic roots are manifest in the Ukrainian National Museum (2453 West Chicago

Avenue), with fine displays of painted Easter eggs and other folk arts, and the Ukrainian Institute of Modern Art (2320 West Chicago). Old-line Galans Restaurant, 2212 West Chicago, serves up a "Kozak feast" of ultra-hearty Ukrainian fare; Ann's Bakery, 2158 West Chicago, sells Ukrainian twist bread and pastries. Now an independent nation, Ukraine was the breadbasket of the former Russian and Soviet empires. The community spirit of the neighborhood's Ukrainian-Americans is captured in an incident related by Richard Lindberg in *Passport's Guide to Ethnic Chicago*. When state regulators informed a local savings and loan in 1964 that it was nearly insolvent due to $360,000 in missing assets, the association's president appealed to depositors "for help. The residents answered the appeal. Borrowing a page from [Frank Capra's] *It's a Wonderful Life*, they streamed into his office with cash gifts, some as high as $1,000." The $300,000 infusion enabled the savings and loan to reopen three days later.

Chicago School master Louis Sullivan designed **Holy Trinity Orthodox Cathedral** (1121 North Leavitt) in 1903 along the traditional lines of Russian churches with his own more delicate variant of that style's bulbous onion domes. The local Ukrainian congregations split in the 1960s on the matter of church calendars. The modern Gregorian calendar is used at **St. Nicholas Ukrainian Catholic Cathedral,**

A Polish bakery on Milwaukee Avenue in Avondale offers many Old World delicacies.

erected in 1914 at Rice and Oakley streets on the model of Kiev's Basilica of St. Sophia with 13 copper-clad domes. Adherents of the old Julian calendar built **St. Volodymyr and Olha Church** on a site two blocks north in 1975. The mosaic over the main entrance portrays the conversion of the Ukraine to Christianity by St. Volodymyr in 988. Actually, Volodymyr was a warrior prince who advanced God's cause with the sword.

Wicker Park's treasure trove of Victorian homes, now much in demand, can be admired on block-long Concord Place running west off Milwaukee Avenue just north of Damen. There are handsome graystones here, and Pierce Avenue to the south boasts another block of fine homes. Paderewski House at 2138 West Pierce owes its name to the fact that the renowned Polish pianist once played there. **Bucktown**, a triangular enclave just west of the Kennedy Expressway and north of Wicker Park, now draws evening visitors with a blossoming assortment of restaurants, coffee shops, bars, and galleries. Goats were raised in Bucktown as early as the 1830's, hence the name (which derives from the male of the species).

West beyond Wicker Park's boundaries in a predominantly Puerto Rican neighborhood, **Humboldt Park** bears the pedigree of its design by William Le Baron Jenney in 1869 and its landscape improvements by Jens Jensen after the turn of

Ilya Rudiak offers everything Russian from matryoshka dolls to Soviet military uniforms at his store on West Devon.

the century. Expansive Humboldt Boulevard and Kedzie Avenue, with their grassy medians, were laid out as part of the green belt intended to circle Chicago in the 1870s. The towering classical column planted in Logan Square is Henry Bacon's **Illinois Centennial Monument,** dedicated in 1918 and circled at its base with sculpted reliefs portraying the state's history.

There's no doubt of Chicago's strong Polish heritage once you're back on Milwaukee Avenue in the **Avondale** community's **Little Warsaw** strip, with its European-accented delicatessens, bakeries, markets, and gift shops. Dozens of varieties of Polish sausages with jawbreaking names hang behind the counters of the delis. **Home Bakery,** operated by the Senkowski family, is among the best-regarded Polish restaurants, which include the Teresa II, Orbis, and Red Apple. Leave your cholesterol calculator at home. Tarnovia sells a weekly dinner pass and dishes up an all-you-can-eat Polish-American buffet. There's also polka-paced nightlife, or for a mellower alternative, visit one of several video shops renting Polish films. Polonia Book Store has the largest stock of Polish-language books in this country, as well as ethnic records and cassettes.

Buying potatoes on Maxwell Street during the Depression. (Chicago Sun-Times)

Something very different from Milwaukee Avenue's ethnic potpourri can be found to the east of Milwaukee Avenue on Clybourn, another of Chicago's few diagonal thoroughfares. This rather faded stretch of factories and warehouses, now christened the **Clybourn Corridor**, has been swept by a whirlwind of retail development since the 1980s. Not all of the light industry has vanished, but most of what's left coexists off the Clybourn main drag with the recently arrived yuppie allures. Shopping as a participant sport is the recreation here at a half-dozen trendy malls, some of which feature other attractions such as cinemas, legitimate theater, and a micro-brewery.

One remnant of the neighborhood's former German days, the **Golden Ox** restaurant, survives near the corridor's south end at North and Clybourn. Weekend nights at the Golden Ox bring zither music to accompany the perennially hearty German fare. The neighboring Crate & Barrel outlet store at North and Halsted is a warm-up act for the parade of conspicuous consumption running up Clybourn. A former Turtle Wax factory houses the 1800 Clybourn Mall, home of well-regarded Remains Theater, which has produced several David Mamet plays, and Goose Island Brewing, where several labels of the house suds are served. Par Excellence provides nine holes of miniature-golf diversion inside 1800 Clybourn, and the shopping is about what you'd expect. That's true also at the Foundry Shopping Center, Market Square, Webster Place (in a former Butternut Bread factory), and other malls on the strip. The Clybourn Corridor speaks for the continuing commercial vitality of Chicago, as well as the fact—with apologies to P.T. Barnum—that there's a shopper born every minute.

■ LINCOLN PARK

Yes, that is a mausoleum at the south end of Lincoln Park, tucked in a grove of trees behind the Chicago Historical Society not far from the splendid bronze statue of Abraham Lincoln by Augustus St. Gaudens. The solitary tomb, near the southwest corner of the city's largest park, shelters the remains of pioneer Chicago hotelkeeper Ira Couch. His determined family went to court to keep the gravesite undisturbed when the rest of the sprawling municipal cemetery was cleared in the years after 1868 to make way for this major link in a proposed urban greenbelt of parks and boulevards.

Only one other burial is known to remain in Lincoln Park. Its site farther north near the Farm-in-the-Zoo is marked with a boulder to commemorate the remarkable life of David Kennison. The last living participant in the Boston Tea Party, Kennison died in 1852—at age 115, by his sometimes disputed account. All the other loved ones resting here suffered the fate described by traveler Sara Jane Lippincott, who praised the park in 1873 as "already very beautiful, with a variety of surface and ornamentation most wonderful," but noted that its entrance "is a little depressing, being through a cemetery, for those old settlers are fast being resettled and reestablished elsewhere. Even the dead must 'move on' in Chicago."

Most of those ghosts surely would bear no grudge once they saw the pleasure that Lincoln Park's wealth of recreational allures provides for millions of Chicagoans and out-of-towners each year. Its beaches, harbors, ponds, picnic groves, bike paths, and sports fields are scattered along the full five-and-a-half-mile (8.9-km) length of the city's largest park, while its southern expanse is home to the perennially popular **Lincoln Park Zoo**, as well as Lincoln Park Conservatory and the museums of the Chicago Historical Society and Chicago Academy of Sciences. A favorite spring-to-fall pastime on Lincoln Park's grassy diamonds is 16-inch (41-cm) softball, a sport virtually unique to Chicago that is played barehanded with a great deal of gusto.

The park itself forms the eastern edge of the lively Lincoln Park neighborhood, where an evening parking spot can be as precious as a cool drink in the desert. Restaurants, theaters, music clubs, and shops abound along the bustling corridors of Lincoln Avenue, Halsted Street, and other thoroughfares between the community's north and south boundaries around Diversey Parkway and North Avenue. Amid the clamor, gracious blocks of older homes supply welcome oases of tranquility, while the DePaul University campus adds a reflective air. Like its Old Town neighbor to the south, Lincoln Park is an expensive address these days after three decades of urban renewal and gentrification.

But some things in life remain free even in this pricey part of Chicago—including the family-thronged North Avenue beach and Lincoln Park Zoo, one of the few major zoos anywhere that charge no admission fee. A gift of two swans from New York's Central Park in 1868 started the zoo's collection, which now totals around 2,000 beasts and birds arrayed on a compact 35-acre site that has been dramatically improved in the last couple of decades by new and renovated houses that reflect the state of the zookeeping art. A particular pride is the **Great Ape House,** where visitors can go nose-to-nose (through thick plate glass) with playful gorilla youngsters from the world's finest captive ensemble of that endangered genetic cousin to the human race. Less exotic creatures from the barnyard are a revelation to big-city kids at the **Farm-in-the-Zoo** south of the main facility.

Renting a paddleboat on the **South Pond** adjoining the farm makes for a pleasant sunny-day putter, and there's a whiff of salty adventure northwest of the pond in the somewhat forlorn-looking replica of a tenth-century Viking longboat that was sailed from Norway for the 1893 World's Columbian Exposition here. On the pond's western shore, the landmark architecture is much more appealing than the forgettable fast food at **Cafe Brauer,** a 1908 Prairie School gem designed by Dwight Perkins that sat idle and rotting for a half-century until a concerted civic effort restored it to beauty and service a few years ago. The Great Hall upstairs is magnificently adorned with tile murals, stained glass, and bronze chandeliers.

Birdwatchers can tune up their waterfowl skills at the zoo's recently refurbished Rookery, where ducks, geese, and other species come and go freely amid the rock garden. Neighboring **Lincoln Park Conservatory** is at its most inviting during four annual shows: azaleas in February and March, lilies and other spring plants in April, chrysanthemums in November, and poinsettias over the Christmas holidays.

Lincoln Park Conservatory is best visited during February and March for its azaleas, April for its lilies, November for its chrysanthemums, or December for its poinsettias.

CHICAGO STORIES

"HINKY DINK" DEMOCRACY

On the morning of the day last December when voters were choosing between Hopkins and Swift a very prominent republican politician, who was a member of the campaign committee, went into the first ward to quietly look for frauds. He pulled up his coat-collar, drew his hat forward and loafed around the polling places just to see what was happening and not to attract attention. In the "Hinky Dink" precinct he was standing apart watching the barrel-house delegation put in enough ballots to offset the entire school-teacher vote. A man with a badge noticed him and called him aside.

"Have you voted yet?" he asked.

"No, not yet."

"Come on over and have a drink."

They went into the headquarters conducted by "Hinky Dink" McKenna [*sic*] and the man wearing the badge stood treat. The two talked for a minute or two about the weather and the probable size of the vote, and then the prominent republican began to edge toward the door. But the other man followed him.

"Here," said he, pushing a half dollar into his hand. "Don't put it off any longer, but go and vote for Hopkins."

The prominent republican was too much amazed to return the money. He began to wonder if he resembled a tramp. It was a good joke, but perhaps the joke was on him. At any rate he didn't tell the story until some time afterward.

LITTLE BILLY

It was a great day for "Little Billy" when, as a member of the arbitration committee of the Longshoremen's union, he went forth to represent the cause of labor.

For a man who works along the docks and who has known the tyranny of a mate on a Mississippi steamer, it is a strange experience to be lifted to sudden eminence and given large responsibilities. The longshoremen drew no lines on color and nationality. "Little Billy," as black as ebony, was a brother so long as he stood for union wages and the rights of the men. And he was just beginning to find out that he was a man. Two years before he had roustabouted on a Mississippi steamer for starvation pay. Finally he concluded it would be better to work in a freight house than carry barrels up-hill, so in company with other adventurous spirits he struck out for Chicago and big pay.

It was big pay compared with what he had been receiving, but, like every other dissatisfied man who finds that he is supported by numbers and organization, "Little Billy" fell in with the movement for higher wages. He wanted 25 cents an hour because all the other men wanted it and because he had become convinced that his work was worth that much. In the strike of 1893 he took part merely as a private in the ranks. He was one of the strikers that chased a transportation agent one night. This agent professed great contempt for the roughly dressed men who unloaded the vessels, and when the strike was declared he purchased two large revolvers and sent word to the strikers that they must not come around his premises. They came one evening, however, to argue with the non-union men and he advanced upon them with both "guns" drawn. The strikers, instead of being terrified, charged upon him, whereupon he threw away his weapons, in order to lighten himself, and ran for his life. They chased him around a freight house and over the railroad tracks. He would have been captured had he not in his desperation jumped into the Chicago River. When he jumped the strikers became frightened and proceeded to scatter. The agent was rescued by a policeman.

This episode was considered a victory for the strikers, and "Little Billy" was especially gratified, as it was the first time he had ever chased a white man. A few days later the men were given the wages they asked. It was a complete victory, and "Little Billy" from that time was a more rampant union man than ever before.

—George Ade, collected from the *Chicago Record,* 1893-1900

The museums of both the Chicago Historical Society and the Chicago Academy of Sciences date back to the 1850s; once rather musty places, they've shaken off the torpor and put a lively step in many of their exhibits. The equestrian statue of Ulysses S. Grant along the park's Cannon Drive might feel more at home if it could gallop the three miles (4.8 km) south to Grant Park, which surprisingly lacks a sculpture of the Civil War commander and U.S. president whose name it bears.

The western fringes of the park are the venue for beguiling residential blocks lined with homes that date back as far as last century's Gilded Age. One of the oldest is the charming frame cottage with decorative shingles and raised basement at 2121 North Hudson. "This is Policeman Bellinger's Cottage, saved by heroic efforts from the Chicago Fire of October 1871," announces a plaque on the building—which was designed by W. W. Boyington, also the architect for the most famous survivor of that conflagration—the Old Chicago Water Tower. The three blocks of **Cleveland Avenue** from Dickens north to Fullerton boast an eclectic mix of handsomely restored townhouses, ranging from an Art Deco facade with a two-story leaded-glass window (No. 2150) and an 1874 Italianate duplex with white Corinthian entrance columns (No. 2234-36), to a Gothic brick jumble with a Georgian Revival porch (No. 2314) and an 1880 dowager with a square bay window and roof turret (No. 2325).

At **440 West Belden,** just east of Cleveland, the decorative Queen Anne design reflects the formative period of Louis Sullivan, who was 27 in 1883 when he executed this first known residential commission for the firm that would become Adler and Sullivan. As counterpoint, the last apartment building designed in Chicago by Modernist Ludwig Mies van der Rohe is the sleek glass-and-aluminum highrise a block north and east at **2400 North Lakeview Avenue** overlooking the park. Just north, two shaded blocks of late-nineteenth-century townhouses form the tiny **Arlington and Roslyn Park District** as designated by the Chicago Landmarks Commission.

The **Wrigley Mansion,** at the corner of Arlington Place and Lakeview, is richly ornamented with terra-cotta, copper, and iron trim. Designed in 1897 by Richard E. Schmidt, it was bought in 1911 by chewing-gum maestro William Wrigley. **Deming Place,** another tree-lined refuge from the clamor of Clark Street shopping, offers such visual enticements as the twin townhouses at No. 466-468 with their huge bay windows and intriguing brickwork patterns. A block north at 503 West Wrightwood, one of the most astounding facades in the city fronts the **Francis J. Dewes House,** erected in 1896 for a German brewer. The Baroque Revival mansion's entrance is flanked by a pair of huge Greek caryatids (actually, one is male) who support a wrought-iron balcony with classical columns and an elaborately decorated frame.

Lincoln Avenue, which darts diagonally northwest through the neighborhood along an eighteenth-century Native American trail, provides a time-tested mix of culture and entertainment. Wise Fools Pub, at 2247 North Lincoln, is a cramped but congenial pure-Chicago bar that features live blues nightly. Victory Gardens and Body Politic, two pioneers in the city's off-Loop theater renaissance, sit side-by-side at 2257 and 2261 North Lincoln. John Barleycorn Memorial Pub, at Lincoln and Belden, disdains the giant-screen TVs of sports bars in favor of projecting slides that show masterpieces of painting and sculpture. The **Biograph Theater** (No. 2433), now regrettably carved into a multiplex like so many vintage cinemas, is famed as the spot where the FBI and Chicago police gunned down the bank robber John Dillinger when he came out of a movie on July 22, 1934. Booksellers Row (No. 2445) stocks a floor-to-ceiling bounty of used books sure to accelerate the pulse of browsing bibliophiles. Across the avenue, Guild Books (No. 2456) focuses on politics, social issues, and contemporary literature spiced by a steady schedule of autographing parties. The Children's Bookstore (back on the east side at No. 2465) caters to families with its play and reading area in the rear. Earl's Pub (No. 2470), a direct descendant of Earl Pionke's legendary Earl of Old Town, varies its musical fare among folk, country, and blues.

Halsted Street, which intersects Lincoln at Fullerton, is a dining and entertainment stalwart that blossomed in a 1980s burst of development. Anchoring this strip's south end are two stylish new theater complexes. The much-acclaimed Steppenwolf theater troupe has settled into a custom-designed complex with a 500-seat mainstage at 1650 North Halsted. The Royal-George Theater Center, 1633 North Halsted, hosts a number of companies on its two stages, complemented by a cabaret, piano bar, restaurant, and wine cellar. Charlie Trotter's, a recent darling of restaurant critics (at 816 West Armitage, just west of Halsted), is an inventive

Famed bank robber John Dillinger was gunned down by law enforcement officials as he exited the Biograph Theater in July 1934.

DILLINGER'S NEMESIS

It happened on a day when Chicago's temperature hit 102 degrees F (40° C), and it was the city's hottest news of 1934. It drew swarms of morbidly curious onlookers to the Biograph Theater where the shooting had taken place and to the Cook County morgue where the famous corpse reposed. The date was July 22, 1934, and the dead desperado was 31-year-old bank robber John Dillinger, the FBI's most-wanted fugitive and "the greatest folk hero of American crime," in the opinion of anthologist Albert Halper.

Dillinger built his tabloid fame in little more than a year during the depths of the Great Depression by planning and executing a succession of bold bank robberies and prison escapes. At the jail in Crown Point, Indiana, on March 3, 1934, he used a razor to carve a fake pistol from a piece of wood, blackened it with shoe polish, and forced his way past a dozen guards while singing, "I'm heading for the last roundup."

He was essentially a loner from a rural Indiana background. As Halper wrote, "Such a lone wolf was destined for betrayal, and a seemingly sympathetic woman in whose house he was hiding out double-crossed him by turning informer." She was a brothel madam named Anna Sage who hoped to avoid deportation to Romania as an undesirable alien by cooperating with the FBI and police. Having tipped off authorities the evening of July 22, she went with Dillinger to the Biograph, 2433 North Lincoln Avenue. Her skirt was orange, but it looked red under the marquee lights, fixing her in history as "The Lady in Red."

FBI agents and police surrounded the Biograph while Dillinger and his betrayer watched Clark Gable go to the electric chair in "Manhattan Melodrama." Emerging from the theater in a straw hat and glasses, he was ordered to halt. Instead, he reached into his right pants pocket for his Colt automatic and dashed in a partial crouch toward the alley next to the Biograph. One FBI shot tore into his left side, while another drilled through his stooped back and out his right eye. Dead on the spot, he was later buried near Indianapolis. A fable persists that some other man was shot by the FBI outside the Biograph, and that Dillinger disappeared with the aid of accomplices. If so, he may well still linger with the likes of Elvis Presley in that twilight land of the celebrated undead.

Arch-gangster John Dillinger posing for the camera with a machine gun and wooden pistol at a family reunion three months before his death in 1934. (Times newspaper, Munster, Indiana)

place where diners can expect the unexpected. The Old Town School of Folk Music, 909 West Armitage, carries on as a steadfast Chicago treasure that gives lessons, workshops, singalongs, and concerts. Back on Halsted, the blues talent is dependably big-league at B.L.U.E.S. (No. 2519) and Kingston Mines (No. 2548). Uncle Tannous (No. 2626), with its indoor patio, ranks as one of the city's most inviting Lebanese restaurants.

The neighborhood got a much-needed infusion of green space in the 1970s with the creation of two-square-block **Oz Park,** bordering on the east side of Halsted between Dickens and Webster; its name salutes the fact that *Wizard of Oz* creator Frank Baum once lived nearby. West of Halsted and south of Fullerton, the **Sheffield Historic District** encompasses most of the DePaul University campus in another sylvan enclave where sturdy but decrepit old housing has been renovated and real-estate prices have soared. Especially worth seeking out is **McCormick Row House District,** tucked into the DePaul campus just south of Fullerton and east of the rapid-transit tracks. The provenance of the privately owned three-story brick row houses, which front on Chalmers Place, dates to the 1880s, when McCormick Theological Seminary decided to augment its income by building and renting out houses. In the original plans, the house at the end of each row was a professor's home. The seminary vacated the DePaul area in the 1970s, but its row-house legacy still sounds a grace note of quiet gentility just steps from the push and shove of Lincoln Park's busy streets.

■ NORTH SIDE MOSAIC

The signs still say "Andersonville," and the Swedish presence lingers in the 5200 block of North Clark Street amid this once strongly Scandinavian neighborhood on Chicago's North Side. The survivors include Wikstrom's and Erickson's delicatessens, where Swedish can still be heard across the counter; Ann Sather's restaurant, one of the few places in Chicago to buy a Ringnes beer from Norway or a Nordic Wolf from Sweden; and the Swedish-American Museum Center, selling an array of handcrafted items. But they share the commercial strip these days with such distinctly non-Scandinavian establishments as the Beirut Restaurant, Byblos I bakery-deli, and Reza's Persian restaurant. Although the Scandinavian and Middle Eastern cultures seem like truly odd bedfellows, they mix without evident incongruity on Clark Street.

The door of John Barleycorn Memorial Pub, at 658 West Belden Avenue, would do justice to any museum collection.

It's like this elsewhere around the North Side, where the city's human mosaic continues to shift away from European-Americans and toward new immigrant waves from the Middle East and southern and eastern Asia. Although it may be unsettling at times for the communities involved, this new melting-pot mix makes for fascinating hopscotch exploration (by car or public transit) from Wrigley Field north to Devon Avenue and beyond. Several enclaves of vintage architecture add extra spice to the excursion.

Wrigley Field, home of the Chicago Cubs, deserves a visit during the April-September baseball season even from non-fans. It is the quintessential old-fashioned ballpark, with seating right on top of the action (but watch out for vision-obstructing posts), real grass, and outfield walls draped in ivy that occasionally snares an extra-base hit. For years, Wrigley was the only major-league park without lights, but the imperative of television ratings brought night games to the field in the late '80s. Scalpers outside the park are sometimes the only source of seats for weekend games, or you can try knocking on the doors of the three-flat apartment buildings that ring the outfield on Waveland and Sheffield, then asking politely if you might join the long-distance bleacherites on the roof. Rapid

In Chicago, sports fans start young.

transit will deliver you directly to the ballpark from the Loop; if you drive, parking may cost as much as your box seat.

Tucked a block north of Wrigley Field in the Wrigleyville community is enchanting **Alta Vista Terrace,** an ensemble of rowhouses in varying styles that looks like a transplant from an idyllic backwater of Boston or London. Built in 1904-05, they form a tiny landmark district that abuts on **Graceland Cemetery** to the north. Graceland is to Chicago what Père Lachaise is to Paris: a burial ground of the rich and famous strewn with an incredible assemblage of funerary monuments. Graceland's premier attraction for grave-gazers is the Getty Tomb, designed in 1890 by Louis Sullivan with exquisitely lacy ornamentation on the upper half of the limestone mausoleum and its bronze gates. The nicely named Nuts on Clark emporium across from Graceland's southern tip stocks a cornucopia of nutmeats and candies.

Due east of Graceland, the two landmark-district blocks of Hutchinson Street between Marine Drive and Hazel Street feature five houses designed by George W. Maher, a colleague of Frank Lloyd Wright. Prairie School motifs are prominent among the more than two dozen notable residences constructed between 1894 and 1919, but there are also Queen Anne and Romanesque Revival beauties. The two-story 1902 Maher commission at 750 West Hutchinson exemplifies his Farson House style with its low double-hip roof and stone-framed entryway. A mile (1.6 km) southeast at the lakefront, Hawthorne Place landmark district in the Lake View neighborhood preserves a cluster of Victorian-era homes, including an Adler and Sullivan design built for insurance magnate George Harvey in 1888 at 600 West Stratford Place.

Overlooking Lake Shore Drive's eight lanes opposite Addison Street stands a magnificent **totem pole** that is actually a replica of a century-old artifact carved by the coastal Kwakiutl Indians of British Columbia. The pole—which portrays the motifs of a sea monster, an upside-down whale with a man on its back, and a thunderbird—was bought in the 1920s by cheesemaker James L. Kraft and given to the Chicago Park District. At the urging of Native Americans from the Pacific Northwest, the original was returned to Canada and replaced by this copy in 1986. North of the totem stretches the nine-hole **Waveland Golf Course,** with lake views only somewhat less spectacular than the ocean vistas of California's Pebble Beach, and a fieldhouse carillon lovingly restored by volunteers. A few blocks inland from the park, north-south Broadway is a main commercial axis of the city's vibrant gay and lesbian community.

North of Graceland, the **Uptown** neighborhood has been down on its luck for decades but is showing some recent signs of rebounding. Home to the city's largest concentration of Native Americans, Uptown also boasts a bustling **Little Saigon** commercial strip along Argyle Street, around 5000 North just west of Lake Shore Drive. Along with a shoulder-to-shoulder lineup of restaurants and shops run by Vietnamese and an earlier core of Chinese, the community is the site of a **Vietnam Museum** (at 954 West Carmen Avenue) recalling that long and melancholy war. This improving neighborhood, as Richard Lindberg puts it in *Passport's Guide to Ethnic Chicago* is a "busy, thriving retail corridor, where hard work and self-reliance carry a great weight. It is an old story with a new twist when 65-year-old refugees eagerly sign up for English classes at nearby Truman College." Even the ABC Exterminating sign on Broadway south of Argyle makes its pitch in Vietnamese.

Two miles (3.2 km) west lies **Lincoln Square Mall**, around Lincoln and Lawrence avenues, the last real vestige of a **Germantown** in Chicago. The commercial enclave is graced by a 96-foot-long (29-m) wall mural depicting a medieval fortress and a peasant village. Teutonic-tinged shops in the mall area include Inge's Delicatessen, Hogen's Restaurant, Huettenbar tavern, Merz Apothecary, and Schmid Imports gift shop. Nearby at 2458 West Montrose is the time-tested Lutz Continental Cafe and Pastry Shop, and farther south on Lincoln Avenue are Dinkel's Bakery and Kuhn's Delicatessen.

No North Side thoroughfare is more of an ethnic kaleidoscope today than the mile-and-a-half (2.4 km) of **Devon Avenue** running west from Ridge Boulevard. This West Rogers Park thoroughfare, at 6400 North, showed a resolutely Jewish face to the world as recently as the 1960s. Now the Indian subcontinent has the most prominent presence along Devon, but there are also Russian, Middle Eastern, Mexican, and other shops and restaurants, as well as the Croatian Cultural Center. Establishments catering to the Jewish community survive at the west end of the strip, among them Gitel's Kosher Pastry Shop and Chicago Hebrew Bookstore. The arrival since the 1970s of new Russian immigrants, mostly Jewish, is reflected in the Cyrillic lettering at the Three Sisters and Kashtan delicatessens. The R. Restaurant, a "free style cafe" at 2954 West Devon, covers several bases with the promise of "Middle East, American, and Russian" cooking—including Georgian-style chiburek dumplings from the Caucasus.

Devon's shifting ethnic spectrum is marked at **California Avenue**, where the

(following pages) Immigrants, but Chicagoans to the core.

honorary street sign pointing west is Golda Meir Boulevard and the eastward name is Gandhi Marg. Popular Indian and Pakistani restaurants—where fixed-price lunch buffets are especially good value—include Viceroy of India, Gandhi, Moti Mahal, and Natraj. A profusion of shops sells videos, saris, jewelry and other imported goods to the Chicago area's 70,000 residents from the Indian subconti-nent. The complexity of this South Asian weave can be gauged by the sign outside Bombay Video at 2634 West Devon: "We carry all languages of India—Hindi, Gujarati, Indi-Punjabi, Tamil, Telugu, Malayalam, Marathi, Bengali, Rajasthani, Pakistani, Pak-Punjabi, Peshto." Devon is a quick, cheap, fascinating trip halfway around the world.

■ HYDE PARK/KENWOOD

The brooding Henry Moore bronze could be a human skull or a mushroom cloud. Twelve feet (3.7 m) high and perched on a base of black polished granite, it occupies the site on the **University of Chicago** campus where one of man-kind's most fateful accomplishments took place on December 2, 1942. Beneath since-demolished football bleachers along Ellis Avenue, a team of physicists led by Enrico Fermi achieved the first self-sustaining chain reaction and so gave birth to the nuclear age. That it happened here reflects the scientific and intellec-tual muscle of this century-old university, the institution which has been the magnet holding together the surrounding Hyde Park neighborhood as a bastion of brainpower—and one of Chicago's most extraordinary neighborhoods.

In what is often described as America's most residentially segregated big city, Hyde Park also stands out as an island of surprisingly stable racial integration. According to the most recent census, the African-American percentage of the pop-ulation here has held steady at 38 percent since a decade earlier, with the small decrease in white residents to 53 percent accounted for by the near-doubling of Asians to 8 percent. Along with the similarly mixed southern section of the Ken-wood neighborhood immediately north, this balanced integration is holding steady amid the virtually all-black canvas of Chicago's expanding South Side ghetto.

Credit for creating this model of racial diversity should be shared among the world-renowned university, determined community groups, and hundreds of

Union Station saw the arrival of many hopeful immigrants in the 1940s, as portrayed in this William Sturm photograph entitled "Christmas in the New World." (Chicago Sun-Times)

Kosher fish market on Devon in the West Rogers Park neighborhood.

East Indian textile shop on Devon.

individual property owners with the gumption to practice what America usually only preaches. Starting with the Quaker-founded Hyde Park-Kenwood Community Conference in 1949, the neighborhood reshaped and solidified itself from the 1950s on through the nation's first major urban-renewal program. Critics have suggested there was a price to pay for all this in the displacement of low-income residents and the economically elitist undertone of the integration efforts. The satirists Mike Nichols and Elaine May once described Hyde Park as "black and white united against the poor." Whatever the truth in such gibes, this bastion of cerebral energy remains one of Chicago's most stimulating corners.

Hyde Park was open countryside a distant half-dozen miles from downtown Chicago in 1853 when developer Paul Cornell bought 300 acres of lakefront land between 51st and 55th streets. There he created a sylvan community that had some of the flavor of a small New England town. It was not until 1889 that Hyde Park would be annexed to Chicago. The founding of the University of Chicago by John D. Rockefeller in 1892 marked the neighborhood's prime watershed, but the next year's staging of the World's Columbian Exposition on the South Side lakefront also had a major impact on development. Today's most visible legacy of that world's fair is the massive **Museum of Science and Industry**, which occupies the Palace of Fine Arts built for the exposition in lakefront Jackson Park. Billed as Chicago's No. 1 tourist attraction, with yearly attendance around 4.5 million, this is the place to descend into a full-scale replica of an Illinois coal mine or a captured World War II German U-boat—two banner headliners among more than 2,000 exhibits. The museum entered the space age in 1986 by opening its **Henry Crown Space Center and Omnimax Theater**, where a 3-D film simulates lift-off and flight in a full-size Space Shuttle mockup. There's now a museum admission charge for the first time, but Thursday remains a free day.

Stretching west from Jackson Park at the southern edge of the U.C. campus is **Midway Plaisance**, a block-wide parkway running a mile (1.6 km) in length, where the Bazaar of Nations provided the 1893 World's Fair's liveliest entertainment. A 250-foot-high (76-m) Ferris wheel revolved above the Midway, and one of the exposition's biggest hits was Little Egypt, a belly dancer who titillated and scandalized Victorian-era tourists in the Streets of Cairo pavilion. The Midway today serves as a year-round student and neighborhood playground—with ice skating and occasional cross-country skiing in winter. Lorado Taft's somber "Fountain of Time" sculpture, in which a hooded figure gazes over a pool at a procession of human figures moving through life, dominates the Midway's western end at the entrance to Washington Park. **Midway Studios**, where the illustrious sculptor did much of his work, functions today as the university's art center, at 6016 South Ingleside Avenue.

The University of Chicago, as the *WPA Guide to Illinois* put it a half-century ago, "sprang fully fledged into the world as a large and splendidly equipped university, its entry smoothed by the oil millions of the Rockefellers." An early student ditty went: "John D. Rockefeller, wonderful man is he,/Gives all his spare change to the U. of C." The "spare change" eventually mounted to $35 million, and grants from Rockefeller foundations over the decades have multiplied that sum many times. The university's first president, Hebraic scholar William Rainey Harper, was only 35 when the campus opened in 1892; he focused on recruiting a first-rank faculty, which has continued to be the institution's pride. Its most remarkable president, Robert Maynard Hutchins, had just turned 30 when he assumed the post in 1929. A dynamic and controversial administrator during his 22-year tenure, Hutchins revolutionized the undergraduate curriculum with his Chicago Plan, which concentrated on general liberal studies for freshmen and sophomores. He introduced study of the Great Books, reorganized the graduate school, and abandoned intercollegiate football as part of his campaign against nonacademic pursuits. Later in life, Hutchins founded the Center for the Study of Democratic Institutions within the Fund for the Republic as a "community of scholars."

In the Eisenhower era, the University of Chicago had something of a reputation locally as a hotbed of radicalism, perhaps a legacy of the impressions left by Hutchins' sweeping reforms of the 1930s. It has always boasted a superb academic record in many fields of research, with the largest number of faculty Nobel laureates of any American university. Because the campus is shadowed by high-crime neighborhoods to the west and south, visitors may detect a fortress mentality on the part of some students. As in the past, the aggregate campus tone is more earnest than exuberant: this is definitely not a party school.

The mixed bag of buildings on the 175-acre U.C. campus reflects a century's worth of commissions involving more than 70 architects, a good many of world stature. Ludwig Mies van der Rohe's pavilion-like **School of Social Services Administration Building**, a 1965 design in black steel and glass, stands at 969 East 60th Street on the south side of the Midway. A block to the east, **Laird Bell Law**

Quadrangle is a splendid 1960 ensemble by Eero Saarinen, also the architect for Woodward Court residence hall at 5825 South Woodlawn. But the heart of the campus continues to be the staunchly late English Gothic original **University of Chicago Quadrangle**, laid out in 1892 by Henry Ives Cobb in emulation of Oxford and Cambridge. During a 1960 campus visit, Saarinen praised the "beautiful, harmonious visual picture" created by the Indiana-limestone complex. "Wandering in the University of Chicago today," he said, "one is amazed at the beauty achieved by spaces surrounded by buildings all in one discipline and made out of a uniform material; where each building—through its common material—is aging in the same way."

The most imposing Gothic Revival structure on campus, **Rockefeller Memorial Chapel**, was built in 1928 with a bequest from the university's founder and renamed in his honor after his death a decade later. The walls of Bertram G. Goodhue's masonry design rise from a base eight feet (2.4 m) thick. Steel is used only in the roof beams, which support an exquisite vaulted tile ceiling. The 72 bells in the 207-foot (63-m) carillon tower are the finest in the city. One of the world's choicest ancient Near Eastern collections, including such impressive artifacts as a huge Assyrian winged bull, is displayed in the museum of the university's **Oriental Institute**. Another notable U.C. cultural facility, the **Smart Museum of Art**, boasts a rich collection in such varied fields as ancient Greek ceramics, sculpture by Auguste Rodin and other modern masters, and furniture by Frank Lloyd Wright. The university's highly regarded Court Theater Company occupies a handsomely functional 1981 building designed by Harry Weese.

Hyde Park Art Center, now in the old Del Prado Hotel (1701 East 53rd Street), carries on as a neighborhood fixture with a respected reputation for giving boosts to the careers of talented young artists; Ed Paschke and his Hairy Who colleagues are among the most notable alumni. The expanding **Du Sable Museum of African American History** brings to life black history and culture on the eastern perimeter of Washington Park. One vanished Hyde Park institution of note, the Compass Bar, occupied the site where a fire station now stands at 55th Street and University Avenue. Its Compass Players, who included Mike Nichols and Elaine May, evolved into the famed Second City satirical troupe. Another local landmark, the **Woodlawn Tap**, soldiers on as a perennial campus hangout at Woodlawn and 55th Street; if you're asking directions, everybody calls it Jimmy's.

"Me and Me" by Chicago artist Ed Paschke, 1992, oil on linen. The Hyde Park Art Center helped boost the reputation of Mr. Paschke and many other talented young artists. (courtesy Phyllis Kind Gallery)

The Hyde Park mecca for Prairie School pilgrims is Frank Lloyd Wright's **Robie House**, described with no false modesty on the Chicago Landmarks Commission plaque outside as "his boldest example of a Prairie House design and one of the most significant buildings in the history of architecture." Now owned by the university and used by its alumni association, the house was designed by Wright in 1909 for a maker of bicycle and auto parts. The citation from the city's earlier Architectural Landmarks Commission sums up Wright's achievement at 5757 South Woodlawn: "A home organized around a great hearth where interior space, under wide sweeping roofs, opens to the outdoors. The bold interplay of horizontal planes about the chimney mass, and the structurally expressive piers and windows, established a new form of domestic design." Free tours of Robie House take place at noon Monday through Saturday, and the superb dining-room set designed by Wright is in the Smart Museum of Art.

A Wright commission from 12 years earlier, **Heller House** (5132 South Woodlawn) gives hints of the coming Prairie School movement in its widely projecting eaves, and in the open feeling of the third story with its molded plaster frieze by sculptor Richard Bock. But the bottom two stories present a closed face to the outside world. North across Hyde Park Boulevard in the landmark Kenwood District, two Wright houses from the start of the 1890s were done by the young architect on a moonlighting (or "bootleg") basis under the name of a friend while he was still employed as chief draftsman by the Adler and Sullivan firm. Wright designed the frame dwelling with deep eaves at 4858 South Kenwood Avenue for insurance broker George Blossom, while its brick-and-stucco neighbor (No. 4848) was commissioned by Warren McArthur.

Kenwood prospered in the last two decades of the nineteenth century as one of Chicago's most desirable addresses, and that era's surviving mansions are a principal pride of the community's integrated beachhead south of 47th Street. The private **Madison Park** stretch of closely set residences, running for three blocks from Woodlawn to Dorchester avenues between 50th Street and Hyde Park Boulevard, is a racially diverse enclave with an almost rural air. On a grander scale, the 42-room mansion at 4901 South Ellis Avenue was built in 1903 for Sears, Roebuck executive Julius Rosenwald, a renowned philanthropist who contributed $3 million to the founding of the Museum of Science and Industry. Kenwood Park, a square-block oasis of green, is still known in the neighborhood as Farmer's Field. It is said that a cow grazed its grass as recently as the 1920s, when life in Hyde Park and Kenwood was obviously more rustic than it is today.

The University of Chicago faculty boasts more Nobel laureates than any other American university.

■ SOUTH TO PULLMAN

George M. Pullman called it "practical philanthropy" when he built a model town in the 1880s to house the families of workers at his **Pullman Palace Car Company complex** on Chicago's Far South Side. The self-contained town, which survives as an illuminating trip back in time, 14 miles (22.4 km) south of the Loop, was built on the notion that employees—Pullman called them "my children"—would be more productive if they lived in neat and sanitary dwellings close to the factory where they toiled. No taverns were allowed, and the single church in the 600-acre (243-ha) town was rented by Pullman management to various denominations. There was no individual home ownership, and residents of the 1,750 rowhouses and apartments paid rent and utilities to the company, at rates calculated to bring Pullman a six percent annual profit.

It seemed at first like a dream community, in idyllic contrast to the city's festering tenements. But the nightmare came in 1894 when an economic depression led Pullman to lay off large numbers of workers and cut the pay of those left by 25 to 50 percent, while refusing to reduce rents in the company town. A strike led by Eugene V. Debs grew into a national labor war that ended in defeat for the union after federal troops were sent to Chicago. But Pullman's notion of "practical philanthropy" was deeply discredited, and he died a bitter man three years later. A 1907 Illinois Supreme Court ruling forced the company to sell all the housing to private owners, and the model town deteriorated to a near-slum before rebounding as a landmark district in 1971.

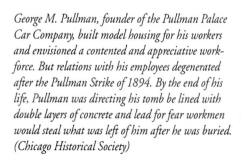

George M. Pullman, founder of the Pullman Palace Car Company, built model housing for his workers and envisioned a contented and appreciative workforce. But relations with his employees degenerated after the Pullman Strike of 1894. By the end of his life, Pullman was directing his tomb be lined with double layers of concrete and lead for fear workmen would steal what was left of him after he was buried. (Chicago Historical Society)

Pullman's rail carriages were the ultimate in late-nineteenth-century travel luxury, as this Pullman club car "La Rabida" demonstrates. (Chicago Historical Society)

Because Pullman remains a vital working-class community, as well as a living museum of social and industrial history, it's well worth making the half-hour drive south on the Dan Ryan and Calumet expressways (exiting at 111th Street). **Pullman Historic District** retains the nineteenth-century small-town feel imparted by architect Solon S. Beman and landscaper Nathan F. Barrett. Thanks to tireless efforts since the 1960s by the Historic Pullman Foundation, which maintains a visitor center at 614 East 113th Street, the company town's main public buildings have been preserved and restored. They include the red-brick **Administration Building and Clock Tower**, which was fronted a century ago by a three-acre manmade lake; the **Florence Hotel**, named for Pullman's favorite daughter and now housing a restaurant that is noted for its Sunday brunch; **Pullman Stables**, whose pair of carved horses' heads at the entrance marked the only place residents could keep their steeds; and **Greenstone Church**, a Gothic Revival gem faced with Pennsylvania serpentine stone.

South of these landmarks, it's a pleasure to stroll the shaded streets of the original Pullman housing tract, still home to working-class families. What you see along St. Lawrence, Champlain, and Langley streets is mostly diminutive townhouses arranged in rows of two to 28; the original plans provided only two free-standing houses (for top managers). As you pass residents relaxing on their stoops, it may occur to you that Chicago's industrial prowess as City of the Big Shoulders was built on the muscle and sweat of countless ordinary working men and women. And you may comprehend their enmity toward the grasping and paternalistic Pullman, who died fearing his grave might be desecrated. In *Fabulous Chicago*, Emmett Dedmon described the 1897 funeral: "It was night when the procession arrived at Graceland Cemetery, where elaborate precautions had been made to assure that Pullman was 'more secure from the encroachment of the living world' than any of 'the Egyptian monarchs supposedly resting under the ponderous weight of the pyramids.'" Pullman's lead-lined mahogany casket, wrapped in tar paper and coated with quick-drying asphalt, was lowered into a pit as large as a living room that had been lined with reinforced concrete 18 inches (45.7 cm) thick. It took two days to fill in the grave, which was topped by crisscrossed steel rails imbedded in yet more concrete.

If you have the time for some hopscotching on the way to Pullman, several other stops can shed light on Chicago's continuing diversity, starting with **Chinatown's** retail strip along Wentworth Avenue less than a mile west of the

Casa Aztlan in the Pilsen neighborhood.

vast McCormick Place convention center. The ongoing vitality of this Chinese-American enclave is symbolized by the colorful **Chinatown Gate** designed by Peter Fung in 1975 to arch across Wentworth just south of Cermak Road. Now counting around 10,000 residents, the densely packed and expanding little neighborhood began shifting here from the south edge of the Loop just before World War I. The imposing building bedecked with red-and-green pagoda towers at 2216 South Wentworth was built in the 1920s by the On Leong Merchants Association, the community's principal *tong* society. Most of Chinatown's numerous restaurants remain bastions of Cantonese cuisine; steamed-dumpling devotees swear by the dim sum at Hong Min and Three Happiness. The strip is further enlivened by Chinese bakeries, groceries, tea and herbal shops, and arts and souvenir emporiums.

It's three miles (4.8 km) straight west from Chinatown to the heart of the city's largest Mexican community in the adjoining **Pilsen** and **Little Village** neighborhoods between 18th and 26th streets. The nation's biggest Bohemian-American settlement in the years before World War II, this area was the political bailiwick of Chicago's only Czech mayor, Anton Cermak, who was fatally shot in Miami while appearing with President-elect Franklin D. Roosevelt in 1933. Now 26th Street also goes by "Avenida Mexicana," and Benito Juarez High School is a pride of the community. Hand-painted wall murals focusing on Mexican history, culture, politics, and religion are a Pilsen trademark along 18th Street and elsewhere.

Rather than detouring to Pilsen, it's possible to head south from Chinatown for a crash course in the Modernist precepts of Ludwig Mies van der Rohe on the **Illinois Institute of Technology** campus, just east of the Dan Ryan Expressway between 31st and 35th streets. Having left Nazi Germany for America, Mies became chairman of the Armour Institute of Technology architecture department in 1938. When Armour and another school merged in 1940 to form Illinois Institute of Technology, Mies embarked on a visually unified design of the new South Side campus. His work on the series of overlapping courts and quadrangles went on until he retired from the IIT faculty in 1958.

The massive structure on the west side of the Dan Ryan at 35th Street is **Comiskey Park**, which opened in 1991 as the new and improved home of the baseball White Sox. Erected with state financing to save the franchise from a threatened move to St. Petersburg, the stadium lacks the gritty South Side feel of its demolished 1910 predecessor. At least the field is real grass, and the sightlines are unimpeded by the forest of pillars that infested the old park. Even North Side Cubs fans are likely to concede the superiority of new Comiskey's ballpark food, a legacy of former White Sox owner Bill Veeck.

Mayor Richard J. Daley, the most famous lifelong White Sox fan, lived within walking distance of old Comiskey in the **Bridgeport** neighborhood immediately west, and his widow still resides in the family's brick bungalow in the 3500 block of Lowe Avenue. One of Chicago's earliest neighborhoods, Bridgeport started out as **Hardscrabble**, a shantytown settlement of Irish laborers who began arriving before 1840 to dig the Illinois & Michigan Canal. Six Chicago mayors—including Hizzoner's son, Richard M. Daley—have hailed from Bridgeport, which has an ethnically diverse population these days. Its Irish taverns were immortalized a century ago by Finley Peter Dunne's "Mr. Dooley" columns in the old *Chicago Daily News*, and **Schaller's Pump** at 37th and Halsted streets boasts a storied reputation as the city's heavyweight political bar.

A prime Bridgeport employer for more than a century was the **Union Stock Yards**, which finally closed in 1971. Warehouses and light industry have filled some of the vacated slaughterhouse space west of Halsted between 39th and 47th streets, where everything was extracted from the pig "except the squeal," and Upton Sinclair found his shocking raw material for *The Jungle*. Standing as a lonely sentinel at Exchange and Peoria is the triple-arched **Old Stone Gate**, erected in 1879 at the original entrance to the stockyards; the design is attributed to John W. Root of Burnham and Root. The **Back of the Yards** neighborhood to the southwest was the first venue for Saul Alinsky's innovative community-organizing efforts just before World War II. Like Alinsky, Sinclair aimed to bring reform. *The Jungle* strove to expose not so much the unsanitary processing of meat as the inhumane working conditions faced by Lithuanians and other immigrants, who were treated like beasts by their stockyard employers. "For the odors in these ghastly charnel-houses there may be words in Lithuanian, but there are none in English," Sinclair wrote. The suffering of his characters was "unredeemed by the slightest touch of dignity or even pathos." As he commented later in assessing the book's impact, "I aimed at the public's heart, but by accident I hit it in the stomach."

(following pages) The curved red roofs of Chinatown make a pleasant contrast to the square values of modern highrise architecture.

SKIMMING THE SUBURBS

IT HAS BEEN CALLED "THE LAND BEYOND O'HARE"—a generic label hung on the sprawling expanses of suburbs that have paved over a great deal of the eight-county greater Chicago metropolitan area radiating 40 miles (64 km) and more north, west, and south across northeast Illinois and into Indiana's northwest corner. Rock-ribbed city dwellers picture the suburbs as a monochromatic wasteland of crabgrass and strip malls where renting a video for the weekend may be the closest thing to live excitement. Suburbanites, who now make up almost two-thirds of the metropolitan population, nurse their own crime-and-grime stereotypes of the city so many have deserted—when they bother to think about Chicago at all. Particularly in the farthest exurban reaches, a trip to the Loop and Michigan Avenue may be a once-a-year (or less) expedition almost as exotic as going overseas. City and suburbs are a pair of neighboring but sometimes very distant mental planets.

In fact, the area's roughly 270 suburbs in Cook, Du Page, Lake, Will, McHenry, and Kane counties (plus Indiana's Lake and Porter counties) are more diverse in some ways than Chicago's 77 designated community areas. Economically, the spectrum runs the gamut from America's top "social status" suburb in a respected annual study (Kenilworth, on the North Shore, per-capita income: $72,620) to the nation's poorest (Ford Heights, 46 miles [73.6 km] south and a social universe away, $4,660 per capita). Many suburbs are ticky-tacky bedroom subdivisions where the trees will need another generation to grow from stick figures into shade givers. But others are almost as old (and nearly as urban in feel) as Chicago itself. For short-time visitors, no single suburb falls into the don't-miss-by-any-means category—with the exception of Oak Park, if you happen to be an architecture enthusiast with a passion for Frank Lloyd Wright. But it's worth investing a day or two, once you've seen enough of the city proper, in excursions by car west or north to expand your appreciation of mid-America's premier metropolis.

Oak Park, boasting the world's largest trove of Wright-designed buildings, is the core of the west-suburban itinerary. If a Wright pilgrimage is your only objective, riding rapid transit to Oak Park is feasible (although the Lake Street line does have crime problems). But driving gives more flexibility for extending the trip to additional Wright houses in River Forest to the west, as well as taking in the sylvan nineteenth-century planned community of Riverside, world-class Brookfield Zoo, and (somewhat farther west) Morton Arboretum in Lisle and legendary Chicago Tribune publisher Col. Robert McCormick's estate of Cantigny near Wheaton.

Oak Park Visitors Center, 158 Forest Avenue, is a useful first stop to buy a detailed *Architectural Guide Map* with photographs of the 25 Wright buildings in Oak Park and the six in River Forest, along with 49 other architecturally distinctive properties in the two suburbs. The visitors center also sells tickets for the Wright Home and Studio Tour and a walking tour of 13 Wright buildings along Forest Avenue. Besides the home and studio, only Unity Temple—his "little jewel"—is normally open to the public. It is possible see the interiors of some others, all private residences, during the annual Wright Plus Housewalk, normally held the third weekend in May.

Wright was a 22-year-old newlywed in 1889 when he built the home, only his second residential design, at 951 Chicago Avenue. His commissions before leaving Oak Park (and his wife and six children, to pursue a love affair in Europe) in 1909 provide a virtually complete record of his progress toward the revolutionary Prairie School of architecture. Observes the *Chicago on Foot* guide by Ira J. Bach and Susan Wolfson:

> You will be surprised at the early designs, especially those before 1900. Steep gables and dormer windows have little resemblance to the style now associated with Wright's name. But the impact of the type of house he had developed by the end of that period continues to be felt today in house designs all over the world. Low roof lines, wide eaves, horizontal planes and casement windows—all are characteristics of the Prairie House.

The Wright legacy overshadows the Oak Park presence of another twentieth century cultural icon who detested playing second banana during his tumultuous life. This western suburb was the **birthplace of Ernest Hemingway** in 1899 and the future novelist's home until he graduated from high school in 1917. Hemingway once branded Oak Park a town of "broad lawns and narrow minds," but he has been forgiven sufficiently that the Ernest Hemingway Foundation of Oak Park prints a brochure mapping out his birthplace, boyhood home, grade school, high school, and other sites with even a slender link to the future Nobel Prize winner. A vivid sense of this macho maestro's formative years is conveyed at the **Ernest Hemingway Museum,** opened in 1991 at the Oak Park Arts Center, 200 North Oak

Park Avenue. The nicely arranged museum displays a copy of the famous "Ernie, dear boy" letter from nurse Agnes von Kurowsky, who tended his World War I wounds in Italy. Telling the young Hemingway she related to him "more as a mother than as a sweetheart," the nurse wrote, "I am afraid it is going to hurt you, but I'm sure it won't harm you permanently." In fact, some critics have traced Hemingway's lifelong suspicion of women to that broken affair.

Four miles (6.4 km) south of Oak Park along the **Des Plaines River, Riverside** was incorporated in 1875 as an early and distinctive example of planned suburbia. Principal designer Frederick Law Olmsted (most renowned for New York City's Central Park) aimed to create a community that represented "the best application of the art of civilization to which mankind has yet attained." Riverside's layout featured curving streets, then a novelty for American suburbs. As Ira J. Bach noted in an earlier edition of the *Chicago on Foot* guide, "It is a great tribute to Olmsted that the first of his suburbs has managed to maintain its rural character for over a century, despite the increase in automobiles and urban growth." The winding streets still serve, as Olmsted described them, "to suggest and imply leisure, contemplativeness, and tranquillity."

There's less tranquillity to be found on a family-thronged Saturday or Sunday

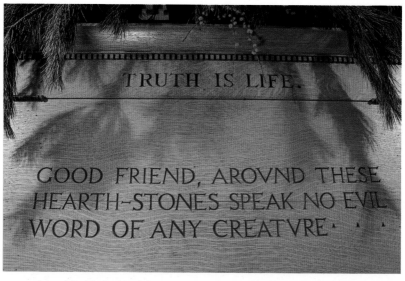

TRUTH IS LIFE.

GOOD FRIEND, AROVND THESE HEARTH-STONES SPEAK NO EVIL WORD OF ANY CREATVRE · · ·

(above) Frank Lloyd Wright studio detail over fireplace at his home in Oak Park.
(opposite) Wright considered the Unity Temple in Oak Park to be his "little jewel."

at **Brookfield Zoo** in the suburb of the same name just west of Riverside. The suburban setting allows the animals to roam in capacious enclosures, a nice complement to Chicago's skillfully designed though rather cramped Lincoln Park Zoo. It's another nine miles (14.4 km) west to **Morton Arboretum,** a 1,500-acre oasis of exotic trees, shrubs, flowers, and herbs that has its prime times in April-May when the magnolias bloom and in October when fall foliage peaks. The arboretum was established in 1922 by Morton Salt Company founder Jay Morton on his Lisle estate, then open countryside but now set smack against the busy East-West Tollway.

Colonel McCormick's **Cantigny estate,** four miles (6.4 km) northwest of the arboretum, is a revelation for its superb gardens, restored 35-room mansion, and First Division Museum retelling that much-decorated outfit's exploits in four twentieth-century wars. If you've meandered this far from Oak Park, the toll road will whisk you back to downtown Chicago by way of the Eisenhower Expressway.

One lesson of the lakeside drive up Sheridan Road from Evanston to Lake Forest is that the rich are still very different from you and me, as evidenced by the scale of their dwellings. This is one of the most expensive and exclusive residential enclaves anywhere, running through Wilmette, Kenilworth, Winnetka, Glencoe, and Highland Park. "I don't suppose there is another such extended parade of opulence on earth," wrote Jan Morris in *Locations,* a 1992 collection of essays. "Nor does it seem, like some lesser exhibitions—like Beverly Hills, California, say, or Palm Beach in Florida—in any way illusory. There is nothing flimsy to the Chicago style."

Once north of Evanston, a diverse community dating back to the Civil War decade with a population 23 percent black, the racial landscape is very white: the 1990 census recorded 130 African Americans among Wilmette's 26,690 residents, 45 among 12,174 in Winnetka, exactly 5 among 2,402 in ultra-posh Kenilworth.

Evanston houses the **national headquarters of the Women's Christian Temperance Union,** without whom the United States might have been spared Prohibition and Al Capone might have stayed a small-time hoodlum. Thanks to bluenoses of the WCTU ilk, Evanston lays claim to the invention of the ice cream sundae. The story goes that the Sunday sale of seltzer water was banned by the city council in the 1880s, taking the fizz out of ice-cream sodas on the Lord's Day. So druggists made the best of it by selling what was left—the ice cream and the syrup—as a "sundae." Although Evanston restaurants are now allowed to sell liquor, this remains a city without taverns. As the home of **Northwestern University,** it offers an ample array of cultural activities, most notably at Pick-Staiger Hall on the lakefront campus.

Near the lake just across the Wilmette border looms one of the area's most eye-popping structures, the **Baha'i House of Worship.** Irreverent undergrads used to call it "the Great Orange Juice Squeezer," but Louis Bourgeois' remarkable nine-sided design (completed in 1953) evokes this ecumenical religion's nineteenth-century Persian origins with its soaring dome and webs of delicate stone tracery. The interior effect beneath the dome is both grand and serene. Another Wilmette attraction, **Kohl Children's Museum,** engages squirming youngsters with a diverting mix of hands-on exhibits.

For a break from North Shore mansion-peeping, **Chicago Botanic Gardens** in the northwest corner of Glencoe shows how much beauty can be created from 300 acres of swampy soil. Developed since the mid-1960s by the Forest Preserve District of Cook County, and managed by the Chicago Horticultural Society, the gardens are scattered on landscaped islands. The varied motifs include three traditional Japanese gardens, a rose garden with 5,000 bushes, a plot designed after Europe's first scientific botanic garden (1545 at Italy's University of Padua),

Ragdale, summer home of architect Howard Van Doren Shaw at the turn of the century, is now an important and much-loved writer's colony in Lake Forest. (Ragdale Foundation)

DOING THE DUNES

It's not virgin wilderness, tucked virtually cheek-to-jowl with the oil refineries and steel mills of Chicago's industrial armpit at the southeastern extremity of the greater metropolitan area. But **Indiana Dunes National Lakeshore**, intertwined with older Indiana Dunes State Park, shelters a network of complex and fragile ecosystems no more than 50 miles (80 km) from the Loop. Almost lost to Rust Belt sprawl before the late Sen. Paul Douglas (D-Ill.) led the fight to bring it under the protection of the National Parks system in 1972, Indiana Dunes has been described as "America's first urban national park." Its 13 miles (20.8 km) of Lake Michigan shore draw crowds of swimmers and sunbathers in the summer months, but deeper pleasures unveil themselves to hikers who take time to seek out the huge sand dunes (as high as 120-foot [36.5-m] Mount Baldy), the bogs and marshes, the diverse plants and animals.

The thousand species of flowering plants and ferns at this meeting point of climatic zones range from prickly-pear cactus to tundra mosses and southern dogwood to northern jack pine. Birdwatchers have catalogued nearly 300 species at Indiana Dunes, and at least 30 species of mammals including weasels and white-tailed deer are believed to inhabit the lakeshore preserve. There's intriguing human history as well at **Bailly Homestead**, established by a French-Canadian fur trader in the 1830s, and **Chellburg Farm**, a restored turn-of-the-century Swedish homestead. For Chicagoans and visitors, this is a bracing cure for the big-city doldrums.

A beautiful winter's day at Indiana Dunes National Lakeshore which has been described as America's first urban national park.

and a learning garden for the disabled. The setting is likewise sylvan in next-door **Highland Park at Ravinia,** the renowned open-air venue for summer concerts ranging from folk to classical. A supreme joy on a breezy July or August evening is picnicking on Ravinia's grassy lawn while the Chicago Symphony Orchestra or some other ensemble supplies the mood music.

North beyond Highland Park and the former Army base of Fort Sheridan lies **Lake Forest,** laid out in 1856 and developed as Chicago's most exclusive suburb "the favorite resort of the better class of Chicago's inhabitants," as one nineteenth-century observer put it. A wistful resident in 1928 could remember when Lake Forest was a "comparatively unsuburban suburb," when few roads were paved, when "everyone kept horses and rode them," and when "there was only one country club." Just a bit of that horsey-set flavor still lingers in Lake Forest, where it's possible on the second Wednesday of each month from April through October to tour **Ragdale,** a turn-of-the-century mansion that serves as a retreat for artists and writers. It was originally the summer home of architect Howard Van Doren Shaw, who named it Ragdale for the aura of "cultivated shabbiness." That's the closest thing to shabby in Lake Forest.

(following pages) Chicago's suburbs sprawl into the sunset.

COMING CLEAN ON THE RIVER

In addition to the lakefront and the architectural splendors of downtown, visitors to Chicago now have another site to add to their list: the Chicago River. Once described by Upton Sinclair as a "great open sewer, a hundred or two feet wide," the still-murky river is attracting ardent patrons. On fair Saturday mornings, docents from the "Friends of the Chicago River" lead two-hour walking tours alongside the historic "Checagou."

The local branch of the recently formed national coalition "Friends of Trashed Rivers," the Friends seek to build awareness of the Chicago as an urban treasure too long taken for granted, even by the city's own residents. Executive director Laurene von Klan notes that more and more people are turning out for the Saturday morning tours. She attributes some of this attention to the publicity the river gained for itself when an underground tunnel collapsed in April of 1992, causing river water to flood the basements of downtown office buildings and closing businesses for days. For years Chicago had built tourist status as the "City on the Lake"—within a few drenched minutes, the river had usurped top billing.

First explored by Jacques Marquette and Louis Joliet in 1673, the 92-mile-long river would in the nineteenth century become the link between the Plains and the East Coast. Once the Illinois and Michigan canal was finished in 1848, it became possible to transport grain, meat, and lumber from the Mississippi to the Atlantic via the Great Lakes. Indeed the city of Chicago probably owes its importance to the river for which it was named. But ever since, the Chicago River has paid a stiff price, suffering the assaults of urban waste and industrial pollution.

The river was perhaps at its lowest point in the late nineteenth century, when industry had enjoyed free rein for some years, and the waterway had become a convenient repository for garbage. In *The Jungle*, Upton Sinclair describes places in the river where "the grease and filth have caked solid, and the creek looks like a bed of lava. Chickens walk about on it, feeding, and many times an unwary stranger has started to stroll across, and vanished temporarily." Ironically, docents note that the tour's biggest draw, the Bubbly Creek tour, owes its popularity to those very days of flagrant pollution. Old Chicago slaughterhouses dumped their refuse unchecked, and over time, intestines and other unused animal parts sank to the bottom of the river. Nowadays, these send up a combination of methane, carbonic acid, and carbon dioxide, which forms little bubbles on the water's surface.

Considerably cleaner than it was 20 years ago, the Chicago River has again become home to fifty species of fish who'd deserted its brown waters, including salmon, perch, and carp. With the help of the Friends, the river may yet enjoy top attraction status from Chicago's tourists—and respect from its citizens.

PRACTICAL INFORMATION

■ AREA CODE

The area code for Chicago is 312. The suburban area code is 708.

■ WHEN TO GO TO CHICAGO

Hit Chicago on a stormy day in midwinter, and you may logically assume that the "Windy City" label applies to the weather—rather than, as is historical fact, to the hot air of civic boosters who hustled successfully to land the 1893 world's fair. When "the Hawk"—a nickname uttered with shivers of respect here—whistles in from the north in January and February, wind-chill factors can plummet into the frostbite range. The thermometer falls to 0° F (-17° C) or lower on seven days in the average January, with -27 °F (-33 °C) (on January 20, 1985) the coldest ever recorded locally. So winter figures to be the least pleasant season for a Chicago pleasure trip, although it is a time of year when music, theater, museums, and restaurants are running at full steam.

Chicago summers have their occasional hot and humid blemishes: five days of 90° F (33° C) or above in the average June, eight in July, five in August. The city's record high is 105° F (42° C) which occurred on July 24, 1934. June qualifies as the rainiest month, but Chicago's annual average precipitation of 33.3 inches

(following pages) Winter ice-sailing on Wolf Lake south of the city.

(84.6 cm)—less than New York's 42.8 (109 cm) though more than San Francisco's 19.7 (50 cm)—is spread rather evenly around the calendar. Snowfall in the average winter adds up to 39.8 inches (101 cm); in the snowiest 24-hour period ever, a memorable 18.1 inches (45.7 cm) paralyzed the city from January 26 to 27, 1967.

■ TEMPERATURE AND PRECIPITATION

	TEMPERATURE				PRECIPITATION	
	Average Daily in F		Average Daily in C		Average Each Month	
	MIN	MAX	MIN	MAX	INCHES	MM
Jan.	18	34	-8	1	1.6	41
Feb.	20	36	-7	2	1.3	33
March	29	45	-2	7	2.6	66
Apr.	40	58	4	14	3.7	94
May	49	70	9	21	3.2	81
June	59	81	15	27	4.1	104
July	65	86	18	30	3.6	91
Aug.	65	85	18	29	3.5	89
Sept.	56	76	13	24	3.4	86
Oct.	45	65	7	18	2.3	58
Nov.	32	49	0	9	2.1	53
Dec.	22	36	-6	2	2.1	53

■ GETTING TO CHICAGO

Many visitors get their first glimpse of Chicago at O'Hare, which brags about being "the world's busiest airport"—although that may sound less like a boast than a consumer warning. More than 60 million passengers a year take off and land at O'Hare's four terminals, so brace yourself for trampling herds reminiscent of Chicago's legendary stockyards—especially when bad weather snarls air traffic and turns concourses into refugee camps.

Because O'Hare is a major hub for two of the nation's biggest airlines, American and United, it has the definite virtue of nonstop service to almost all U.S.

MOTHER O'HARE

O Mother O'Hare, big bosom for our hungry poets, pelvic saddle for our sexologists and Open Classroom theorists—O houri O'Hare, who keeps her Perm-O-Pour Stoneglow thighs ajar to receive a generation of frustrated and unreadable novelists—

But wait a minute. It may be too early for the odes. Has it ever been duly noted that O'Hare, which is an airport outside Chicago, is now the intellectual center of the United States?

Curious, but true. There at O'Hare, on any day, Monday through Friday, from September to June, they sit . . . in row after Mies van der row of black vinyl and stainless-steel sling chairs . . . amid soaring walls of plate glass . . . from one tenth to one third of the literary notables of the United States. In October and April, the peak months, the figure goes up to one half.

Masters and Johnson and Erica Jong, Kozol and Rifkin and Hacker and Kael, Steinem and Nader, Marks, Hayden and Mailer, Galbraith and Heilbroner, and your bearmarket brothers in the PopEco business, Lekachman & Others—which of you has not hunkered down lately in the prodigious lap of Mother O'Hare!

And why? Because they're heading out into the land to give lectures . . . . Giving lectures in the heartland is one of the lucrative dividends of being a noted writer in America. . . . All the skyways to Lectureland lead through O'Hare Airport. In short, up to one half of our intellectual establishment sits outside Chicago between planes.

At a literary conference at Notre Dame, I . . . ran into a poet who is noted for his verse celebrating the ecology, née Nature. He lives in a dramatic house nailed together completely from uncut pieces of hickory driftwood, perched on a bluff overlooking the crashing ocean. . . . I remarked that this must be the ideal setting in which to write about the ecological wonders.

"I wouldn't know," he said. "I do all my writing in O'Hare."

—Tom Wolfe, "The Intelligent Coed's Guide to America"
in *Mauve Gloves and Madmen, Clutter and Vine*, 1976

cities of consequence and an increasing number of foreign destinations. A spanking-new international terminal opened in 1993 to replace the "temporary" facility that operated from the ground floor of a parking garage for the previous decade. The general O'Hare information number is (312) 686-2200.

If you're traveling light, the least expensive way to cover the 18 miles (28.8 km) between O'Hare International Airport and the Loop is the Chicago Transit Authority's rail service, which runs frequently from beneath Terminal 4 and takes 35 to 40 minutes. But you can't haul the airport's rental baggage carts onto the CTA platform, and there's no space to store luggage on the rapid-transit trains. Taxis take 40 to 60 minutes to get downtown, depending on time of day and Kennedy Expressway conditions; a share-the-ride program can cut the cost of a cab. Continental Air Transport, (312) 454-7799, runs buses from O'Hare to hotels and other stops downtown, the Near North Side and northwest suburbs; fares are roughly half of what a taxi costs. Beware of hustlers for unlicensed cabs and limousines.

Flustered fliers may find less of a hassle at Chicago's second airport, Midway, which gets not much more than a tenth the passenger traffic of O'Hare. Midway, (312) 767-0500, is located about eight miles (12.8 km) southwest of the Loop in a bungalow neighborhood.

Chicago is also a hub for Amtrak rail service from recently renovated Union Station, at Jackson and Canals streets on the western edge of the Loop. The Amtrak information number is (800) 872-7245. For intercity bus riders, Greyhound's

The tunnel connecting the United Airlines terminals at O'Hare is a public light sculpture in its own right.

main Chicago station is at 630 West Harrison Street a bit southwest of downtown, (312) 781-2900.

■ GETTING AROUND TOWN

Chicagoans grouse about rising fares and what some riders perceive as deteriorating service on their Chicago Transit Authority. But visitors from the many U.S. cities less well-endowed with public transportation are likely to marvel at the CTA's extensive network of buses and trains. The rapid-transit segment, which celebrated its centennial in 1992, is known as the "L"—short for elevated, even though parts of some lines run in subways or down the middle of expressways.

Many CTA routes operate 24 hours a day, crisscrossing the city and serving a number of bordering suburbs. Riding the L and buses at night can be risky if you are unfamiliar with high-crime neighborhoods. For a different slant on the city, a daytime ride on the Ravenswood L circles the Loop's skyscrapers before heading north and west through a variety of commercial and residential neighborhoods to the end of the line at Lawrence and Kimball. On Sundays and holidays from May

Chicago has been the rail hub of the nation for over one hundred years with Union Station as its terminal.

through September, the CTA's special Culture Bus service links museums and other landmarks on three routes starting at the Art Institute of Chicago; a single ticket allows unlimited riding for the day.

CTA buses require exact change (with $1 bills accepted). Buying a pack of 10 tokens at banks, currency exchanges, supermarkets, and some L stations provides a small saving on rapid-transit and rush-hour bus fares.

For CTA information, call (312) 836-7000; a detailed route map is available.

It's usually easy to find a taxi in Chicago—except during wretched weather when you really need one. In the central city, simply hail an unoccupied cab on the street; to call for a pickup from outlying neighborhoods, the main companies include Checker/Yellow, (312) 829-4222; Flash, (312) 561-1444; and American United, (312) 248-7600. Fares rise periodically, and all cabs are metered.

Whether you'll want a car in Chicago depends on your itinerary. In the central city, trying to negotiate dense traffic jams and find a parking spot for less than a prince's ransom is sure to have you cursing the invention of the internal-combustion engine. The best means of private transportation in the Loop and environs is your own two feet. To visit outlying neighborhoods or suburbs, however, an automobile is often the only practicable way to go. All major and many off-brand rental-car agencies operate in Chicago; you're likely to get a better rate by reserving in advance through the toll-free numbers in your Yellow Pages. Taxes on rental cars total at least 18 percent.

■ ACCOMMODATIONS

You can search a long time in Chicago without finding the hotel hunter's dream of an elegant and intimate hideaway centrally located and charging a mere pittance. This is a high-priced metropolis, after all, not a fantasyland.

But you can get a lot more hotel room for your dollars, as in most big cities, by scheduling your visit over a weekend and shopping around via toll-free 800 numbers for the best deals (as much as 50 percent off rack rates—with breakfast, champagne, parking, or other amenities sometimes thrown in). Both the Chicago Office of Tourism and the Hotel-Motel Association of Illinois publish brochures listing weekend and other discounts. Cut-rate bets may be off on weeks of the half-dozen biggest annual conventions.

Parking in downtown Chicago has always been a nightmare. This novel "elevator parking facility" in 1941 proved to be too slow in operation. (Chicago Historical Society)

Many of Chicago's most vaunted (and most expensive) hotels are located within an easy walk of the Magnificent Mile. The Loop and its southern fringe contain a number of older properties that have benefited greatly from renovation over the past decade. Motels along commercial strips in outlying city neighborhoods are a less expensive option for visitors with a car. And the suburbs offer budget lodging down to the Motel 6 level—if you don't mind daily commuting as part of your vacation. The Chicago International Hostel (312) 262-1011 is a frugal option for the young-at-heart near Loyola University on the North Side.

Chicago lacks the network of commercial bed-and-breakfast inns that enrich the tourist fabric of cities like San Francisco. But it is possible to book a room in a private home or apartment through time-tested Bed and Breakfast Chicago (312) 951-0085, which represents about 70 properties. A couple can expect to pay $60 to $95 per night for a room with breakfast, $80-$130 for a self-contained apartment.

Because hotels are a matter of personal taste and budget, any short list of top bets is a risky undertaking subject to debate. Each of the two dozen places that follow has some special virtue, even if nothing more than particularly good value for location. There are dozens of other commendable lodgings, and advance reservations almost always make sense. The coding at the end of each listing indicates the property's price range (Note that the plague of occupancy and other local taxes will add 12.4 percent or more to the bill.):

B=Budget (under $90); M=Moderate ($90-$130);
E=Expensive ($130-$175); L=Luxury ($175 and up).

Best Western River North. Free parking is a bonus at this recently refurbished motel-style spot handily located for River North's galleries and Michigan Avenue's shops. 125 W. Ohio St. (River North neighborhood), (312) 467-0800 or (800) 727-0800. M

Blackstone. Impending renovation should put new bounce in the step of a venerable property where lakeside rooms overlook Grant Park's Buckingham Fountain. There's both live theater and top-flight jazz on the premises. 636 S. Michigan Ave. (South Loop), (312) 427-4300 or (800) 622-6330. M

Chicago Hilton and Towers. Palatial lobbies dripping with marble and chandeliers set a tone of grandeur in what was once the world's largest hotel. The rooms are now considerably fewer and more spacious. 720 S. Michigan

(previous pages) Most of Chicago's outdoor leisure activity takes place along the Lake Michigan waterfront.

Ave. (South Loop), (312) 922-4400 or (800) 445-8667. L

Claridge. An air of European gentility and reasonable rates commend this 172-room hotel in a 1930s building on a tree-shaded Gold Coast street. 1244 N. Dearborn Pkwy. (Gold Coast), (312) 787-4980 or (800) 245-1258. M

Comfort Inn-Chicago. Reliable comfort at rack rates under $100 a night adds up to a value-hunter's best bet (with precious parking) along a bustling commercial strip four miles (7.2 km) north of the Loop. 601 W. Diversey Pkwy. (Lincoln Park), (312) 348-2810 or (800) 228-5151. B

Days Inn Lake Shore Drive. The amenities are predictable, but the terrific views of next-door Lake Michigan—plus an outdoor swimming pool—make the center-city Days Inn a summertime family magnet. 644 N. Lake Shore Drive (Streeterville), (312) 943-9200 or (800) 942-7543. M

The Drake. High tea in the Palm Court lobby epitomizes the grande-dame graciousness at this favored Chicago haunt of Very Important Persons. 140 E. Walton Place (Magnificent Mile), (312) 787-2200 or (800) 553-7253. L

Essex Inn. Grant Park's museums are near neighbors to an affordable hotel with a heated pool. 800 S. Michigan Ave. (South Loop), (312) 939-2800 or (800) 621-6909. M

Hotel Florence in Pullman no longer takes overnight guests but provides a popular eating establishment and a small museum of Pullman memorabilia.

Fairmont. Perhaps the most stylish of the city's newer luxury hotels, this sleek 45-story tower clad in Spanish pink granite is a business executive's favorite. 200 N. Columbus Drive (New East Side), (312) 565-8000 or (800) 527-4727. L

Forum. Good value and middle-of-everything location are watchwords at a nothing-fancy place that gets high marks for its helpful staff. 525 N. Michigan Ave. (Magnificent Mile), (312) 944-0055 or (800) 327-0200. M

Four Seasons. Tucked into 17 stories of a Post-Modernist tower deep in the heart of the shop-till-you-drop zone, this no-comforts-spared dazzler garners many discerning votes as best in town. 120 E. Delaware Place (Magnificent Mile), (312) 280-8800 or (800) 332-3442. L

Knickerbocker. Recent renovation has brightened the clubby Knickerbocker's 256 rooms. The 14th floor boasts Prohibition-era secret doors leading to a central stairwell for quick escapes out of the speakeasies. 163 E. Walton Place (Magnificent Mile), (312) 751-8100 or (800) 621-8140. E/L

Lenox House Suites. Murphy beds fold into the wall for more daytime space, and the kitchenette setup can cut dining costs for Chicago visitors staying longer than a couple of days. 616 N. Rush St. (Magnificent Mile), (312) 337-1000 or (800) 445-3669. M

Midland. Full breakfast is included in the rates at this handsomely renovated heart-of-town hotel shadowed by the Sears Tower. 172 W. Adams St. (Loop), (312) 332-1200 or (800) 621-2360. E

Nikko. This sleek Japanese beachhead on the north bank of the Chicago River boasts a traditional Oriental garden and a half-dozen suites with *tatami* sleeping rooms. 320 N. Dearborn (River North), (312) 744-1900 or (800) 645-5687. L

Omni Ambassador East. Home of the reincarnated Pump Room, the 275-room Ambassador East is a trip back in time to Chicago's Gilded Age. 1301 N. State Pkwy. (Gold Coast), (312) 787-7200 or (800) 843-6664. L

Palmer House Hilton. This rambling downtown giant boasts a pedigree stretching more than a century, bolstered by a recent renovation that put the sparkle back into its opulent public rooms. 17 E. Monroe St. (Loop), (312) 726-7500 or (800) 445-8667. E

Park Hyatt. Located just west of the Old Chicago Water Tower, the 255-room Park Hyatt plays its elegance in a muted key. 800 N. Michigan Ave. (Magnificent Mile), (312) 280-2222 or (800) 233-1234. L

Radisson Suite Hotel O'Hare Airport. Plenty of space and amenities are major selling points for a relative newcomer to the O'Hare orbit. 5500 N. River Road, Rosemont (O'Hare), (708) 678-4000 or (800) 333-3333. E

Raphael. It's hardly a country inn, but this neighbor of the skyscraping John Hancock Center gives guests a bracing taste of European intimacy and charm at sensible prices. 201 E. Delaware (Magnificent Mile), (312) 943-5000 or (800) 821-5343. M/E

Richmont. The European character here extends to the compact size of most guest rooms, but the location and rates are right on target. 162 E. Ontario (Magnificent Mile), (312) 787-3580 or (800) 621-8055. M/E

Ritz-Carlton Chicago. Managed by Four Seasons, this bastion of elegant appointments and service has a separate Water Tower Place entrance to whisk fortunate guests to the leafy 12th-floor lobby. 160 E. Pearson St. (Magnificent Mile), (312) 266-1000 or (800) 332-3442. L

Sheraton Plaza. Remodeling has spruced up this converted condominium complex splendidly located for prowling North Michigan Avenue. 160 E. Huron St. (Magnificent Mile), (312) 787-2900 or (800) 325-3535. E

Sofitel. This Midwest outpost of the upscale French chain has the most distinctive character of any O'Hare hotel. 5550 N. River Road, Rosemont (O'Hare), (708) 678-4488 or (800) 258-4888. E

Stouffer Riviere. Chicago's newest luxury hotel is located at the corner of State Street and Wacker Drive, right between the Loop and Magnificent Mile. 1 West Wacker Drive, (312) 372-7200. E

■ TASTES OF CHICAGO

Most Chicagoans do know how to use a knife and fork, although you might wonder from watching them tuck into the city's trademark delicacies. Deep-dish pizza, Chicago's most heralded contribution to the American palate, is best savored as a hands-on experience. Even more so are some other grasp-and-chew foods—hot dogs, barbecued ribs, Italian beef sandwiches—for which Chicagoans take inordinate pride in doing it their way. Getting a Chicago-style hot dog just right—down to the poppy-seed bun and the celery salt (but never, ever, catsup)—is a matter of no small skill and artistry. Nathan's, that hot dog hall-of-famer from New York, couldn't cut the mustard here.

Finger food may be a local headline act, performed with gargantuan gusto by two million or more frenzied feeders at the start of each summer during the Taste of Chicago festival in Grant Park. But the real story of Chicago dining in the 1990s is the ever-expanding depth and breadth of ethnic diversity simmering among the 7,000 restaurants in this melting-pot metropolis. From Afghan to Vietnamese with dozens of nationalities in between, Chicago dishes up a culinary global tour as exhaustive and rewarding as you'll find anywhere in North America.

The annual Taste of Chicago Festival may be enjoyed while on the job or off.

It's an astonishing transformation for the erstwhile meat-and-potatoes bastion of the Midwest, where the ingrained beef bias was captured deliciously in Lucius Beebe's 1951 *Holiday* magazine article headlined "Name Your Cut!" Beebe, a trencherman as well as railroad buff, branded Chicago "the beef citadel of the world." The city, he wrote, "lives by beef, and the best food you can get in any Chicago restaurant, with few exceptions, is some part of a steer raised on the distant ranges of Texas, Colorado, or Nebraska."

Longtime mecca for carnivores was the legendary Stock Yard Inn, "a temple of T-bone," as Beebe called it. Patrons at the inn's Sirloin Room selected their cut from a great ice-filled altar in the center of the restaurant, stamped the steak with one of the miniature branding irons from the nearby charcoal brazier, and dispatched it to the kitchen. That marked the summit of Chicago gourmet dining two generations ago, when seldom was heard a discouraging word about cholesterol. The Stock Yard Inn, like the South Side yards themselves, is merely a Chicago memory today. And while it is still possible to get a slab of grilled meat in the City of the Big Shoulders, the decline and fall of beef can be gauged by comparative figures from two useful diners' resources: in a typical recent month, *Chicago* magazine's restaurant guide recommended seven places for vegetarian dishes, seven for seafood, a mere five for steaks. The *Zagat Chicago Restaurant Survey*'s 1992-93 edition listed 36 seafood spots, 26 Thai, and just 21 steakhouses. Top steak venues, if you care to indulge, include Morton's (four locations), Gene & Georgetti, the Palm, and Eli's.

Thanks in part to all the storefront ethnic fare, Chicago dining tends to be light on the wallet—if not always light on the stomach. Zagat, which bases its ratings on reports from thousands of volunteer gourmets, ranks this as the most fair-valued of major U.S. dining markets: an average customer tab of $22 for the 750-plus Chicago area places covered. Comparative figures are $34 for New York, $28 for Los Angeles, $26 for San Francisco, $25 for Miami. "There's no question that Chicago leads all Zagat big cities in unadorned, salt-of-the-earth eating," says the guide. Heading Zagat's Top 100 "Bangs for the Buck" list is Walker Bros., a local-institution pancake house with three north suburban locations. Whatever your budget, a blossoming summer delight is the scores of Chicago restaurants that set up their gardens or sidewalks for outdoor dining, a pleasure almost unheard of during the red-meat era.

This selective menu of recommended Chicago restaurants merely nibbles at the banquet of possibilities in one of America's richest and most varied cities for dining. Each month's *Chicago* magazine contains incisive reviews of about 150 area restaurants. The *Zagat Chicago Restaurant Survey* pocket guide digests opinions of frequent diners on several hundred places. Dining reviews appear in the Friday activities sections of the *Chicago Sun-Times* and *Chicago Tribune*, as well as the Sunday *Sun-Times*.

■ RESTAURANTS

Reservations are always a good idea at restaurants that accept them. A call ahead also can confirm opening hours and credit-card policy. Restaurants do change chefs and go out of business, so no set of listings can be entirely up-to-date. Price categories are coded at the end of each listing:

B=Budget ($12 or less per person); M=Moderate ($12-$25); E=Expensive ($25-$40); D=Deluxe ($40 and up).

American

Al's No. 1 Italian Beef. Chin-dripping beef sliced paper-thin, heaped onto soft Italian bread, and slathered with juice. 1079 W. Taylor St. (Little Italy), (312) 226-4017; also 169 W. Ontario St. (River North), (312) 943-3222. B

Army & Lou's. Spacious South Side soul-food spot is renowned for its gumbos, short ribs, fried chicken, cornbread. 420 E. 75th St. (Grand Crossing), (312) 483-3100. M

Blue Mesa. Local pioneer of the hybrid Santa Fe cuisine pleases a yuppie crowd with first-rate fajitas and knockout margaritas. 1729 N. Halsted St. (Lincoln Park), (312) 944-5990. M

Gene & Georgetti. Carnivores and spaghetti hounds keep the faith at this longtime steakhouse where brusque service is considered part of the charm. 500 N. Franklin (River North), (312) 527-3718. E

Gladys' Luncheonette. Bustling soul-food diner dishes up top value along with rib-sticking fare. 4527 S. Indiana Ave. (Grand Boulevard), (312) 548-4566. B

Gold Coast Dogs. Lunchtime swarms testify to the primacy of these Chicago-style dogs on poppy-seed buns. 418 N. State St. (River North), (312) 527-1222; 2100 N. Clark St. (Lincoln Park), (312) 327-8887. B

Gordon. Chefs seem to come and go at Gordon, but the sophisticated contemporary American cooking manages to maintain an enviably high standard. 500 N. Clark St. (River North), (312) 467-9780. D

John Barleycorn Memorial Pub. One of Chicago's well known pubs with a beautifully ornate door that deserves a look or two. 658 W. Belden Ave. (Lincoln Park), (312) 348-8899.

Lawry's The Prime Rib. Savor the ornate setting in a former McCormick mansion while making the only basic menu decision—which cut of the excellent prime rib to order. 100 E. Ontario St. (Magnificent Mile), (312) 787-5000. E

Lou Malnati's. Reliable purveyor of Chicago-style deep-dish pizza. 441 N. Wells St. (River North), (312) 828-9800; several suburban locations. B/M

Printer's Row, immediately south of downtown, is home to several fine restaurants.

Metropolis 1800. Drop-dead casual-chic setting showcases fashionably inventive fare. 1800 N. Clybourn Ave. (Clybourn Corridor), (312) 642-6400. M/E

Morton's. The elite meet to eat meat in this time-tried spot that gets tons of votes as Chicago's best steakhouse. 1050 N. State St. (Magnificent Mile), (312) 266-4820. Also suburban locations in Highland Park, Rosemont, Westchester. E/D

The 95th. Happily, the quality of the regional American food is not inversely proportional to the view from 1,000 feet up in the John Hancock Center. 875 N. Michigan Ave. (Magnificent Mile), (312) 787-9596. D

Pizzeria Uno/Pizzeria Due. Bring patience or come at an off-hour to these neighboring shrines where Chicago's redoubtable deep-dish pizza was born. (Magnificent Mile/River North). Uno: 29 E. Ohio St., (312) 321-1000. Due: 619 N. Wabash Ave., (312) 943-2400. B/M

Prairie. A personal favorite, Prairie features ingredients from America's heartland creatively prepared and served in a dining room that evokes Frank Lloyd Wright's Prairie Style. 500 S. Dearborn St. (South Loop), (312) 663-1143. E

Printer's Row. Down the block from Prairie, chef-owner Michael Foley's neighborhood pioneer likewise does inventive cooking in Midwestern ways. 550 S. Dearborn St. (South Loop), (312) 461-0780. E

Robinson's No. 1 Ribs. Barbecue front-runner, boasting slow-smoking process that lowers fat content. 655 W. Armitage Ave. (Lincoln Park), (312) 337-1399. B/M

Shaw's Crab House. The bounty of superlative seafood in this bustling place starts with such basics as exemplary oysters on the half shell and Maryland crab cakes. 21 E. Hubbard St. (Magnificent Mile/River North), (312) 527-2722. E

Twin Anchors. No-nonsense neighborhood perennial purveys meaty baby-back ribs and terrific jukebox tunes. 1655 N. Sedgwick St. (Old Town), (312) 266-1616. M

Walker Bros. Original Pancake House. The delectably fresh, cholesterol-be-damned breakfast fare brings legions of flapjack fans to this north suburban institution. 153 Green Bay Road, Wilmette (North Shore), (708) 251-6000. Other locations in Arlington Heights, Glenview, Lincolnshire. B

Latin American

Abril. Family-filled taqueria serves up huge portions of Mexican standards plus some less-expected menu items. 2607 N. Milwaukee Ave. (Logan Square), (312) 227-7252. B/M

Caribbean Delight. OK, so Jamaica is hardly Latin. Relax and enjoy the spicy goat curry, jerk chicken, oxtail stew, and other island specialties. 7303 N. Damen Ave. (West Rogers Park), (312) 743-2900. M

Chano Chano. Terrific homemade tortillas form the base for an array of authentically Mexican fillings at this lively taqueria. 3901 W. 26th St. (Little Village/Pilsen), (312) 522-0041. B/M

Hat Dance. It may look like a Hollywood soundstage, but Hat Dance serves first-rate food spun inventively from Mexican ingredients. 325 N. Huron St. (River North), (312) 649-0066. M

Rinconcito Sudamericano. Seafood stands out at this Peruvian storefront, but the intriguing Andean fare ranges as far as beef heart and tripe stew. 1954 W. Armitage Ave. (Bucktown), (312) 489-3126. M

Tania's. *Lechon asado* (roast pork) and other Cuban specialties mingle with Spanish favorites in a lively place with dancing to Latino rhythms. 2659 N. Milwaukee Ave. (Logan Square), (312) 235-7120. M

El Tinajon. The little-known cooking of Guatemala is featured at this homey storefront. 4638 N. Western Ave. (Ravenswood), (312) 878-5862. B/M

Topolobampo/Frontera Grill. Serious regional Mexican fare sparkles in these same-kitchen siblings steered by the genius of chef-owner Rick Bayless. Topolobampo is more upscale. 445 N. Clark St. (River North), (312) 661-1434. M/E

Eclectic

Bistro 110. It's not pure Paris, but here's a fashionably bustling spot for a break from all the nearby shopping. The wood-burning oven plays a starrring role. 110 E. Pearson St. (Magnificent Mile), (312) 266-3110. M/E

Charlie Trotter's. The eponymous chef-owner of this much-praised townhouse restaurant stirs Asian flavors into European recipes for an experimental American cuisine superbly on target. 816 W. Armitage Ave. (Lincoln Park), (312) 248-6228. D

The Eccentric. Oprah Winfrey is the celebrity presence for a French-Italian-English pastiche that delivers the goods on the plate in an exuberant setting. 159 W. Erie St. (River North), (312) 787-8390. E

Jackie's. Chef Jackie Shen mixes French and Asian flavors for an intense dining experience. 2478 N. Lincoln Ave. (Lincoln Park), (312) 880-0003. D

Yoshi's Cafe. West and East meld marvelously at chef-owner Yoshi Katsumura's cozy Pacific Rim restaurant where subtlety is the hallmark. 3257 N. Halsted (Lake View), (312) 248-6160. D

French

Ambria. Perhaps Chicago's finest restaurant, certainly a grand-night-out experience blessed by chef Gabino Sotelino's light and unerring touch. 2300 N. Lincoln Park West (Lincoln Park), (312) 472-5959. D

Cafe Provençal. Suburban-style French inn carries on admirably in the spirit of its late chef-founder Leslee Reis. 1625 Hinman, Evanston (North Shore), (708) 475-2233. D

Carlos'. Nouvelle French flies high at this small but firmly entrenched north suburban temple of lighter-is-better gastronomy. 429 Temple Ave., Highland Park (North Shore), (708) 432-0770. D

Everest Room. Ambrosial Alsatian-accented fare from chef Jean Joho puts this 40th-story eyrie in Chicago's financial canyon at the pinnacle of the city's dining pyramid. 440 S. La Salle St. (South Loop), (312) 663-8920. D

Le Francais. The legendary Jean Banchet is gone, but new chef-owners Roland and Mary Beth Liccioni are keeping this sumptuous suburban showplace in five-star form. 269 S. Milwaukee Ave., Wheeling (Northwest Suburbs), (708) 541-7470. D

Jimmy's Place. There's a Japanese lilt to chef Kevin Shikami's contemporary French cooking in a slightly out-of-the-way setting embellished with opera posters and recordings. 3420 N. Elston Ave. (Logan Square), (312) 539-2999. D

Kiki's Bistro. Good value for French country fare lures crowds who savor such standards as gloriously rare roast leg of lamb. 900 N. Franklin St. (River North), (312) 335-5454. M/E

Le Titi de Paris. Relocated in Arlington Heights, chef-owner Pierre Pollin creates reliable French classics with an aura of assured elegance. 1015 W. Dundee Road, Arlington Heights (Northwest Suburbs), (708) 506-0222. E/D

La Tour. Sophisticated food, silken service, and splendid views of the Old Chicago Water Tower make this a prime candidate for that special romantic occasion. 800 N. Michigan (Magnificent Mile), (312) 280-2230. D

Greek

Courtyards of Plaka. Ambiance a cut above the Greektown crowd is matched by Greek cooking that goes a step beyond the typical. 340 S. Halsted St. (Near West Side), (312) 263-0767. M

Greek Islands. Although it may have lost some competitive edge, Greek Islands still does a high-spirited job of dispensing good-value Hellenic food. 200 S. Halsted St. (Near West Side), (312) 782-9855. There's a suburban Greek Islands in Lombard. M

Papagus Greek Taverna. Less heavy Hellenic fare in non-Greektown location with an array of *mezedes,* the Aegean equivalent of small-portion tapas. 620 N. State St. (River North), (312) 642-8450. M

Parthenon. One of the oldest and most reliable Greektown competitors, featuring an 11-course family-style feed for serious diners. 314 S. Halsted St. (Near West Side), (312) 726-2407. B/M

Santorini. Accent on seafood in whitewashed Greektown setting with a touch of class. 138 S. Halsted St. (Near West Side), (312) 829-8820. M

Italian

Carlucci. Exemplary Northern Italian dishes—from staples like osso buco to such novelties as carpaccio of goose—are set off to fine advantage in two striking rooms. 2215 N. Halsted (Lincoln Park), (312) 281-1220. Another location in suburban Rosemont. E

La Locanda. Risotto is one of the best choices in this smartly decorated spot that draws a stylish crowd. 334 W. Chicago Ave. (River North), (312) 335-9550. E

Rosebud on Rush New red-sauce celebrity is drawing rave reviews for its central Italian fare. 55 E. Superior (Magnificent Mile), (312) 266-6444. E

Scoozi! It's easy to imagine Fellini filming the jampacked seekers of la dolce vita who flock to the trendy but tasty country-Italian menu. 410 W. Huron St. (River North), (312) 943-5900. M/E

Spiaggia. The high-Italian food now matches the exquisite setting at this expense-account favorite. 980 N. Michigan Ave. (Magnificent Mile), (312) 280-2750. D

Informal dining on seafood is available at the Navy Pier.

(opposite) Berghoff on West Adams in the Loop is Chicago's oldest restaurant.

Trattoria No. 10. An erstwhile downtown boiler room has been transformed into a fair imitation of a time-seasoned trattoria, where pastas are among the top choices. 10 N. Dearborn (Loop), (312) 984-1718. E

Vivere. Formerly the Florentine Room of the venerable Italian Village, Vivere boasts a dazzling post-modern decor and regional cooking with a light touch. 71 W. Monroe St. (Loop), (312) 332-4040. E

Other European

Ann Sather. Swedish dishes from fruit soup to meatballs dot the menu of this homespun favorite with two North Side locations. 5207 N. Clark (Andersonville), (312) 271-6677; 929 W. Belmont (Lake View), (312) 348-2378. B/M

Berghoff. Your crusty waiter is as likely to be Hispanic as Teutonic these days, but the Berghoff soldiers on as a century-old stalwart of German heartiness. 17 W. Adams St. (Loop), (312) 427-3170. There's a new Berghoff clone in River North. M

Bohemian Crystal. Bread dumplings, sauerkraut and mounds of meat swathed in gravy give hearty Czech-style satisfaction in a Du Page County suburb. 639 N. Blackhawk, Westmont (Western Suburbs), (708) 789-1981. M

Galans. Amid the neighborhood's new wave of urban pioneers, Galans sticks to its unassuming ways with belt-popping Ukrainian dishes. 2210 W. Chicago Ave. (Ukrainian Village), (312) 292-1000. B/M

Home Bakery. Cheap Polish food and lots of it keep crowds coming for pierogi, borscht, stuffed cabbage, and other Middle European delicacies. 2931 N. Milwaukee Ave. (Avondale), (312) 252-3708. B

La Paella. Glorious garlic soup and plentiful paella are two hallmarks of this Spanish outpost where fish cheeks figure on the menu. 2920 N. Clark St. (Lincoln Park), (312) 528-0757. E

Middle Eastern/African

Addis Abeba [sic]. The former Moulibet is Chicago's premier practicioner of Ethiopia's exotic cuisine, which uses the tangy *injera* bread as eating utensil. 3521 N. Clark St. (Lake View), (312) 929-9383. M

Cafe Phoenicia. Cheerful service in an airy setting adds zest to the well-prepared Middle Eastern food. 2814 N. Halsted St. (Lake View), (312) 549-7088. M

Hashalom. This Israeli-Moroccan hybrid is a melting pot of Middle Eastern and North African flavors. 2905 W. Devon Ave. (West Rogers Park), (312) 465-5675. B/M

Konak. Tasty Turkish food in a carpet-adorned setting does justice to one of the world's most notable cuisines. 5150 N. Clark St. (Andersonville), (312) 271-6688. M

Reza's. Large and lively Persian storefront dispenses vast portions of authentic Iranian fare, including succulent quail. 5255 N. Clark St. (Andersonville), (312) 561-1898. B/M

Sayat Nova. Tried-and-true Armenian spot dependably does the standards, from hummus to borek and kebabs to couscous. 157 E. Ohio St. (Magnificent Mile), (312) 644-9159. Northwest suburban location in Des Plaines. M

Asian

Arun's. Thai dining takes a leap above typical storefront levels with well-informed service and exquisite presentation. 4156 N. Kedzie Ave. (Irving Park), (312) 539-1909. E.

Benkay. The Japanese equivalent of haute cuisine is serenely and superbly served at this dining complex in the Hotel Nikko. 320 N. Dearborn St. (River North), (312) 836-5490. E/D

Emperor's Choice. Cantonese classics, especially seafood, are at the top of their form here. 2238 S. Wentworth Ave. (Chinatown), (312) 225-8800. M

Gin Go Gae. The large number of Korean diners in this two-room storefront testifies to the quality at this ethnic stalwart. 5433 N. Lincoln Ave. (Ravenswood), (312) 334-3895. M

Hau Giang. A top choice among the Vietnamese spots clustered in a North Side Oriental enclave, Hau Giang does wonderfully filling noodle soups. 1104 W. Argyle St. (Uptown), (312) 275-8691. B/M

The Helmand. Chicago's only Afghan restaurant is a surprisingly stylish place where spicy meat dishes highlight the menu. 3201 N. Halsted St. (Lake View), (312) 935-2447. M

Hong Min. The dim sum lunch is a prime draw at this no-frills Cantonese mainstay. 211 W. Cermak Road (Chinatown), (312) 842-5026. B/M

Klay Oven. Upscale quality (and prices) distinguish the intricately seasoned Indian Mogul cooking here. 414 N. Orleans St. (River North), (312) 527-3999. M/E

Matsuya. Sushi plays a starring role at Matsuya, but the rest of the good-value Japanese menu also sparkles. 3469 N. Clark St. (Lake View), (312) 248-2677. M.

Siam Cafe. This time-tested place ranks among the best of the city's many budget-level Thai restaurants. 4712 N. Sheridan Road (Uptown), (312) 769-6602. B/M

T'ang Dynasty. Lavishly appointed restaurant with attentive service ranges across several Chinese regional cuisines. 100 E. Walton St. (North Michigan Avenue), (312) 664-8688. M/E

Viceroy of India. Here's a reliable winner among the welter of Indian/Pakistani storefronts along West Devon. 2516 W. Devon Ave. (West Rogers Park), (312) 743-4100. M

■ NIGHTLIFE

Chicago has always been "that toddling town," where the 1922 songwriter Fred Fisher even "saw a man dance with his wife." The arts and entertainment choices run the full gamut from highbrow to no-brow. The free *Reader* newspaper, published each Thursday, features extensive listings of performances and clubs. Thorough listings also appear each Friday in the two metropolitan dailies, the *Sun-Times* and the *Tribune*. Theater-goers can save as much as 50 percent on day-of-performance tickets at the several Hot Tix locations, (312) 977-1755. There's an array of commercial, dinner, non-profit, and experimental theater beyond the notable companies mentioned here.

■ THEATER COMPANIES

Body Politic/Victory Gardens. Space-sharing pioneers of Chicago's off-Loop theater renaissance dating back two decades and longer, with wide-ranging repertoires. 2257 N. Lincoln Ave. (Lincoln Park), (312) 871-3000.

Court Theater. 5535 S. Ellis Ave. Mainly revivals of classics, on the University of Chicago campus. (Hyde Park), (312) 753-4472.

Goodman. Sturdy perennial with a polished reputation for classical and contemporary works. 200 S. Columbus Drive (Loop), (312) 443-3800.

Next. Challenging scripts that might have a hard time finding a stage elsewhere. 927 Noyes Ave., Evanston (North Shore), (708) 475-1875.

Eddie Clearwater, one of Chicago's blues legends, does his thing at the Grant Park Blues Festival.

Remains. A focus on original work from American playwrights by a company born more than a decade ago in a storefront. 1800 N. Clybourn Ave. (Clybourn Corridor), (312) 335-9800.

Second City. Mecca of revue and improvisational comedy still going strong on mainstage, with second-banana E.T.C. troupe in smaller room. 1616 N. Wells St. (Old Town) (312) 337-3992. Suburban company in Rolling Meadows.

Steppenwolf. Nationally known for the power of its meaty productions, some of which have been successfully exported to Broadway. 1650 N. Halsted (Lincoln Park), (312) 335-1650.

Wisdom Bridge. Innovative stagecraft in a mix of styles on city's Far North Side. 1559 W. Howard St. (Rogers Park), (312) 743-6000.

■ C L A S S I C A L   M U S I C   A N D   O P E R A

Chicago Opera Theatre. First-rate productions in English at a North Side church auditorium. 2936 N. Southport Ave. (West Lake View), (312) 663-0048.

Chicago Symphony Orchestra. One of world's premier orchestras, playing from September to May at Orchestra Hall, plus outdoor summer performances at the Ravinia Festival on the North Shore. 220 S. Michigan Ave. (Loop), (312) 435-6666.

Grant Park Symphony Orchestra. Free summer concerts at Petrillo Bandshell in lakefront Grant Park. Columbus Drive and Jackson Boulevard (Loop), (312) 819-0614.

Lyric Opera of Chicago. Town's toughest cultural ticket for star-studded September-January season at Civic Opera House, 20 N. Wacker Drive (Loop), (312) 332-2244.

■ D A N C E

Ballet Chicago. City's only resident classical ballet troupe, founded in 1988. No permanent stage. (312) 993-7575.

Hubbard Street Dance Chicago. Contemporary dance success story in a city where companies come and go. Various stages. (312) 663-0853.

■ F I L M

Facets Multimedia. Enticing array of revivals, retrospectives, experimental and foreign films in two barebones screening rooms. 1517 W. Fullerton Ave. (Clybourn Corridor), (312) 281-4114.

Film Center of the Art Institute. Classic revivals and exotic current releases. Columbus Drive and Jackson Boulevard (Loop), (312) 443-3733.

Fine Arts Theater. Multiplex with a welcome difference, showing a lively mix of foreign and independent movies on its four screens. 418 S. Michigan Ave. (Loop), (312) 939-3700.

Music Box Theater. Beautifully restored 1920s moviehouse that shows art and revival releases, and hosts Chicago International Film Festival each October. 3733 N. Southport Ave. (Wrigleyville), (312) 871-6604.

■ C O M E D Y

Funny Firm. Less intimacy, more celebrities in this 300-seat club. 318 W. Grand Ave. (River North), (312) 321-9500.

Second City. Mecca of revue and improvisational comedy still going strong on mainstage with second-banana E.T.C. troupe in smaller room. 1616 N. Wells St. (Old Town), (312) 337-3992.

Zanies. Time-tested 100-seat venue that books big names and local up-and-comers. 1548 N. Wells St. (Old Town), (312) 337-4027.

■ J A Z Z

Andy's. Near-Loop mainstay of mainstream jazz, with sessions at lunch as well as evenings. Blues on Friday nights. 11 E. Hubbard St. (River North/Magnificent Mile), (312) 642-6805.

Gold Star Sardine Bar. Big-name musicians in a cramped highrise space with free admission. 680 N. Lake Shore Drive (Streeterville), (312) 664-4125.

Green Mill. First-rate jazz and more, including poetry slams, inside Prohibition-era gangster hangout. 4802 N. Broadway (Uptown), (312) 878-5552.

Joe Segal's Jazz Showcase. Stylish setting for impresario Joe Segal, Chicago's grand old man of mainstream jazz. 636 S. Michigan (South Loop), (312) 427-4300.

Moosehead Bar & Grill. Unpretentious jazz venue relocated from South Loop. 240 E. Ontario (North Michigan Avenue), (312) 649-9113.

■ B L U E S

Blue Chicago. Good starter spot for folks who've never heard the blues live before. 937 N. State St. (Near North), (312) 642-6261.

Blue Chicago on Clark. Sibling of the State Street joint, and likewise a top choice for blues beginners. 536 N. Clark St. (River North), (312) 661-0100.

B.L.U.E.S. Cramped room and small stage, but top-flight Chicago performers at what may well be the North Side's best blues club. 2519 N. Halsted St. (Lincoln Park), (312) 528-1012.

B.L.U.E.S. Etcetera. Younger sister of B.L.U.E.S., with more space and comfort as tradeoffs for a bit less crackle. 1124 W. Belmont Ave. (Lake View), (312) 525-8989.

Buddy Guy's Legends. 754 S. Wabash Ave. Ample elbow room and occasional performances by guitar maestro Guy, a part-owner. (South Loop), (312) 427-1190.

Checkerboard Lounge. A living museum of Chicago blues, in a South Side neighborhood that may be intimidating. 423 E. 43rd St. (Grand Boulevard), (312) 624-3240.

Rosa's. Adventuresome booking, friendly atmosphere in an out-of-the-way location. 3240 W. Armitage Ave. (Humboldt Park), (312) 342-0452.

Wise Fools Pub. Cozy North Side perennial with eclectic booking policy. 2270 N. Lincoln Ave. (Lincoln Park), (312) 929-1510.

■ ROCK

Avalon Niteclub. Alternative acts with a mix of big-name bookings in 500-seat

Jazz at Andy's Club

space hard by the L tracks. 959 W. Belmont Ave. (Lake View),
(312) 472-3020.

Biddy Mulligan's. Several shades of rock and blues as well, with a neighborhood feel. 7644 N. Sheridan Road (Rogers Park), (312) 761-6532.

Cubby Bear. No-decor venue for rockers and others across from Wrigley Field. 1059 W. Addison St. (Wrigleyville), (312) 477-7469.

Fitzgerald's. Roadhouse flavor in a working-class suburb. 6615 W. Roosevelt Road, Berwyn (Western Suburbs), (708) 788-2118.

Lounge Ax. Stimulating mix of alternative rock, reggae, folk, country. 2438 N. Lincoln Ave. (Lincoln Park), (312) 525-6620.

Wild Hare. Reigning spot for reggae and Afro-Caribbean acts. 3530 N. Clark St. (Lake View), (312), 327-4273.

■ TOURS

There are plenty of Chicago enterprises eager to give visitors a guided overview of the city or a focused look at some special subject. Here's a sampler:

American Sightseeing. Repertoire of 10 narrated bus tours. (312) 427-3100.

Chicago Architecture Foundation. Wide-ranging selection of authoritative architecture tours by foot, bus, and boat. (312) 922-3432.

Chicago Motor Coach Company. Hour-long narrated tours aboard a red London-style double-decker bus. (312) 922-8919.

Friends of the Chicago River. Docent-led walking tours along various stretches of the river. (312) 939-0490. (See page 212 for more information.)

Gray Line of Chicago. Narrated bus tours lasting two to seven hours. (312) 427-3107.

Here's Chicago! One-hour multimedia introduction to the city in the Water Tower Pumping Station, Pearson St. and Michigan Ave. (312) 467-7114.

Mercury Skyline Cruises. Ninety-minute sightseeing voyages on the lake and river. (312) 332-1353.

Shoreline Marine Sightseeing. Departures from the Shedd Aquarium/Field Museum dock for half-hour Lake Michigan cruises. (312) 222-9328.

Untouchable Tours. Two-hour bus circuit of Prohibition-era gangster sites. (312) 881-1195.

Wendella Sightseeing Boats. River and lake cruises of one to two hours, by a company founded in 1935. (312) 337-1446.

■ MUSEUMS

There are enough enjoyable museums in the Chicago area for a month of rainy days. Including the recommended spots that follow, the *Chicago's Museum* guidebook, written by Victor J. Danilov and published by Chicago Review Press, covers more than 150 area museums and other cultural attractions.

Adler Planetarium. By far the best place in Chicago to see the stars, given the city's glaringly bright streetlights. 1300 S. Lake Shore Drive (South Loop), (312) 322-0300.

Art Institute of Chicago. As good as any art museum in the world, and always striving to be even better. S. Michigan Ave. at Adams St. (Loop), (312) 443-3600.

Balzekas Museum of Lithuanian Culture. A fascinating repository of the history and culture of this newly independent Baltic state. 6500 S. Pulaski Road (Marquette Park), (312) 582-6500.

Brookfield Zoo. Splendid suburban zoo highlighted by Tropic World's rainforest habitats from three continents and the Seven Seas Panorama's dolphin show. 3000 S. Golf Road, Brookfield (Western Suburbs), (708) 485-0263.

Chicago Academy of Sciences. Once stodgy, now full of lively interactive exhibits including a first-rate Children's Gallery. 2001 N. Clark St. (Lincoln Park), (312) 871-2668.

Chicago Botanic Garden. Well worth the suburban drive up the lakeshore for its array of artfully designed habitats. Lake-Cook Road, Glencoe (North Shore), (708) 835-5440.

Chicago Children's Museum. Stimulating hands-on exhibits tucked amid the commercial bustle of North Pier Terminal. 435 E. Illinois St. (Streeterville), (312) 527-1000.

Chicago Historical Society. Essential stop for a lively and informative gloss on how this city became what it is. 1629 N. Clark St. (Lincoln Park), (312) 642-4600.

Alexander Calder's "Flamingo" in Federal Center Plaza is one of the Loop's many public sculptures.

"What is strange to us today will be familiar tomorrow."—*Mayor R. J. Daley, 1967.*

Du Sable Museum of African American History. Originally a family venture by Margaret and Charles Burroughs, now one of the nation's premier museums of African-American heritage. 740 E. 56th Place (Hyde Park), (312) 947-0600.

Field Museum of Natural History. Spectacular Hall of Dinosaurs and a universe of other world-class exhibits on the world around us. S. Lake Shore Drive at Roosevelt Road (South Loop), (312) 922-9410.

Garfield Park Conservatory. Magnificent botanic legacy of the civic-improvement flurry that accompanied the 1893 World's Columbian Exposition. 300 N. Central Park Blvd. (East Garfield Park), (312) 533-1281.

International Museum of Surgical Sciences. Illuminating if occasionally gruesome survey of medical progress. 1524 N. Lake Shore Drive (Gold Coast), (312) 642-6502.

Lincoln Park Conservatory. A grand, century-old showcase for palms, ferns, cacti, and an array of beautiful blooms. 2400 N. Stockton Drive (Lincoln Park), (312) 294-4770.

Lincoln Park Zoo. Nonpareil Great Ape House and host of other conservation-minded exhibits—with free admission. 2200 N. Cannon Drive (Lincoln Park), (312) 294-4660.

May Weber Museum of Cultural Arts. Fascinating folk art from around the world, with a gift shop selling authentic artifacts. 299 E. Ontario St. (Streeterville), (312) 787-4477.

Mexican Fine Arts Center Museum. Pioneering museum of its kind in the Midwest, featuring visual and performing arts. 1852 W. 19th St. (Pilsen), (312) 738-1503.

Morton Arboretum. Almost 5,000 kinds of trees and shrubs arrayed along four hiking paths and an eight-mile driving circuit. Route 53, Lisle (Western Suburbs), (708) 968-0074.

Museum of Broadcast Communications. From Jack Benny to Oprah Winfrey, an entertaining and enlightening window on radio and television. Chicago Cultural Center, Michigan Ave. at Washington St. (Loop), (312) 629-6000.

Museum of Contemporary Art. Another standout in its field, providing a provocative showcase for today's art and gearing up for a new facility by the middle of the decade. 237 E. Ontario St. (Magnificent Mile), (312) 280-5161.

Museum of Contemporary Photography. Columbia College's showcase of photography as an art and documentary form. 600 S. Michigan Ave. (South Loop), (312) 663-5554.

Museum of Holography. Billed as the world's most complete center for the three-dimensional projection of images. 1134 W. Washington St. (Near West Side), (312) 226-1007.

Museum of Science and Industry. Working Illinois coal mine, captured World War II German submarine, and several visits' worth of other well-designed exhibits. S. 57th St. at Lake Shore Drive (Hyde Park), (312) 684-1414.

Oriental Institute Museum. Marvelous Middle Eastern artifacts reflecting 75 years of archeology by this University of Chicago school. 1155 E. 58th St. (Hyde Park), (312) 702-9520.

Polish Museum of America. Vast collection of Polish-American art, folklore and history now stranded in the old neighborhood. 984 N. Milwaukee Ave. (River West), (312) 384-3352.

Shedd Aquarium. State-of-the-art Oceanarium opened in 1991, plus simulated coral reef and almost 200 traditional exhibit tanks. 1200 S. Lake Shore Drive (South Loop), (312) 939-2438.

Smart Museum of Art. Both intimate and elegant, showcasing University of Chicago collections that span several millenia. 5550 S. Greenwood Ave. (Hyde Park), (312) 702-0200.

Spertus Museum of Judaica. Joys and sorrows of the Jewish experience, ranging from a rich display of ceremonial treasures to the Zell Holocaust Memorial. 618 S. Michigan Ave. (South Loop), (312) 922-9012.

Swedish American Museum Center. Focus on the Scandinavian immigration to the Midwest, with a good museum store. 5211 N. Clark St. (Andersonville), (312) 728-8111.

Terra Museum of American Art. One wealthy man's inspired vision of American art from the mid-19th to early 20th century. 666 N. Michigan Ave. (Magnificent Mile), (312) 664-3939.

Ukrainian National Museum. Painted Easter eggs, wood carvings, and many more folk art objects from another newly independent land. 2453 W. Chicago Ave. (Ukrainian Village), (312) 276-6565.

■ BOOKSTORES

Chicago, known for its literary renaissance in the early decades of this century, remains rich in bookstores. All the chains and discounters are here, of course, but the real joy for bibliophiles is the array of homegrown specialists. If you're an addicted browser, an ideal companion is *The Book Lover's Guide to Chicagoland* by Lane Phelan, published in 1992 by Brigadoon Bay Books. It covers more than 400 area bookstores. Following is a browser of notable Chicago bookshops.

Polonia Bookstore, the largest Polish bookstore in America, is located on Milwaukee Avenue in Avondale.

Abraham Lincoln Book Shop. Civil War and other eras of U.S. history. 357 W. Chicago Ave. (River North), (312) 944-3085.

Act I Bookstore. All aspects of legitimate theater. 2632 N. Lincoln Ave. (Lincoln Park), (312) 348-6757.

African American Book Center. African history, black American culture and fiction. 7524 S. Cottage Grove Ave. (Avalon Park), (312) 651-0700. Two other locations.

American Indian Books. Native American fiction and non-fiction. 2838 W. Peterson (West Rogers Park), (312) 761-5000.

Archicenter Bookstore. Architecture with a focus on Chicago. 330 S. Dearborn St. (Loop), (312) 922-3431.

Barbara's Bookstore. Community-involved bookseller in business since 1963. 1350 N. Wells St. (Old Town), (312) 642-5044. Three other locations.

Barnes & Noble. Wide variety of titles, fiction and non-fiction. 659 W. Diversey Ave. (Lake View), (312) 871-9004.

Regular customer Anatoly Krif, a recent Moscow émigré, sits in front of Russian American Books on West Devon, one of Chicago's many specialty bookstores.

Book Box—Shake, Rattle & Read. Movies and the entertainment industry, as well as cookbooks. 4812 N. Broadway (Uptown), (312) 334-5311.

Booksellers Row. Used and antiquarian volumes, including review copies. 2445 N. Lincoln Ave. (Lincoln Park), (312) 348-1170. Also at 408 S. Michigan Ave. (Loop), (312) 427-4242.

Centuries & Sleuths Bookstore. History and mystery under one roof. 743 Garfield, Oak Park (Western Suburbs), (708) 848-7243.

Chicago Hebrew Bookstore. Judaic literature in English, Hebrew, Yiddish. 2942 W. Devon Ave. (West Rogers Park), (312) 973-6636.

Chicago Historical Society Museum Bookstore. Rich lode on Chicago's past and present. 1629 N. Clark St. (Lincoln Park), (312) 642-4600.

The Children's Bookstore. More than 20,000 kid-friendly titles. 2465 N. Lincoln Ave. (Lincoln Park), (312) 248-2665.

57th Street Books. Impressive stock of more than 50,000 new titles. 1301 E. 57th St. (Hyde Park), (312) 684-1300.

Grand Tour World Travel Bookstore. Labor of love by well-traveled owner Bob Katzman. 3229 N. Clark St. (Lake View), (312) 929-1836.

Guild Books. Political and social focus, hosting authors and involved in community. 2456 N. Lincoln Ave. (Lincoln Park), (312) 525-3667.

Kroch's & Brentano's. Chicago's best-known old-line bookstore, and one of its best-stocked. 29 S. Wabash Ave. (Loop), (312) 332-7500. Seventeen other locations.

Marshall Field's. Finest remaining department store book department in the country. 111 N. State St. (Loop), (312) 781-4284.

Mystery Loves Company. Mystery, true crime, horror, espionage. 3338 N. Southport Ave. (Lake View), (312) 935-1000.

O'Gara and Wilson Booksellers. Chicago's oldest bookstore, founded in 1882, with a vast stock and a scholarly slant. 1311 E. 57th St. (Hyde Park), (312) 363-0993.

People Like Us Books. Gay and lesbian literature. 3321 N. Clark St. (Lake View), (312) 248-6363.

Polonia Book Store. Largest Polish bookstore in America, some titles in English. 2886 N. Milwaukee Ave. (Avondale), (312) 489-2554.

Powell's Bookstore. Used books in all fields, renowned in University of Chicago neighborhood. 1501 E. 57th St. (Hyde Park), (312) 955-7780. Locations also at 828 S. Wabash and 2850 N. Lincoln.

Prairie Avenue Bookshop. America's most comprehensive architectural bookstore. 711 S. Dearborn St. (South Loop), (312) 922-8311.

Rand McNally Map Store. Maps and travel guides. 444 N. Michigan Ave. (North Michigan Avenue), (312) 321-1751. Also at 150 S. Wacker Drive (Loop), (312) 332-2009.

Russian American Books. In addition to a large selection of Russian books, Russian audio tapes, videos, and gifts are sold here. 2746 W. Devon Ave. (West Rogers Park), (312) 761-3233.

Rizzoli Bookstore. Art and gift books are specialties in elegantly paneled setting. Water Tower Place (Magnificent Mile), (312) 642-3500.

Sandmeyer's Bookstore. Travel, children's books, fiction. 714 S. Dearborn St. (South Loop), (312) 922-2104.

The Savvy Traveller. City's most complete selection of travel books, as well as gear and gadgets. 50 E. Washington St. (Loop), (312) 263-2100.

Stuart Brent Books. Reflects the character of its namesake proprietor, whom the novelist Saul Bellow has called "the Orpheus of Chicago booksellers." 670 N. Michigan Ave. (North Michigan Avenue), (312) 337-6357.

Waterstone's. Newer addition to the superstore book trade. 840 N. Michigan Ave. at Chestnut St. (Magnificent Mile), (312) 587-0808.

Women & Children First. Chicago's leading feminist and lesbian bookstore. 5233 N. Clark St. (Andersonville), (312) 769-9299.

■ INFORMATION SOURCES

The Chicago Office of Tourism distributes free brochures and other information at visitor centers in the Chicago Cultural Center (Michigan Avenue and Randolph Street downtown) and the Here's Chicago lobby (163 East Pearson Street off North Michigan Avenue). To call the Office of Tourism, dial (312) 280-5740; from outside Illinois, (800) 487-2446. Another agency, the Chicago Convention and Tourism Bureau, is headquartered at McCormick Place Convention Hall, (312) 567-8500. Help for foreign travelers is available at the International Visitors Center, 520 North Michigan Avenue, (312) 645-1836.

For current recorded information on events, call the Mayor's Office of Special Events Hotline, (312) 744-3370; Chicago Fine Arts Hotline (free exhibits and performances), (312) 346-3278; Chicago Music Alliance (classical music and opera), (312) 987-1123; Concert Line (popular music), (312) 666-6667; Dance Hotline, (312) 419-8383; Jazz Hotline, (312) 427-3300; Soul Hotline, (312) 288-7685.

Both of Chicago's metropolitan daily newspapers, the *Sun-Times* and the *Tribune*, are filled with information on events and activities of interest—particularly in the weekend sections published as part of the Friday editions and the arts-and-entertainment sections on Sunday. Exhaustive weekly cultural and nightlife listings can be found in the free *Reader* newspaper, distributed each Thursday. The monthly *Chicago* magazine lists a host of performances and exhibits, as well as capsule reviews of numerous recommended restaurants. The *Chicago Daily Defender* has a long history as the city's principal African-American newspaper. The free *Windy City Times* focuses on the gay and lesbian communities.

■ RADIO STATIONS

Popular Chicago radio stations on the AM band (with frequency and format) include: WIND (560, Spanish language); WMAQ (670, news); WGN (720, variety, talk, sports); WBBM (780, news); WSCR (sports talk); WLS (890, talk); WLUP (1000, talk); WJJD (1160, oldies).

Among major stations on the FM band are: WBEZ (91.5, National Public Radio days, jazz nights); WNIB (97.1, classical); WXRT (93.1, rock); WLIT (93.9, adult contemporary); WYTZ (94.7, pop hits); WNUA (95.5, jazz); WBBM (96.3, top 40); WLUP (97.9, rock); WFMT (98.7, classical); WUSN (99.5, country); WPNT (100.3, adult contemporary); WKQX (101.5, rock); WTMX (101.9, adult contemporary); WWBZ (103.5, rock); WJMK (104.3, oldies); WOJO (105.1, Spanish); WCKG (105.9, rock); WGCI (107.5, urban contemporary).

■ SPORTS

In 1876, the same year that Gen. George A. Custer was shut out at Little Big Horn, the ancestors of today's Chicago Cubs (then called the White Stockings) won the championship in the National League's very first season of baseball. Chicago has carried a passionate torch for its professional sports teams ever since, even though that fledgling flight of high fortune turned out to be prologue to many more seasons dampened by disappointment than garlanded by glory. Today's prime exception to this heartbreak history is the phenomenal success of the Chicago Bulls, winners of the National Basketball Association's 1991 and 1992 championships. Described below are the city's professional baseball, football, basketball, and hockey teams, all followed avidly by modern Chicagoans.

"Red" Grange (second from left), one of many Chicago sports legends, at a Chicago Bears game after signing on with the team in 1925. (Underwood Photo Archives)

■ BASEBALL

Chicago Cubs

Wrigley Field, the picture-perfect old-fashioned baseball park of ivy-covered out-field walls and mostly afternoon games, manages to draw more than 2 million fans each season—a testament to the unquenchable allegiance of Chicagoans in the face of athletic adversity. After its founding in 1876, the club was bought by the Wrigley family who owned it until 1981, when the National League club was bought by the Tribune Company.

In recent years Cubs fans have admired modern-day heroes the likes of Ryne Sandberg and Andre Dawson: Sandberg has won more Gold Glove awards than any other second baseman, and Andre Dawson, 1987's Baseball Writers' Association's Most Valuable Player, led the team to the National League playoffs in 1989. But despite the valiant efforts of its stars, the Cubs have failed to win a World Series since the Stanley Steamer era in 1908. Their last World Series appearance, in a losing effort, coincided with the end of World War II in 1945.

Nonetheless, even Cubs detractors would agree that Wrigley Field, with its hand-operated scoreboard, gives spectators a taste for baseball's history: the seventh-inning stretch is greeted with an off-key "Take Me out to the Ballgame" as sung by

It seems all Chicagoans are sports enthusiasts, whether they're settling down for a game at Wrigley Field or watching the ballgame from a rooftop nearby.

Hall-of-Fame sports announcer Harry Caray. (Appropriately, Pat Pieper, the originator of the "Play ball!" order, was another Wrigley Field announcer.) In spite of giving in to pressure from the broadcast media to play night games (the Cubs were the last team to introduce floodlights and play night games, in 1988) a majority of the Cubs' home games are still played in daylight hours.

Home: Wrigley Field, 1060 West Addison Street
Information: (312) 404-2827 for schedule
             (312) 831-CUBS for tickets in Illinois
             (800) 347-CUBS for tickets outside Illinois
Season: April through September

Chicago White Sox

Although a mutual animus has always divided South Side fans of the White Sox from the Cubs' North Side partisans, the city's two baseball teams are yoked in a tradition of championship futility. Founded in 1901 by Charles Comiskey, the White Sox last won the World Series in 1917, back when the first doughboys were sailing to France to make the world safe for democracy. The "Black Sox" betting scandal disgraced the 1919 World Series losers, and the Sox have appeared in the post-season classic just once since then: yes, a defeat by the Dodgers in 1959.

The American League's White Sox play in a spanking-new stadium which was built to save the team from being kidnapped to Florida in the late '80s. The new park has all the conveniences of a modern stadium—unobstructed views, monitors throughout the walkways so that not a moment of the game will be missed —but home-team home runs are still applauded with fireworks launched from behind the scoreboard.

Home: Comiskey Park, 333 West 35th Street
Information: (312) 924-1000 for schedule information
             (312) 831-1769 for tickets
Season: April through September

Transportation to the Parks

Both teams are best reached by public transportation. Wrigley Field is reached by the Howard Street L line: take the B train to Addison Street. Comiskey Park can be reached on an A or B Dan Ryan L train to 35th Street.

■ FOOTBALL

Like their baseball counterparts, the **Chicago Bears** have a long history in the sport. George Halas, organizer of the American Professional Football Association (later to become the NFL) founded the Bears and coached the redoubtable "Monsters of the Midway" in the 1930s and '40s. Also like their baseball brethren in disappointing seasons, "da Bears" have reached the Super Bowl only once since its inception in 1967. That glorious 46-10 triumph in January 1986, when William "Refrigerator" Perry became a household name and coach Mike Ditka was certified a genius, led not to another pigskin dynasty but only to disappointment. Quarterback Jim McMahon moved to the Philadelphia Eagles in the 1989 season; since 1990 the position has been filled by Jim Harbaugh. Ditka lost his job after the 1992 season, leaving Bears fans with new head coach Dave Wannstedt and a fresh infusion of hope.

Hope, indeed, is the fuel that keeps Chicago fans clicking through the turnstiles season after roller-coaster season.

> Home: Soldier Field, 425 East McFetridge Drive
> Information: (312) 663-5100 for tickets and information. Subscription sales account for most tickets; however, they can occasionally be obtained from subscribers at the stadium before games.
> Season: August (pre-season) through December (January if in playoffs)
> Transportation: Take the Jeffery Express (Number 6) bus to Roosevelt Road and Lake Shore Drive. The stadium is just south of the Field Museum of Natural History.

■ BASKETBALL

After drafting Michael Jordan in 1984, the **Chicago Bulls** had a star to lead an otherwise merely mortal crew of players. In spite of Jordan's talents, the Bulls continued to come up short. The disparity between Jordan's abilities and those of his supporting cast was perhaps never more clear than in the 1986 double-overtime playoff with the Boston Celtics, in which Jordan scored 63 points and the Bulls still lost.

The advent of a new decade, however, ushered in a new spirit and a new coach, Phil Jackson. Under Jackson's leadership, Jordan has led the team to consecutive

Michael Jordan is fouled by the Knicks' Gerald Wilkins during the 1992 Eastern Conference Finals. (photo by Rob Brown)

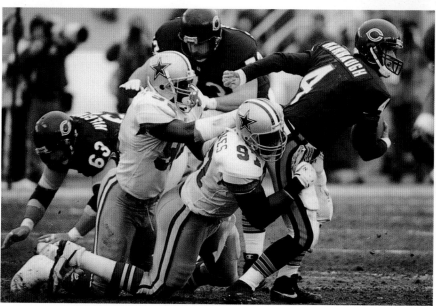

Mike Ditka (top) ponders strategy in his last season as Bears coach, while quarterback Jim Harbaugh (above) resists a tackle by Dallas defense.

championship years in 1991 and 1992. Jordan also shares the court with Scottie Pippen, a star in his own right; both played on the Barcelona "Dream Team" at the 1992 summer Olympics. And Michael Jordan continues to break the records: he holds the NBA record for the highest career scoring average, and has been the season's scoring leader for the past six years.

Blessed with the unparalleled talents of Jordan, the world's most famous athlete of the moment, the Bulls delight a succession of audiences at the cavernous old Chicago Stadium, which is due to give way by mid-decade to a state-of-the-art arena being built nearby on the West Side. Tickets to these games are hard to come by—it's standing-room-only at Chicago Stadium—so if connections get you a Bulls ticket, count yourself among the blessed of Chicago fandom.

Home: Chicago Stadium, 1800 West Madison Street
Information: (312) 943-5800 for tickets and game times
(usually 7:30 P.M.)
Games are broadcast on WMAQ, AM 670.
Season: November to May

■ HOCKEY

No Chicagoans are more rabidly devoted to their team than the hockey-loving followers of the **Chicago Blackhawks**, who share Chicago Stadium with the Bulls. The prospect of their first Stanley Cup title in three decades was dangled and then snatched away in 1992 when the Pittsburgh Penguins swept four straight games in the final series. As it is, three National Hockey League championship trophies repose in the Blackhawks' case—for the 1934, 1938, and 1961 seasons.

The team enjoyed its heyday in the '60s, when the Ross Trophy (for leading scorer in the NHL) was won by Blackhawk Bobby Hull in '60, '62, and '66, and Stan Mikita in '64, '65, '67, and '68. The Blackhawks may well see another successful era: current goalie Eddie Belfour, winner of both a Calder Trophy (for rookie of the year) and a Vezina (for best goalkeeper), seems to have inherited the mantle of superior goalkeeper from '70s Blackhawk Tony Esposito, winner himself of several Vezina trophies. And Chicago fans are hopeful.

Home: Chicago Stadium, 1800 West Madison Street
Information: (312) 783-5300 (games usually start at 7:30 P.M.)
Season: October through April

SAY IT AIN'T SO, JOE

One potentially great Chicago team which has unfortunately gone down in infamy in the annals of baseball history: the Chicago White Sox, pennant winners in 1917 and 1919 and World Series winners in 1917:

*T*he White Sox had a fine infield, good catching, pitching as good as Boston's, and in the outfield one of the best hitters who ever lived—Shoeless Joe Jackson. Joseph Jefferson Jackson, of Brandon Mills, South Carolina, couldn't read or write, but he certainly could hit, as attested to by his .356 lifetime batting average —third highest in history, right behind Ty Cobb's .367 and Rogers Hornsby's .358. Jackson hit over .370 four times, once over .400, but never won a batting title because Ty Cobb or George Sisler always ended up just a bit higher.

Joe Jackson's illiteracy was widely known and a frequent subject for laughter. People chuckled at various versions of the widely repeated story that in restaurants he would always wait for another ballplayer to order first, since he couldn't read the menu, and then say, "I'll have what he's having."

continues

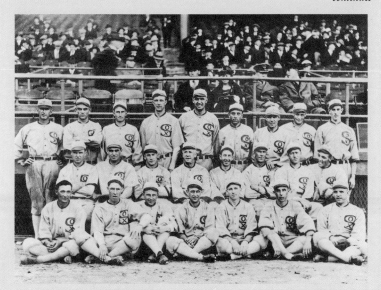

The White Sox team of 1919, the year of the scandal.

Shoeless Joe Jackson had the third-highest lifetime batting average in history.

Shoeless Joe knew people made fun of him, and he didn't like it. Once he hit a long triple and, as he stood on third base, someone in the crowd raised snickers by shouting, "Hey Joe, can you spell 'cat'?" Joseph Jefferson Jackson looked over, squirted a stream of tobacco juice in the heckler's direction, and yelled back, "How about you, big shot—can you spell 'shit'?"

The Chicago White Sox were heavy favorites to win the World Series in 1919, just as they had won it two years earlier. The Cincinnati Reds, National League pennant winners, were a good team, led by center fielder Edd Roush and third baseman Heinie Groh, but on paper the Reds seemed to be no match for the powerful White Sox.

However, in an upset reminiscent of the 1914 Miracle Braves and the 1906 Hitless Wonders, the Reds trounced the White Sox, five games to three. (From 1919 through 1921 the World Series was extended to a five out of nine basis instead of the usual four out of seven.) There were ugly rumors that everything was not as it appeared to be, but such talk was typically dismissed as irresponsible if not downright unpatriotic.

Almost a year later the story broke: eight of the White Sox (thereafter to be known as the Black Sox) had been bribed by gamblers to lose the Series. Those implicated were first baseman Chick Gandil (evidently the ringleader), pitchers Eddie Cicotte and Lefty Williams, outfielder Happy Felsch, shortstop Swede Risberg, utility infielder Fred McMullin, and third baseman Buck Weaver, who knew about the fix but may or may not have participated in it.

And, yes, Shoeless Joe Jackson. As Shoeless Joe was leaving the courthouse in Chicago after confessing his involvement, a small boy, tears in his eyes, is reported to have tugged at his sleeve. "Say it ain't so, Joe," he pleaded.

Apocryphal or not, it was an entire nation that was praying it wasn't so. When it turned out to be all too true, the shock rocked the country. All those involved were banished from baseball for life. But a disillusioned public wondered about the extent of the corruption: if a World Series could be fixed, how many other games were being thrown? With confidence in the integrity of the game shattered, baseball itself was on trial.

—Lawrence S. Ritter and Donald Honig,
The Image of Their Greatness, 1992

RECOMMENDED READING

The non-fiction, fiction, and guidebooks mentioned here only skim the riches of writing about Chicago from its earliest days until the present. Some of the earlier works remain in print in paperback editions.

■ NON-FICTION

Addams, Jane. *Twenty Years at Hull-House*. Insightful memoirs of the Hull House founder. New York: Macmillan, 1910.

Asbury, Herbert. *Gem of the Prairie*. Gangsters and the rest of Chicago's demi-monde. New York: Alfred A. Knopf, 1940.

Condit, Carl. *The Chicago School of Architecture*. Definitive work on the 1875-1925 architectural golden era here. Chicago: University of Chicago Press, 1964.

Cromie, Robert. *A Short History of Chicago*. Brisk waltz through two centuries. San Francisco: Lexikos, 1984.

Cronon, William. *Nature's Metropolis: Chicago and the Great West*. How Chicago shaped America's midcontinent and in turn was defined by the wide-open spaces to the west. New York: W. W. Norton, 1991.

Dedmon, Emmett. *Fabulous Chicago: A Great City's History and People*. Lively spin on larger-than-life personalities, by a redoubtable newspaperman. New York: Atheneum, 1981.

Farber, David. *Chicago '68*. Portrait of a tumultuous watershed year. Chicago: University of Chicago Press, 1988.

Granger, Bill and Lori. *Fighting Jane: Mayor Jane Byrne and the Chicago Machine*. Life and times of the city's first woman mayor. New York: Dial, 1980.

Hayner, Don, and Tom McNamee. *Metro Chicago Almanac*. Irresistible smorgasbord of everything you always wanted to know about the Second City. Chicago: Chicago Sun-Times/Bonus Books, 1991.

Hayner, Don, and Tom McNamee. *Streetwise Chicago: A History of Chicago Street Names.* More delicious facts. Chicago: Loyola University Press, 1988.

Heise, Kenan, and Ed Baumann. *Chicago Originals.* Colorful characters, decade by decade. Chicago: Bonus Books, 1990.

Honig, Donald, and Lawrence S. Ritter. *The Image of Their Greatness: An Illustrated History of Baseball from 1900 to the Present.* Play-by-play history of America's legend-filled sport, with great old black-and-whites. New York: Crown, 1992.

James, Henry. *Letters of Henry James.* New York: Scribner, 1920.

Kaufman, Mervyn. *Father of Skyscrapers, a Biography of Louis Sullivan.* The tempestuous life of the Chicago School genius. Boston: Little, Brown, 1969.

Kipling, Rudyard. "From Sea to Sea," *Letters of Travel.* New York: Scribner, 1889.

Kleppner, Paul. *Chicago Divided: The Making of a Black Mayor.* How Harold Washington won the 1983 mayoral election. De Kalb, Illinois: Northern Illinois University Press, 1985.

Lewis, Lloyd, and Henry Justin Smith. *Chicago, the History of Its Reputation.* Sweet story from two legendary *Chicago Daily News* men. New York: Harcourt Brace, 1929.

Lowe, David. *Lost Chicago.* Vivid photographic look at the heritage that has been torn down. Boston: Houghton Mifflin, 1975.

Mayer, Harold M., and Richard C. Wade. *Chicago: Growth of a Metropolis.* Magisterial illustrated survey of the city's development. Chicago: University of Chicago Press, 1969.

McPhaul, John J. *Deadlines and Monkeyshines, the Fabled World of Chicago Journalism.* Tales from the Front Page Era. Englewood Cliffs, New Jersey: Prentice Hall, 1962.

Rakove, Milton L. *Don't Make No Waves, Don't Back No Losers: An Insider's Analysis of the Daley Machine.* Behind the scenes of Hizzoner's empire. Bloomington: Indiana University Press, 1975.

Rowe, Mike. *Chicago Blues: The City and the Music.* The evolution of a Chicago trademark. New York: Da Capo Press, 1975.

Royko, Mike. *Boss: Richard J. Daley and His Era.* Superlative model of what an urban biography should be. Chicago: Dutton, 1971.

Schoenberg, Robert J. *Mr. Capone: The Real—and Complete—Story of Al Capone.* The latest look at Scarface Al. New York: William Morrow, 1992.

Spear, Allan H. *Black Chicago: The Making of a Negro Ghetto, 1890-1920.* The roots of the city's racial anguish. Chicago: University of Chicago Press, 1967.

Terkel, Studs. *Division Street: America.* Chicagoans talk to the master listener. New York: Pantheon, 1967.

Travis, Dempsey J. *An Autobiography of Black Chicago.* Stirring account of African-American community life here by an civic-minded real-estate man. Chicago: Urban Research Institute, 1981.

Wille, Lois. *Forever Open, Clear and Free: The Struggle for Chicago's Lakefront.* Engaging history of a vital and ongoing battle. Chicago: University of Chicago Press, 1972, 1991.

Wolfe, Tom. *Mauve Gloves and Mad Men, Clutter and Vine.* Commentary on American cities, including essays on Chicago. New York: Farrar, Strauss & Giroux, 1976.

■ FICTION

Ade, George. *Fables in Slang.* Satirical parables by a pioneering Chicago newspaper columnist born in Indiana. Chicago: H. S. Stone, 1900.

Algren, Nelson. *The Man With the Golden Arm.* Poetry and humor in novel of West Division Street saloon life by a writer who loved and hated his Chicago. Garden City, New York: Doubleday, 1950.

Bellow, Saul. *Humboldt's Gift.* Closest thing to Chicago novel in oeuvre of city's most famous post-World War II writer, a Nobel Prize laureate. New York: Viking, 1975.

Looking north from the Sears Tower.

Brooks, Gwendolyn. *Annie Allen.* Pulitzer Prize volume of poetry by leader of city's literary Black Renaissance in 1960s and '70s. New York: Harper, 1949.

Dreiser, Theodore. *Sister Carrie.* Early Chicago-set novel by the relentless social realist. New York: Doubleday, 1900.

Dunne, Finley Peter. *Mr. Dooley in Peace and War.* Chicago-Irish saloon wit of a century ago, collected from Dunne's famous newspaper columns. Boston: Small, Maynard, 1898.

Farrell, James T. *Young Lonigan.* First and most forceful volume of Farrell's South Side Irish trilogy. New York: Vanguard, 1932.

Ferber, Edna. *The Girls.* Three-generation novel spanning Chicago history from 1840s into twentieth century. Garden City, New York: Doubleday, 1921.

Lardner, Ring. *You Know Me Al.* Letters to a friend back home from a major-league baseball naif in the wicked big city of Chicago. New York: Doran, 1916.

Maugham, W. Somerset. *Stories of Hawaii and the South Seas.* Honolulu: Mutual Publishing, 1921.

Sandburg, Carl. *Chicago Poems.* City of the Big Shoulders, and much, much more. New York: Holt, 1916.

Sinclair, Upton. *The Jungle.* Muckraking classic that exposed exploitation of immigrant Chicago stockyard workers—and vile sanitary conditions of the slaughtering process. New York: Doubleday, Page, 1906

Smith, Patricia. *Life According to Motown.* Award-winning Chicago poet writes about growing up in Chicago. Chicago: Tia Chucha Press, 1991.

Wright, Richard. *Native Son.* New American tragedy of Bigger Thomas, a black man "whipped before you were born." New York: Harper, 1940.

■ GUIDEBOOKS

Bach, Ira J., and Susan Wolfson. *Chicago on Foot.* Thirty-one walking tours with architectural focus. Chicago: Chicago Review Press, 1987.

Bach, Ira J., editor. *Chicago's Famous Buildings.* Illustrated briefs on 164 landmarks and notable buildings. Chicago: University of Chicago Press, 1965, 1980.

Camp, Paul A., and Carolyn McGuire, editors. *Zagat Chicago Restaurant Survey.* Meaty frequent-diner consensus on hundreds of restaurants. New York: Zagat Survey, 1992.

Danilov, Victor J. *Chicago's Museums.* Quick look at more than 150 museums and other cultural attractions. Chicago: Chicago Review Press, 1991.

Heise, Kenan, and Mark Frazel. *Hands On Chicago: Getting Hold of the City.* Spotlight on neighborhoods and personalities. Chicago: Bonus Books, 1987.

Lindberg, Richard. *Passport's Guide to Ethnic Chicago.* History and attractions, from Irish to Native American. Lincolnwood, Illinois: Passport Books, 1993.

Molloy, Mary Alice. *Chicago Since the Sears Tower.* Nuts and bolts on downtown buildings erected since 1975. Chicago: Inland Architect Press, 1988.

Pacyga, Dominic A., and Ellen Skerrett. *Chicago: City of Neighborhoods.* Fifteen social essays and driving tours. Chicago: Loyola University Press, 1986.

Phalen, Lane. *The Book Lover's Guide to Chicagoland.* Where the bookstores are. Hoffman Estates, Illinois: Brigadoon Bay Books, 1992.

Wurman, Richard Saul. *Chicago Access.* Color-coded walking tours on block-by-block basis. Dunmore, Pennsylvania: Harper Perennial, 1991.

I N D E X

COMPASS AMERICAN GUIDES

WRITTEN FOR THE "LITERATE TRAVELER," this series of guides conjures up the images, explores the myths and legends, and reveals the spirit of America, its cities and states, and Canada.

Compass American Guides are available in general and travel bookstores, or may be ordered directly by calling 1-800-733-3000; or by sending a check or money order, including the cost of shipping and handling, payable to: Random House, Inc. 400 Hahn Road, Westminster Maryland 21157. Books are shipped by USPS Book Rate (allow 30 days for delivery): $2.00 for the 1st book, 50¢ for each additional book. Applicable sales tax will be charged. All prices are subject to change. Or ask your bookseller to order for you.

> *"Books can make thoughtful (and sometimes even thought-provoking) gifts for incentive travel winners or convention attendees. A new series of guidebooks published by Compass American Guides is right on the mark."*—SUCCESSFUL MEETINGS *magazine*
>
> Consider Compass American Guides as gifts or incentives for VIP's, employees, clients, customers, convention and meeting attendees, friends and others. Quantity discounts and customized editions are available.

Chicago   Veteran newsman and inveterate Chicagoan, Jack Schnedler, who writes regularly for the *Chicago Sun-Times,* captures the essence of this brawny, exuberant city, covering its history from swamp to skyscrapers, its architecture and urban essences.
Author: Jack Schnedler—Photographer: Zbigniew Bzdak
ISBN 1-878867-28-8; 320 pp; Price $16.95 (paper). ISBN 1-878867-29-6; Price: $24.95

Las Vegas   Deke Castleman's rollicking introduction to the capital of glitz, with a tale of fifty hotels, a celebration of tacky museums, a guide to quick weddings and sign language, and, of course, a system for playing slots, craps, blackjack, poker, and other games of chance.
Author: Deke Castleman—Photographer: Michael Yamashita
ISBN 1-878867-18-0; 304 pp; Price $14.95. Second edition.

Los Angeles   A hip and fast-moving tour of Los Angeles with special attention to those places where movies were filmed, movie stars lived and loved, and legends were born.
Author: Gil Reavill—Photographer: Mark S. Wexler
ISBN 1-878867-17-2; 324 pp; Price $14.95.

San Francisco and the Bay Area   San Francisco has something for everyone, whether your taste runs to cappuccino or dim sum, to downtown honky tonk or Davies Symphony Hall. Special emphasis on the surrounding Bay Area, from the Napa Valley to the markets of the East Bay.
Author: Barry Parr—Photographer: Michael Yamashita
ISBN 1-878867-16-4; 400 pp; Price $14.95. Second edition.

Arizona   From hidden canyons to museums of archaeology, from the civilized pleasures of Phoenix to jagged wildlands, author Larry Cheek reveals Arizona's scenic, cultural, and historical attractions and colorful eccentricities.
Author: Larry Cheek—Photographer: Michael Freeman
ISBN 1-878867-32-6; 288 pp; Price $16.95. Second edition.

Colorado   Champagne powder and cattle ranches, deserts and mountains, clean civilized cities, and classic American small towns—author Klusmire describes them all with wit, folksy humor, and a native's insight.
Author: Jon Klusmire—Photographer: Paul Chesley
ISBN 1-878867-07-5; 318 pp; Price $14.95 (paper). ISBN 1-878867-20-2; Price $22.95 (cloth)

Hawai'i   Some credit Hawai'i's magic to climate and scenery, others to its handsome people and spirit of *aloha*—but all are stirred by its royal history and its connection to the cultures of Polynesia. This guide helps you discover Hawai'i's magic for yourself.
Author: Moana Tregaskis—Photographers: Wayne Levin and Paul Chesley
ISBN 1-878867-23-7; 364 pp; Price $15.95 (paper). ISBN 1-878867-24-5; Price $22.95 (cloth)

Montana   Love of land and sky runs deep in Montana. Mountain ranges with names like the Crazies and the Sapphires. Legendary rivers—the Madison, Big Hole, and Yellowstone. Curiouser creeks—Froze-to-Death, Stinking Water, and Hellroaring. High plains, once home to buffalo, still offer wide vistas to the eye and soul. This land of the Big Sky may well be the last best place.
Author: Norma Tirrell—Photographer: John Reddy
ISBN 1-878867-10-5; 320 pp; Price $14.95 (paper). ISBN 1-878867-13-X; Price $22.95 (cloth)

New Mexico   Space, light, purity—New Mexico has cast a magical spell of mystery over its inhabitants for centuries. Rich in history, New Mexico has seen the sophisticated Anasazi culture, Spanish conquistadors searching for gold, 16th century colonists, and Pancho Villa. This truly is a Land of Enchantment.
Author: Nancy Harbert—Photographer: Michael Freeman
ISBN 1-878867-06-7; 336 pp; Price $15.95 (paper). ISBN 1-878867-22-9; Price $22.95 (cloth)

Utah   Unspoiled as the day Brigham Young proclaimed "this is the right place," this land of red-rock canyons and snow-capped mountains offers glorious scenery and a glimpse of the magnificent cliff-dwellings of the ancient Anasazi Indians. Special emphasis on outdoor recreation.
Author: Tom & Gayen Wharton—Photographer: Tom Till
ISBN 1-878867-31-8; 352 pp; Price $16.95. Second edition.

Wyoming   High, wide, and handsome, a land where tales of Indians, pioneers, gun slingers, cattle barons, cowboys and other characters of the Old West still cling to life. Nat Burt, son of pioneering dude ranchers, roams the state where the myth of the cowboy was born.
Author: Nathaniel Burt—Photographer: Don Pitcher
ISBN 1-878867-04-0; 392 pp; Price $14.95 (paper). ISBN 1-878867-03-2; Price $22.95 (cloth)

Canada   Veteran journalist Garry Marchant approaches the second largest country in the world as not one, but six different nations. Special sections on the Inuits, Canadian sports, rail hotels, 'Newfies,' Quebecois culture and the Calgary Stampede.
Author: Garry Marchant—Photographer: Ken Straiton
ISBN 1-878867-12-1; 308 pp; Price $14.95

■ ABOUT THE AUTHOR

JACK SCHNEDLER HAS BEEN TRAVEL EDITOR of the *Chicago Sun-Times* since 1982. His travel section has won an assortment of awards, including the Lowell Thomas Award as North America's best newspaper travel section. He has worked in a variety of positions ranging from sportswriter to arts-and-books editor for four newspapers: the *Chicago Daily News,* the *Miami Herald,* the *Washington Star,* and the *Chicago Sun-Times.*

Schnedler spent one year as a professor of journalism at Northwestern, and he is featured as a travel authority on WGN radio in Chicago. His wife, Marcia Schnedler, is a nationally syndicated columnist and the author of two guidebooks.

■ ABOUT THE PHOTOGRAPHER

ZBIGNIEW BZDAK IS A CHICAGO-BASED photographer whose photography has appeared in *Americas, Reader's Digest,* and many other publications. His photographs of the first exploration team to navigate successfully the Amazon River were published by *National Geographic, Outside,* and Alfred A Knopf. In 1991 he won a Communication Arts Magazine Award of Excellence for his photography in *Living in Wyoming,* Rockridge Press, Inc. He is currently a staff photographer for the *Times* in Indiana.